Troubleshooting and repairing digital video systems

Troubleshooting and repairing digital video systems

Robert L. Goodman

TAB Books
Division of McGraw-Hill, Inc.

New York   San Francisco   Washington, D.C.   Auckland   Bogotá   Caracas   Lisbon   London   Madrid
Mexico City   Milan   Montreal   New Delhi   San Juan   Singapore   Sydney   Tokyo   Toronto

©1995 by **McGraw-Hill, Inc.**
Published by TAB Books, a division of McGraw-Hill, Inc.

pbk   1 2 3 4 5 6 7 8 9 DOC/DOC 9 9 8 7 6 5

Library of Congress Cataloging-in-Publication Data
Goodman, Robert L.
    Troubleshooting and repairing digital video systems / Robert L.
Goodman.
      p. cm.
    ISBN 0-07-024040-X (p)
    1. Microprocessors—Maintenance and repair. 2. Digital video-
-Maintenance and repair. I. Title.
TK7895.M5G65   1995
621.388—dc20   94-48316
                                                            CIP

Acquisitions editor: Roland Phelps
Editorial team: Joanne Slike, Executive Editor
                David M. McCandless, Editor
Production team: Katherine G. Brown, Director
                Ollie Harmon, Coding
                Jeffrey M. Hall, Computer Artist
                Wanda S. Ditch, Desktop Operator
                Jodi Tyler, Indexer
Design team: Jaclyn J. Boone, Designer   EL3
            Katherine Stefanski, Associate Designer   024040X

In loving memory of my late wife Jackie

Contents

8   Troubleshooting computer monitors   267

Acknowledgments

This book contains information compiled from various sources over many years. I sincerely thank the following companies and personnel for this information, drawings, and photos.

Sencore	Al Bowdin, George Gonos, Don Multerer, Larry Schnabel, Paul Nies
Texas Instruments Inc.	Bob Fuller
GE and RCA Thomson Electronics	J.M. Surprise - J.W. Phipps
GTE/Consumer Electronics	E.M. Nanni
Global Specialties Corp.	Gail DeGrand
Hewlett-Packard	Reinhard Hamburger
Zenith Electronics	Ron Meltzer
JVC Corp.	Paul E. Hurst
B & K Dynascan Corp.	Myron E. Bond
Intel Corp.	Mike Peak
Sony Corp. Of America	Howard L. Katz
Tandy Corp. (Radio Shack)	Dave Gunzel
Quasar Corp.	Charlie Howard
Tektronix, Inc.	Martin Middlewood
E & L Instruments, Inc.	Frank W. Gregrio

Introduction

Microprocessors are incredibly versatile devices that represent extraordinary opportunities for any technician who develops an expertise with them. This book helps you to develop that expertise and will also offer actual case history problems that others have found.

You'll learn how to troubleshoot and repair microprocessors found in consumer electronic systems. The electronics technician can readily put this book to practical use, because it's designed to help you dig right into microprocessor operating systems and quickly locate and solve problems with a "hands-on" technique. And the chapters are packed with proven electronic troubleshooting procedures that I have perfected over a period of more than 40 years in the electronics field.

Digital devices & microprocessors

1

THIS CHAPTER BEGINS WITH A BRIEF OVERVIEW OF BASIC digital logic operations and various microprocessor system information, including digital signal pulses, logic gates and levels, details of the digital logic states, and truth tables.

Next, you will see how logic gates function in digital electronics. This section is a primer to help you understand and troubleshoot complex microprocessor systems covered in later chapters.

The chapter concludes with some basic microcomputer information and various sections that make up microprocessor systems in consumer electronic products. You will learn about bits and bytes, data buses, memories, and flowcharts.

Digital signals & pulses

Digital signals, which make the microprocessor run, are pulses whose various states are discrete intervals apart. The typical digital signal (note the scope trace in Fig. 1-1) in digital electronics is a binary signal. A *binary* signal is a voltage or current that carries information in the form of changes between two different states that are a discrete interval apart. One of these states is called the *logic 0* state; the other is called the *logic 1* state. For voltage signals, the logic 0 state is typically at ground potential, whereas the logic 1 state varies between +3 and +5 V. For current signals, the logic 0 state is typically the absence of current (0 mA), and the logic 1 state is generally set at approximately 20 mA.

■ **1-1** *Typical digital signal pulses.*

To visualize these logic off-on or high-low states, refer to the square-wave pulse train in Fig. 1-2. These states may also be referred to as zeros (0's) and ones (1's). A gate input, to be valid, must be positive (high) or grounded (low). Thus, a key point to remember is that any gate can have only one or two possible states for its input or output logic mode when operating correctly. For identification, one state is called *one* (1), the other *zero* (0).

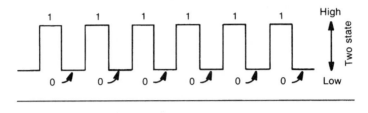

Various states
*Zero and ones
*Off and on
*Low and high

■ **1-2** *Digital logic pulse states.*

Almost all modern digital logic circuits are now transistor-transistor logic (TTL). Thus, the input devices for the gates are transistors and not diodes or resistors. These gates are called DTL (diode-transistor logic) and RTL (resistor-transistor logic). Digital circuits at the block diagram level are much simpler than analog circuits that technicians are used to troubleshooting. The TTLs are two-state devices with precisely defined logic levels. The pulse drawing in Fig. 1-3 indicates the high and low states for TTL. When you work with static logic levels, you can use the logic probe, voltmeter, or scope to detect high and low states. The pulse drawing indicates that 0–0.8 Vdc is low, and 2.4–5 Vdc is high for TTL circuitry. The region in between is known as the *undetermined* state, which, in logic systems troubleshooting, usually indicates a circuit fault.

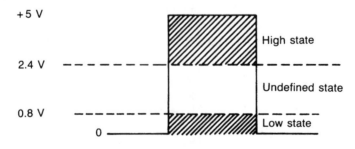

■ **1-3** *High and low states for a TTL pulse.*

Each high pulse and each low pulse has a positive-going edge and a negative-going edge. The TTL gate circuits then detect these transitions, and these edges are used as the actuating signal. Only the positive-going or negative-going edge is required to make the next logic device go into operation.

Digital devices

Basically, a *digital device* can be defined as any device that operates on or manipulates binary information. "Binary" refers to an operation with two states. Binary coding can be represented by any two-state device: for example, a lamp that is on or off; a computer card that is punched or not punched; a magnetic core magnetized north or south; two different voltage levels, current levels, or frequencies; and, as you have already seen, 0 (low) and 1 (high).

In digital electronics, devices manipulate binary information in the form of voltage levels: +5 V for the logic 1 state, and near ground potential for the logic 0 state. A logic state can change in less than 2 nanoseconds (ns). Even faster times have been achieved, and the cost of digital devices is going down. Speed and low cost have made digital devices completely dominate electronics. Some digital devices discussed in this book are gates, counters, decoders, flip-flops, buffers, multiplexers, memories, and microprocessors.

The logic gate

Probably the least complex digital device is the logic gate. A *gate* is a circuit with two or more inputs and one output. Digital information at the output depends on the combination of digital information at the inputs. The term "gate" has various meanings in electronics, but we consider only the digital gate device. The AND, OR, NAND, and NOR gates are the most common. A more complicated gate developed from NOR or NAND gates is the exclusive-OR gate.

The logic circuits

A *gating circuit* is a circuit in which a gate is used to control the passage of a digital signal, which may be a single pulse, a group of pulses, or a train of pulses.

A *logic circuit* is an electronic circuit that provides an input-output relationship corresponding to a Boolean algebra logic function.

A *memory* is any device that can store logic 0 and logic 1 states in such a manner that a single bit or group of bits can be accessed and retrieved. Memory elements can be constructed from groups of gates called *flip-flops*.

Truth table concepts

Truth tables will help clarify logic gate operations. Truth table information shows the relationship of all output logic levels of a digital circuit to all possible combinations of input logic levels in a way that completely gives all circuit functions. (Input or output logic levels, in this book, mean logic 0 and logic 1 states, which in many digital devices contain voltage levels of 0 V and +5 V, respectively.) Another definition is that a truth table shows the relationship of all output logic 0 and logic 1 states of a digital circuit to all possible combinations of input logic 0 and logic 1 states so as to characterize completely all circuit functions.

Figure 1-4 shows a digital circuit with three inputs (A, B, and C) and four outputs (Q1, Q2, Q3, and Q4). The truth table gives the relationship between the inputs and outputs of a logic device. This relationship is simple because the inputs and outputs can only be 0's or 1's. Because there are two possible states for each of the three inputs, there are eight different sets of inputs, which are also shown in Fig. 1-4.

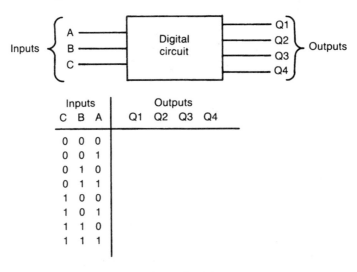

Inputs			Outputs			
C	B	A	Q1	Q2	Q3	Q4
0	0	0				
0	0	1				
0	1	0				
0	1	1				
1	0	0				
1	0	1				
1	1	0				
1	1	1				

■ **1-4** *A logic circuit with a partial truth table.*

The logic states of the four outputs depend on which digital gate circuits are used. You cannot complete a truth table for a given set of inputs until you know the specific circuit gates involved or the name of the specific logic device.

A truth table is used because it is a simple shorthand representation of a digital circuit. It is much easier to devise a truth table than to explain how a specific digital circuit operates. The more inputs and outputs that exist, the more obvious the advantage a truth table has over a written description. Truth tables are used to represent digital circuits in the same way as architects use blueprints for buildings.

The digital gate functions can be used in many ways, but the truth table for the gate will always be the same. A truth table is a basic characteristic of a gate. It does not depend on how a gate is used.

Logic gate operations

The OR gate

The symbol and truth table for the OR gate are in Fig. 1-5. In the OR gate, the unique state occurs when both input A and input B are at logic 0. This observation is important whenever you want to remember the truth table for an OR gate.

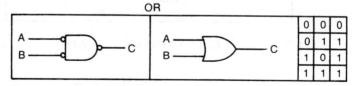

OR

0	0	0
0	1	1
1	0	1
1	1	1

■ **1-5** *OR gate symbol with truth table.*

The NOR gate

In a NOR gate, the output is logic 1 only when all inputs are logic 0; the output is logic 0 if any input is logic 1. The symbol and truth table for the 2-input NOR gate is shown in Fig. 1-6.

Note the small circle on the tip of the cone in the NOR gate symbol (also found in the NAND gate symbol). For the NOR gate, you can consider the inputs as those of an OR gate and invert the output. A 2-input NOR gate can be made from a 2-input OR gate and a single inverter. Or a 2-input OR gate can be made from a 2-input NOR gate and an external inverter. Inversion, or complementation, can

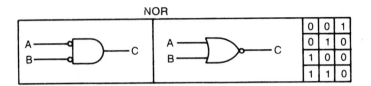

■ 1-6 *NOR gate symbol with truth table.*

be represented by either the inverter symbol or the small circle before or after a gate or digital device symbol.

The exclusive-OR gate

The exclusive-OR gate can be easily defined by looking at its symbol and truth table in Fig. 1-7. This gate is closely related to the OR gate and is sometimes called an inclusive-OR gate by computer programmers. The only difference between the two occurs when inputs A and B are both at logic 1. For the OR gate, the output is logic 1; for the exclusive-OR gate, the output is logic 0. When multiple-input OR gates are used, the exclusive-OR gate is usually a 2-input gate.

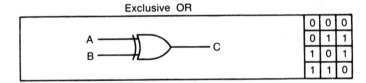

■ 1-7 *Exclusive-OR gate symbol with truth table.*

Exclusive-OR gates are common and can be purchased as integrated circuit (IC) chips containing four such gates on a single chip. Or, you can build a single exclusive-OR gate from three 2-input NAND gates and a pair of inverters. From the truth table for the NAND gate and inverter, you can easily show that this circuit produces the truth table for an exclusive-OR gate.

AND-or-INVERT gate

The AND-or-INVERT gate is a composite gate circuit found in many microcomputer systems. It actually consists of AND gates and a single NOR gate. Such gates are available with two per IC chip. When you use an AND-or-INVERT gate, you must specify how many AND gates are included and how many inputs each AND gate possesses. For example, a 3-wide 2-input AND-or-INVERT gate has

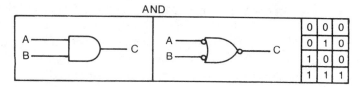

AND

0	0	0
0	1	0
1	0	0
1	1	1

■ **1-8** *AND gate symbol with truth table.*

three AND gates, and each has two inputs. The symbol and truth table for an AND-or-INVERT gate are shown in Fig. 1-8.

The NAND gate

The NAND gate is a binary, logic coincidence circuit or device that can perform the NAND (negative AND) logic operation. The NAND gate behaves like an AND gate whose output is negated: NAND is shorthand for NOT AND. The symbol and truth table for a NAND gate are shown in Fig. 1-9.

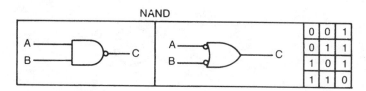

NAND

0	0	1
0	1	1
1	0	1
1	1	0

■ **1-9** *NAND gate symbol with truth table.*

Understanding logic functions

Most logic circuits are made up of circuit elements called "gates," of which two types are generally used. Now with large-scale integration (LSI) techniques, these gates are used in various combinations to build some very complex circuits, including flip-flops, encoders, decoders, and, most important, microprocessor chips. Although most logic circuits now use ICs, older circuits, and some simple logic functions, are made with common transistors and diodes.

Logic ICs, however complex, usually use two basic elements, known as NAND and NOR gates, in various combinations to build complex logic arrays, which may contain hundreds of gates, to perform some complex control functions. In modern circuitry, large arrays are quickly being replaced by the versatile programmable microprocessor. Even with a microprocessor, however, several logic gates, and at times discrete logic circuits, are often used to process the input and/or output signals (data) from the microprocessor chip.

Logic in the real world involves making AND or OR decisions. An example of an AND decision is shown in Fig. 1-10. This illustration of AND logic says that you will go swimming if the temperature is higher than 75° and a pool is available. If either or both inputs are not positive, then you would not go swimming.

The AND thinking process can now be simplified as shown in Fig. 1-11. If both inputs are true, the output is true.

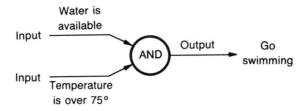

■ **1-10** *A real-world AND logic decision.*

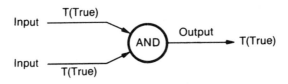

■ **1-11** *A generalized AND logic decision.*

The AND function

Figure 1-11 can now be electronically shown with the AND logic block. AND logic gate ICs are not commonly available for reasons that will be obvious a little later in this chapter. The AND function, however, is quite useful in actual circuits. Figure 1-12 is the symbolic representation of the AND logic function. Note that it is a rectangle with a rounded end.

■ **1-12** *The AND logic symbol.*

Now let's see how digital circuits actually operate electronically. Electronics circuits will not function with "trues" (T) or "falses" (F). Instead, they operate with voltage "highs" and "lows." A "high" is a voltage greater than the "low" voltage—usually several volts greater. For example, one family of logic devices uses +5 V as logic high and 0 V as logic low.

When working with a logic gate, you need a truth table to show the output condition for various input conditions. Figure 1-13 is the AND logic gate and its truth table. The inputs are labeled A and B, and the output is labeled C. A logic 1 output at C is generated only when input A is logic 1 and input B is logic 1. For simplicity, logic high is usually expressed as a 1 or logic 1, and logic low is expressed as 0 or logic 0.

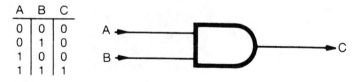

A	B	C
0	0	0
0	1	0
1	0	0
1	1	1

■ **1-13** *The AND symbol with truth table.*

The AND logic function can also be built up with diodes and transistors, as shown in Fig. 1-14. With diodes, inputs A and B must be logic high for output C to be high. If either or both inputs are low, the diode(s) will be forward biased and output C will be logic low. The transistor circuit requires both transistors to be conducting to have a logic high output at C. If either or both inputs are logic low, the transistors will be cut off and output C will be low.

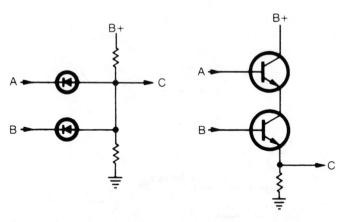

■ **1-14** *Discrete AND logic circuits.*

About the only common equivalent to the AND logic function available in logic gate ICs is the NAND gate. NAND is a contraction of NOT AND. NOT, as used in logic, means "negated," which actually means "inverted." The special symbol 0 is used for the negated or NOT function. In Fig. 1-15, the NAND gate is the now familiar AND gate with the negation symbol.

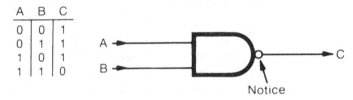

A	B	C
0	0	1
0	1	1
1	0	1
1	1	0

■ **1-15** *A NAND logic symbol with truth table.*

If you compare the AND truth table in Fig. 1-13 with the one for the NAND function, you will find that the same input conditions produce exactly opposite outputs. Thus, the true condition of logic high states on inputs A and B produces a logic low or 0 output at C.

The OR function

In Fig. 1-16, the OR function indicates that if either input is true, then the output is true. Also, if both inputs are true, the output is true. The electronic symbol of the OR function is shown in Fig. 1-17. Note that the truth table for the logical OR function indicates that a logic 1 (high or true) on either (A or B) or both inputs produces a logic 1 on output C. Also notice that logic 0 on both inputs produces a logic 0 output voltage.

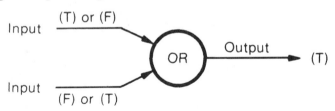

■ **1-16** *Generalized OR logic decision.*

A	B	C
0	0	0
0	1	1
1	0	1
1	1	1

■ **1-17** *An OR symbol with truth table.*

Diodes and transistors are often used to implement the logic OR function. Figure 1-18 shows an example of OR logic circuitry. If the anodes of either diode or both diodes (A or B) input are logic 1, the C output will be logic 1. Analogously, a logic 1 base drive to either or both transistor bases produces a logic 1 output at C.

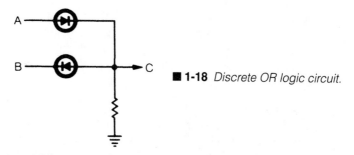

■ **1-18** *Discrete OR logic circuit.*

The NOR function

The complex symbol ○ on the output produces the logic symbol for the NOR gate in Fig. 1-19. Analogously to the AND/NAND comparison, the same logic 1 inputs to the NOR gate produce the opposite outputs from the OR gate: output C is logic 0.

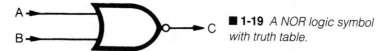

■ **1-19** *A NOR logic symbol with truth table.*

Some negative logic

Let's see why NANDs and NORs are used rather than ANDs and ORs. The phase inversion, or negation, is a useful asset in circuit design and operation. You can use a NAND gate to perform the NOR function, and a NOR gate for the NAND function.

Sometimes you might have to NAND or NOR logic low inputs. These logic gate ICs can be used in a backwards way to implement what is known as negative logic. The term "negative logic" means that the true logic state is logic 0, or logic low. Examine the truth table of Fig. 1-20, which is for the negative logic NOR function, to see that it matches the NAND truth table in Fig. 1-15.

A	B	C
0	0	1
0	1	1
1	0	1
1	1	0

■ **1-20** *Negative logic NOR function with truth table.*

Now consider this example where the circuit design is such that the true inputs at A and B are logic 0's. In this case, the output C will be logic 1 (true) when either or both inputs (A and B) are logic 0. Thus, the NAND gate performs the negative logic NOR function for logic 0 true signals.

When you see a symbol that looks like Fig. 1-20, you will know by the circles at the inputs that it is a negative logic NOR gate. If you check the device type number on the diagram, you will probably find that it is really a NAND gate. This is a way of showing that the NAND gate is performing the negative logic NOR function.

Similarly, note that the symbol in Fig. 1-21 is a negative logic NAND gate. To be sure, check the truth table. The logic 1 output is present only when input A and input B are at the logic 0 level. Thus, the negative logic NAND function can be implemented with a NOR gate.

A	B	C
0	0	1
1	0	0
0	1	0
1	1	0

■ **1-21** *Negative logic NAND gate with truth table.*

The inverter function

A triangle with the negating ○ on the input or output (see Fig. 1-22) is an *inverter*, which is used to easily convert a logic 0 to a logic 1, or vice versa. This symbol also indicates an inverter section of a standard IC package. In this case, only one input lead is available, so no double terminal numbering is required. Or you might see either type of gate used in a configuration as in Fig. 1-23. If you examine the truth tables for the NAND and NOR gates, you will find that this configuration makes either gate an inverter or negator. In other words, a logic 1 input produces a logic 0 output, and vice versa. Thus, if one or more logic signal inputs to a gate have incorrect logic polarity (high or low) to produce the desired output, you can use a spare gate of either type to invert the signal.

■ **1-22** *Inverter logic symbol diagram.*

Types of gates

Buffer

From Fig. 1-24, you can see that two inverters can be connected to form a noninverting element to buffer or isolate signals. Figure 1-25

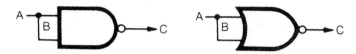

■ 1-23 *Gates used as inverter gates.*

■ 1-24 *Two inverters connected as noninverting buffer.*

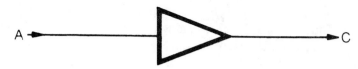

■ 1-25 *Buffer logic symbol.*

shows the buffer symbol. Note that there is no negating ○. Thus, the input and output have the same polarity. The buffer is also available in multiple-circuit ICs known as buffer ICs.

The enabled & tri-state gates

A diagram that shows one or more gates with an added input (see Fig. 1-26) is called an *enabling* input. In other words, you must apply an enabling voltage of the correct polarity to this gate to get an output. The ○ indicates that the enabling voltage must be a logic 0. Enabling inputs without the 0 require a logic 1 voltage to be enabled. Some of these devices are called *tri-state*, which means that when they are not enabled, the output line is a high impedance, which effectively disconnects it from the external circuit. Figure 1-27 illustrates that NAND and NOR gates can be enabled in the same way by adding an enable line.

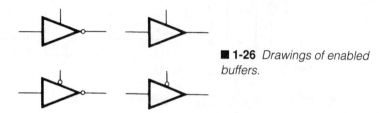

■ 1-26 *Drawings of enabled buffers.*

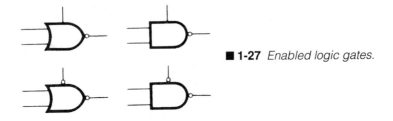

■ **1-27** *Enabled logic gates.*

Flip-flop gates

Two gates of either type can be cross-connected to make a bistable flip-flop. In Fig. 1-28, the output of each gate is connected to one of the inputs of its companion gate. This configuration is known as an *RS flip-flop*. It has two inputs: S (set) and R (reset). The two outputs are Q and $\overline{Q}$ (known as Q bar or not Q). The bar can be used to negate any signal.

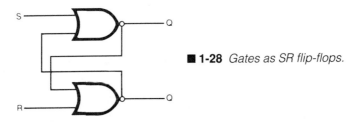

■ **1-28** *Gates as SR flip-flops.*

In the RS flip-flop, a logic 1 pulse or steady-state voltage on the S input sets the Q line to logic 1; hence, the $\overline{Q}$ line goes to logic 0. Input to the R line sets Q to logic 1, so the Q output goes to logic 0. SR flip-flops are also standard IC packages. When the package version is used, it is drawn as shown in Fig. 1-29. These devices are used for pulse storage, latching, square-wave generators, and many other things.

S	R	Q	$\overline{Q}$
0	0	*	*
1	0	1	0
0	1	0	1
1	1	*	*

*Invalid Output

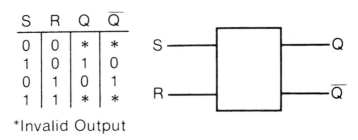

■ **1-29** *SR flip-flops and truth tables.*

14

The JK & D flip-flops

JK and D flip-flops are two of the more common packages of complex IC chips. In the JK flip-flop, the S and R inputs are sometimes available. J and K inputs that have them will inhibit setting or resetting the flip-flop according to the logic states on these lines.

The D flip-flop normally is used to store the input logic state (data storage). A logic high on the D input is clocked in as a logic high on the Q output. (Sometimes Q is not available.) More complex versions have SR input, enables, and so on, but all are takeoffs of the basic SR type.

Combined logic elements

I will now describe some of the techniques designers use to draw logic circuits. They are often used in simplified schematics and block diagrams to clarify circuit operation. In Fig. 1-30, no text is included because the points should now be obvious. These examples and others will suggest themselves to the devious mind of a designer, but you should now be able to determine the required outputs with given input signals for these "hybrid" symbols. And, more importantly, what you've learned from this chapter will allow you to trace and troubleshoot all but the most exotic logic circuits.

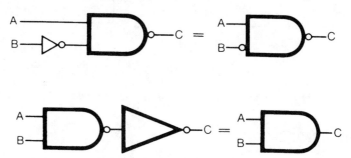

■ **1-30** *Combined logic element gates.*

Logic IC families

There are two general families and several subfamilies of logic. One family is known as *bipolar logic*. The IC logic elements of this family use monolithic integrations of conventional bipolar transistors. Most common in this family is TTL of which there are some fast-operating, low-power subfamilies. Most of these devices are powered by +5 V. A logic high output is a voltage greater than 2.4 V, and a logic low output is a voltage less than 0.8 V. This 1.6 V guard band between the high and low output and input voltages provides noise immunity. More noise immunity is provided by well-filtered, regulated 5-V power supplies.

The second family is MOS logic. And again there are several sub-families: NMOS, PMOS, CMOS/MOS. Usually MOS logic is characterized by low power consumption (much lower than bipolar logic), good noise immunity, less-stringent power-supply requirements, limited output drive capability, and susceptibility to static-discharge damage. This last item is especially important to the service technician. You must observe special precautions when handling MOS devices to keep from damaging them.

The transmission gate

One logic element is unique to the CMOS/MOS logic family. It is known by various names, such as "bilateral switch," "switching gate," or "transmission gate." The symbol for this device has not yet been standardized. This gate truly acts as an electronic switch when it is activated or turned on by a logic high voltage on its gate. When the transmission gate is on, current, or signal, will go in either direction, just as it would in a mechanical switch. Some of the symbols for this gate are shown in Fig. 1-31.

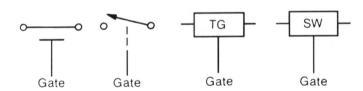

| Gate | Gate | Gate | Gate |

■ **1-31** *Various symbols for transmission gate.*

Microprocessors

The 4-bit microprocessor was introduced in the late 1960s, but the modern microprocessor chip was developed and produced by Intel, a company that at the time was specializing in semiconductor devices. Today, many manufacturers offer various types of microprocessor chips. Several test instruments have microprocessors as the heart of the system: for example, oscilloscopes, video analyzers, and digital multimeters. The microprocessor chip used in the Sencore SC61 scope will be covered in Chapter 3. When the microprocessor first hit the market, it sold for over $100 each. Now, many microchips cost about $10, and the price will no doubt keep going down.

Microprocessor operation

The microprocessor chip is a single IC with all of the control and processing parts found in a digital computer; however, we are interested in the microprocessor as a controller rather than a digital computer. The microprocessor is being used more as a control device than as a computer.

Modern digital systems consist of many functional blocks, such as gates and flip-flops, that perform simple logic functions. The overall system operation depends on how these units are selected and on how they are connected. Now it is feasible to perform many logic functions within a single LSI chip containing thousands of logic elements. These ICs are called *memories*. By controlling the information fed these memories, you can determine what logic functions the system will perform. A block diagram of this system is shown in Fig. 1-32.

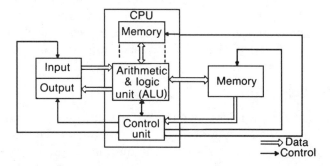

■ **1-32** *Block diagram of computer.*

Now if there were a way to control the operation of a system, you could then build a universal system. The function that this system would perform would depend on how you "programmed" it—that is, how you fed information into the memory. The microprocessor makes this universal system possible. Therefore, you can design a system not with gates and flip-flops but by programming the microprocessor and memories to do the same things that gates and flip-flops do.

The microprocessor technique has many advantages. Data for programming memories have been fully developed by makers of digital computers, so putting a program into memory is easy. Another big plus is that design changes can be made by just changing the program rather than by rewiring and making connection changes in the system. A microprocessor-based system actually has a wiring diagram that can easily be altered without changing a single con-

17

nection. All changes can be performed in the information stored in the memories.

Some microchip limitations

The microprocessor is not the answer to all digital design problems. Two major limitations are the size of the system and the speed of operation. Some systems have only one or two simple IC chips. In this case, not much would be gained by replacing these systems with a microprocessor. When microchips first became available, it was estimated that you must use from 50 to 100 small-scale ICs before it was economical to replace the system with a microprocessor unit. As the cost drops, however, this situation will change.

Another limitation of the microprocessor is its speed. The microprocessor is just not as fast as the regular digital computer. Thus, microprocessors cannot handle the large amounts of data in short time periods as full-sized digital computers do. Except for these limitations, the microprocessor-based system will do anything that a digital computer or a system of discrete logic elements can do.

Technical terms

At first, it might be difficult for you to understand how a microprocessor can perform all of these functions in such a short time. When you first start delving into microsystems, the terminology will not mean much and will be confusing. Thus, it is difficult to read about how microprocessors operate, if you don't understand the language.

Two terms you need to know are "hardware" and "software." *Hardware* is not too difficult because it refers to physical devices such as IC chips, readouts, and interconnecting cables. *Software* is the program or set of instructions that tells the computer what to do. In addition, numbers and instructions that have no actual existence but are stored in hardware, such as IC memory chips, are called software.

Computer block basics

The programmable computer consists of four functional elements: memory, arithmetic and logic unit, control unit, and input-output device.

Memory

The memory stores the data. Data might be the actual numbers the computer works with or the numbers called instructions, which tell the rest of the computer what to do. See Fig. 1-33.

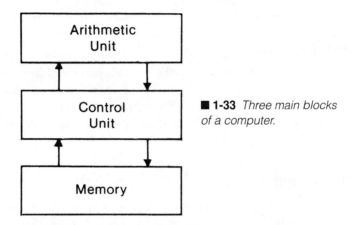

■ 1-33 *Three main blocks of a computer.*

In microprocessors, the memories are called semiconductor devices and may be of two types.

☐ *Read-only memory* (ROM) has information fed into it that cannot be easily erased. Instructions that do not change are usually stored in ROM.

☐ *Random-Access memory* (RAM) is usually used for temporary storage (sometimes called scratch-pad info) of data or instructions that are likely to be changed. You may write data into it or read data out of it, depending on control signals.

Arithmetic & logic unit

The arithmetic and logic unit (ALU) can perform simple arithmetic operations, such as adding two numbers or comparing one number with another to see which is larger. Complex mathematical or control operations are performed by a series of very simple operations.

Control unit

The control unit is usually referred to as the brain of the computer because it coordinates the operation of all computer elements in the proper sequence. The control unit obtains its various instructions from memory chips. A sequence of instructions is called the *program*. The control unit is synchronized by a clock signal that keeps all of the elements of the computer operating with the proper timing sequence.

In a microprocessor, the ALU, the control unit, and some memories are usually grouped under the name *central processing unit* (CPU). As shown in Fig. 1-32, separate memories or separate parts of a memory are used for storing programs and data.

Input-output devices

The basic elements described to this point make up the computer, but to make it operate, you must have a way to put data into it and take other data out of it. Therefore, some type of input-output device is required. It could be as simple as a light switch or as complex as a keyboard or memory disk unit.

How the computer operates

One reason why the computer is hard for a novice to understand is that the computer performs all operations by sequentially performing many simple steps. The computer operation can be explained by the analogy of a person with a calculator, a pad of paper, and a pencil. The person corresponds to the control unit, the calculator to the ALU, and the pencil and paper to the memory circuits.

This comparison can be used to write a program to add the number 2 to the number 3. The first thing you need is a set of instructions. These instructions will be stored in memory, so you must write them on a piece of paper. Remember that a computer has no judgment other than what you program into it, so you must be careful to include all necessary steps.

With a calculator, the following steps are required to add the number 2 to the number 3:

1. Press the CLEAR key.
2. Enter the first number into the calculator.
3. Press the + key.
4. Enter the second number into the calculator.
5. Press the = key.
6. Read the total and write it down.

To locate any of these instructions, you only have to go to the proper line. The line number is called the *address* of the instruction. For example, 3 is the address of the instruction "Press the = key." Looking at the list of instructions, you see that the numbers to be added are not specified, so take another piece of paper and write A = 2 and B = 3.

These numbers are the numerical data that you will work with. To arrive at 2, go to line A; therefore line A is the address of the number 2.

Now you can write a program to add 2 and 3. This program will have three basic procedures:

☐ You must obtain, or fetch, the instructions.
☐ You must obtain, or fetch, the data or numbers to be added.
☐ You must act on, or execute, each instruction.

The computer program steps

The computer program will have more steps than you might suspect because the computer must be told every step that it has to perform. It cannot do any reasoning on its own. Here are the program steps.

1. Fetch the instruction on line 1.

2. Execute this instruction—actually press the CLEAR key.

3. Fetch the instruction on line 2. This instruction tells you to enter the first number, but it does not tell you what the number is.

4. Fetch the number on line A. Now you know that the first number is 2.

5. Execute the instruction on line 2—press key 2 on the calculator.

6. Fetch the instruction on line 3.

7. Execute the instruction on line 3—press the + key.

8. Fetch the instruction on line 4. This tells you to enter the second number, but it does not tell you what the number is, so go onto the next step.

9. Fetch the number on line B. Now you know the number required is 3.

10. Execute the instruction from line 4—press key 3.

11. Fetch the instruction on line 5.

12. Execute the instruction on line 5—press the = key.

13. Fetch the instruction from line 6.

14. The last step is to execute the instruction from line 6. You would read the total 5 and write it down. We must say where to write it: for example, line C on the second piece of paper.

In this comparison, the calculator, the human operator, the pencil, and the paper are hardware. The instructions, numbers, and program are software.

You should now have a better understanding of a computer program. Remember that although a computer is fast, some time is required for each step. Thus, when complicated problems or complex control procedures must be performed, the speed of the computer/microprocessor is most important.

Binary numbers

In a computer system, all data is represented by binary numbers. A binary number is one that has only two possible values—0 and 1. In the microprocessor system, a 1 is represented by some voltage, usually +5 V; a 0 is represented by an absence of voltage. Binary numbers are used because it is much easier to build an electronic system that can tell the difference between a voltage and no voltage than to build a system that can distinguish one voltage from another.

The binary number system is easy to use. Generally, in microprocessors the data representing numbers is carried on eight lines. Each line has some voltage or no voltage. If it has voltage, the line is carrying a logic 1. If it has no voltage, the line is carrying a logic 0. Binary numbers are added as follows:

$$0 + 0 = 0$$
$$0 + 1 = 1$$
$$1 + 1 = 10$$

The number 10 in binary notation is called "one-oh," and is equal to the decimal number 2. The following tabulation shows that logic levels on the eight lines (called a *bus*) of the microprocessor can be used to represent decimal numbers.

$$00000001 = 1$$
$$00000010 = 2$$
$$00000011 = 3$$
$$00000100 = 4$$

Bytes & bits

A voltage or no voltage on each of the eight lines of the bus is referred to as a *bit* of information. Thus, the eight-line bus will carry

8 bits of information at any time. These 8 bits of data are called a *byte* of data.

Data is carried on the bus one bit after another. At one time, the data on the bus might be 00000010, which is decimal number 2. At the next moment, the line levels could well be 00000100, which is the decimal number 4. This type of data transmission is usually called *bit parallel*, *byte serial* transmission, because 8 bits are carried in parallel at one time and the bytes are carried one after another.

With most computer systems, bytes of data can travel in both directions on the bus. Sometimes data is fed into the microprocessor, and sometimes it is fed out of the microprocessor.

Before the microprocessor can work with the digital data, there must be a place to store it. The device used to store digital data is the memory IC chip.

Memories

One way to visualize how a memory works is to think of a set of small boxes or cubbyholes. Figure 1-34 shows a set of 16 boxes, each of which may contain either a logic 1 or a logic 0. Each box is indicated by the letter of the column and the number of the row that it is in. For example, in the drawing, a 1 is in box B2. This designation is called the *address* of the box containing the 1. Microprocessor memories are generally arranged so that each address applies to eight boxes where 1 byte of data can be stored.

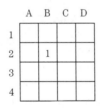

■ **1-34** *Illustration of how memory logic is stored.*

Figure 1-35 is a simplified block diagram of a 256-byte memory. It is arranged internally so that at each address there is an 8-bit byte of data. Just what the data happens to be depends on what is stored at a particular address. In this case, the memory has an eight-line address bus.

By placing logic 1's and 0's on these address lines you can specify 256 different addresses in the memory. Thus, when a particular address is specified by the signal on the address lines, the information stored at that particular address will appear on the output bus.

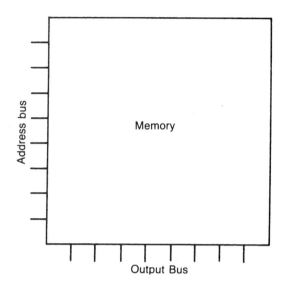

■ **1-35** *Simplified block diagram of a 256-byte memory.*

Read-only memory (ROM)

Several types of memory IC chips are available. The simplest is the read-only memory (ROM). This memory can only be read. The data info is permanently stored in the chip when it is built.

ROMs are used whenever the data to be stored will not have to be changed. One application might be to transform a binary number into a bit pattern to operate a printer.

In the binary number system, the decimal number 1 is written as 00000001. In the American Standard Code for Information Interchange (ASCII), the bit pattern required to make a typewriter/printer print the character 1 is 00110001. For this transformation, the byte 00110001 is stored at the address 00000001. When you use the binary number to address the memory, the correct ASCII byte appears at the output of the memory. ROMs are used whenever a fixed data pattern is to be stored.

The programmable ROM (PROM)

A much more flexible type of memory is the *programmable read-only memory* (PROM). This ROM may be programmed for whatever is required. When it is built at the factory, it has no data stored in it; by using special equipment, you can store required data in the chip. After the data is stored in the memory, it cannot be changed.

Newer PROMs have been developed with a small quartz window. By directing an ultraviolet light through this window, you can erase the data stored in the memory and place new data in storage.

The read-write memory

Probably the most versatile type of semiconductor memory is the *read-write memory* or random-access memory (RAM). With RAM, data storage is not permanent. You can place—that is, write—data into the memory. You can also read out data that is stored in memory.

RAMs have a connection that determines if data will be written into or read out of the memory. This terminal may also be identified as the *read-write terminal*. When a logic 0 is applied to it, the data that happens to be on the output bus will be stored in the memory at the address designated by the byte on the address lines. When a logic 1 is applied to the read-write terminal, the data that is stored at the address designated by the byte on the address lines will appear on the output bus.

Both RAMs and ROMs are used in microprocessor systems. Some memories are actually contained in the same IC chip that contains the rest of the system microprocessor.

Flowcharts

When first encountering microprocessors, you might ask, "just how can a device that is basically a computer perform with software the same functions that have usually been performed with hardware in conventional systems?" To use the microprocessor effectively, you must combine the skills of the hardware designer and the computer programmer. The computer programmer works with instructions rather than with circuits. A device that is used is the *flowchart*, which is a list of the functions that the computer must perform. The flowchart is to the programmer what the block diagram is to the technician troubleshooting complex circuits.

Although different symbols are used in flowcharts, only three will give you a good start in understanding these charts. The first symbol in Fig. 1-36 is a rectangle with rounded ends. It is used to mark the program start and stop. It is needed because the computer must be told when to start and when to stop a program.

The next flowchart symbol in Fig. 1-36 is a rectangle, which is used to represent one or more instructions that the computer must follow. In a well-drawn flowchart, there will usually be a rectangle for each instruction. In some flowcharts, a single rectangle might represent a complete set of instructions. These rectangles are very much like block diagrams.

The diamond-shaped symbol in Fig. 1-36 tells you the difference between a software-based system and a hardware-based system. It designates a point in the program where the system must make a decision. The decision is based on something that the computer system can determine. For example, the computer could be asked to compare two numbers to determine which is larger. Depending on which number is larger, one set of instructions will be followed.

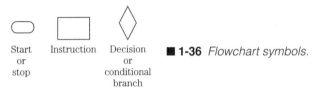

| Start or stop | Instruction | Decision or conditional branch | ■ **1-36** *Flowchart symbols.* |

Troubleshooting tree charts

A *troubleshooting tree,* unlike a flowchart, is a graphical way of showing the sequence of tests to perform on a system under test. These tree charts are often drawn as flowcharts in which the results of each test determine what step is to be taken next. Troubleshooting trees can save you considerable time and effort when repairing microprocessor-based units.

Figure 1-37 shows a portion of the troubleshooting tree for a Hewlett-Packard model HP 3455A digital voltmeter. Theoretically, it should lead you to the instrument's fault by the actions taken and decisions made along the tree. Unfortunately, it doesn't always happen. A perfect troubleshooting tree must consider all possible failures—a difficult, if not impossible, task for the person working up the tree to meet. Also, the troubleshooting trees tend to be fairly generalized and lack the specifics desired for making tests and decisions. Few troubleshooting trees provide practical data about how a specified test or check relates to what the circuit does or is supposed to do. If the troubleshooting tree fails to point you to the actual fault, you may be left at a dead end. But it could be your best way to start, anyway.

Good troubleshooting trees seldom lead to a dead end. They provide a logical, well-directed sequence of tests and measurements that require a minimum level of understanding for the circuit under test. They often include advanced techniques, such as signature analysis, to make it easier to identify the problem. In

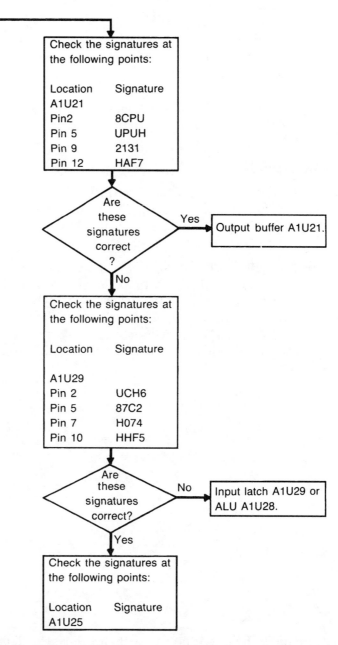

■ 1-37 *Typical troubleshooting tree used in equipment incorporating signature analysis.* Hewlett-Packard

troubleshooting a microprocessor-based device, you can use even the poorer troubleshooting trees to localize a failure area in the system and save considerable time and effort.

For more experienced troubleshooters, working from product block diagrams can give you the right amount of information to understand how the different parts of the circuit work together. A system's theory of operation and its troubleshooting trees do not relate as closely to the hardware. The schematics often provide too much detailed information, making it difficult to see the total microprocessor system picture.

Toggle flip-flop

The toggle or "T" flip-flop is one in which the output state changes each time a single pulse (clock, trigger, toggle, strobe or flip-flop, etc.) is applied. The basic toggle flip-flop is shown in Fig. 1-38 and its logic symbol is shown in Fig. 1-39.

The basic toggle flip-flop of Fig. 1-38 is very similar to a clocked JK. The J and K inputs are both continuous high level and the clock input could be a strobe, enable, etc. When connected in this manner, the Q and $\overline{Q}$ outputs change with each clock (or other similar) input. The circuits in this flip-flop are usually contained in one chip and the layout is normally simplified to the logic symbol shown in Fig. 1-39.

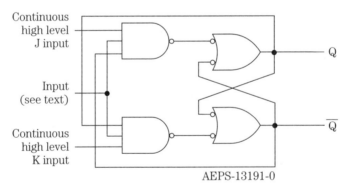

AEPS-13191-0

■ **1-38** *Basic toggle flip-flop*

Type D flip-flop

The D flip-flop will propagate the same data bit information that is, at its D (data) input, prior to the clock pulse, to the Q output on the leading edge of the clock or strobe pulse. If the data input in 1 (high-level), the Q output becomes 1 on the leading edge of the next clock or strobe. If the data input is 0 (low-level) the Q output becomes 0 on the leading edge of the next clock or strobe. The basic D flip-flop is shown in Fig. 1-40.

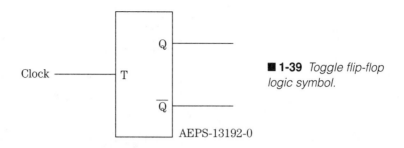

■ **1-39** *Toggle flip-flop logic symbol.*

AEPS-13192-0

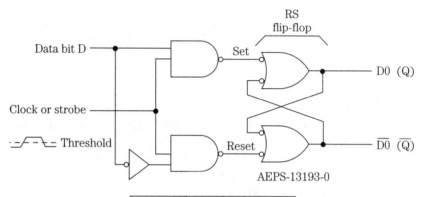

AEPS-13193-0

| Data bit | After clock pulse | |
input	Q output	Q̄ output
H	H	L
L	L	H

■ **1-40** *Basic D flip-flop.*

The basic D flip-flop of Fig. 1-40 shows that if the data bit is high (1), the DO output becomes high (1) during the leading edge of the clock or strobe. Once the clock rises to the flat portion of the pulse, data is loaded; however, if new data is applied, the new data cannot be loaded until the leading edge of the next clock pulse. The D flip-flop has the advantage that the trailing edge of one clock pulse can apply the data (from another circuit) and the leading edge of the next clock pulse can load the data. When the data bit is high, the high going clock (or strobe) causes a low input to the set side of the RS flip-flop (a complementary input is applied to the reset side). This low causes a high DO which, when fed back together with the high reset, causes the Q̄ side to produce a low DO. If the data bit is low, the inverter insures that the circuit action produces a high DO and low DO.

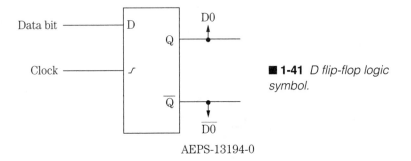

Data bit —— D

Q

Clock —— ⌐⌐

Q̄

DO

D̄O

AEPS-13194-0

■ **1-41** *D flip-flop logic symbol.*

Again, the circuit in this flip-flop are normally contained in one IC and the layout is normally simplified to the logic symbol shown in Fig. 1-41.

Latch flip-flop

The latch flip-flop is a single level output flip-flop that is used as a temporary memory or storage device. Typical examples are shown in Fig. 1-42.

Monostable multivibrator

30

A monostable multivibrator is a circuit having only one stable state. It can be triggered to change the state, but once triggered it remains in the triggered state for a time period that is dependent upon its own RC timing circuits. Monostables are used to convert short duration triggers into pulses of specific duration. With the proper input circuits it can use one edge of a long duration pulse to generate a pulse of specific duration. This circuit is also called single-shot, one-shot, or start-stop. Figure 1-43 shows the basic monostable circuit using two different IC gates.

The monostable shown in Fig. 1-43 is used to produce a short duration pulse as soon as activity is detected. The short duration, high-level pulse which is generated by differentiating the activity pulse is applied to U9D-9 and produces a high-level pulse at U8D-14.

This pulse is coupled back, through the timing RC network, as a re-generative feedback which lasts for 0.5 milliseconds. The resulting 0.5 millisecond pulse is applied to the Cd side of various counter flip-flops to clear them to a particular state at the very beginning of a decoding cycle.

In many instances the monostable circuits are contained in one IC. In this case, the symbol is normally simplified to that shown in Fig. 1-44.

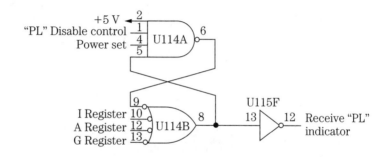

A

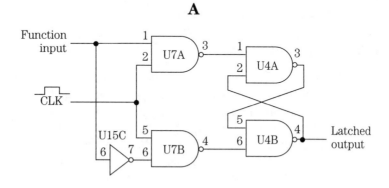

B

Function input	CLK	U7A-3	U7B-4	U4A-3	U4B-4
Don't care*	0	1	1	0	1
1	1	0	1	1	0
0	1	1	0	0	1
1	1	0	1	1	0

* Initial state latched output is 1.

AEPS-13195-0

■ **1-42** *Typical latch flip-flop*

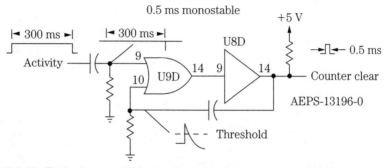

■ **1-43** *Typical monostable circuit.*

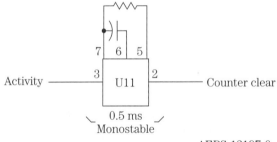

Activity — U11 — Counter clear

0.5 ms
Monostable

AEPS-13197-0

■ **1-44** *Monostable logic symbol.*

Astable multivibrator

An astable multivibrator is a free-running circuit that generates pulses which can be used as the synchronizing clock or other type of timing signal. This circuit normally consists of two or more inverters with a feedback RC network to determine the operating frequency. Figure 1-45 shows the slow scan astable used in the "Pulsar" VHF Mobile Radio-telephone to provide the channel search clock (when searching for an idle channel).

The astable shown in Fig. 1-45 uses the 120 UF feedback capacitor and the 1.8K resistor to determine the channel search clock frequency. After the radio set is locked-on the new channel, the astable is disabled by grounding the enable line and the clock output line remains at a steady high-level.

Slow scan astable

+5 V   +5 V   +5 V

1.8K   1.8K   1K

120

13 U4F 12   9 U4D 8   11 U4E 10

Channel
search
clock

Enable

AEPS-13198-0

■ **1-45** *Typical astable multivibrator (frequency 12 Hz).*

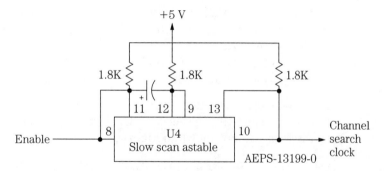

■ **1-46** *Typical astable logic symbol.*

In some instances the astable circuits are contained in one IC chip. In this case, the layout is usually simplified to the logic symbol shown in Fig. 1-46.

Schmitt trigger

The Schmitt trigger is a fast acting, two-stage pulse generator. It produces a constant amplitude pulse for as long as the input exceeds a threshold dc value. The pulse rise and fall time is extremely fast due to the regenerative feedback characteristics of the device. The Schmitt trigger can be used as a pulse shaper, threshold detector, activity checker, etc.

Shown in Fig. 1-47 is a typical Schmitt trigger built from gates contained in two different ICs.

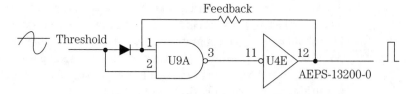

■ **1-47** *Typical Schmitt trigger circuit.*

In the circuit of Fig. 1-47, a high-level signal is applied to U9A-2; however, U9A-1 cannot become high until the diode is forward biased. The diode becomes forward biased when the threshold level is reached and at this time a low-level signal appears at U9A-3. This low level signal is inverted in U4E to produce a high-level output. Feedback is provided to produce a snap-action and provide a fast rise leading edge. Once the input falls below threshold, the diode cuts off to produce the trailing edge of the pulse. Again, feedback causes a rapid decay in the trailing edge. The circuit of Fig. 1-47 converts an accurate-frequency AC sinewave into an accurate-frequency pulse which can be used as a timing clock.

As in some other circuits, the Schmitt trigger circuit might be contained in a single IC. In this case, the layout is normally simplified to the logic symbol shown in Fig. 1-48.

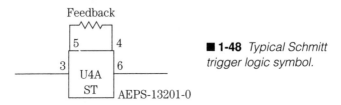

■ **1-48** *Typical Schmitt trigger logic symbol.*

Exclusive OR gate

The exclusive OR gate is a circuit that is used to compare two different inputs and provide an output that is determined by the relation of the two inputs. This circuit produces a low-level output whenever both inputs are identical; however, it will produce a high-level output if both inputs are not identical. The exclusive OR gate can be used in such applications as: comparator circuit; error checker; buffers; and parity generators.

Figure 1-49 shows a typical exclusive OR gate circuit built using gates and inverters from three different ICs.

In the circuit shown in Fig. 1-49, received data is being compared to data stored in the identity (ID) storage register. In this instance a low level ERROR signal is present as long as both data inputs are identical (received data matches stored data). For example, when both data bits are identical neither of the two AND gates are satisfied and both AND gates produce low-level signals to the OR gate; resulting in a low-level ERROR output (low output equals no error when applied to another logic circuit). However, if received data is 1 (high-level) and ID data is 0 (indicating a mismatch), then AND gate U6A is satisfied and produces a high-level at pin U6A-3; resulting in a high-level ERROR output (high output equals error when applied to another logic circuit). Conversely, if received data is 0 (low-level) and ID data is 1 (indicating a mismatch), then AND gate U6B produces a high-level at pin 6; resulting in a high-level ERROR output.

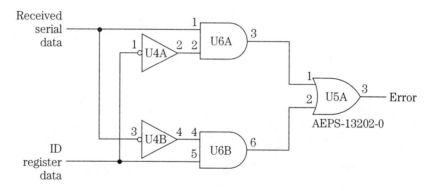

Received serial data	ID reg. data	Error output
0	0	0
1	0	1
0	1	1
1	1	0

■ **1-49** *Exclusive OR using AND/OR/INV.*

Received serial data ─── 1
ID register data ─── 2)) U24A 3 ─── Error

AEPS-13203-0

■ **1-50** *Typical exclusive OR logic symbol.*

As in other logic circuits, the exclusive OR circuit might be fully contained in a single IC. In this case, the layout is normally simplified to the logic symbol shown in Fig. 1-50.

Most times, the IC package contains more than one exclusive OR and the logic designer might not use the whole chip as exclusive ORs. In some of these cases the designer will use the remaining exclusive OR circuits for functions which include inverters and buffers. Figure 1-51 shows how these circuits might appear. Note that the inverter is pulled-up (connected to high-level), whereas, the buffer is tied-down (connected to low-level).

In the inverter circuit, whenever the two inputs are identical (pin 5 input is 1) the output at pin 6 is low-level (input is inverted). However, in the buffer circuit, whenever the two inputs are identical (pin 8 input is 0) the output at pin 10 is low-level (input is not inverted).

Inverter   Buffer

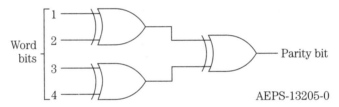

■ **1-51** *Exclusive OR used as inverter and buffer.*

In parity generators it is necessary to generate an extra bit (parity bit) which is included in the binary word. There are basically two types of parity; odd and even. If odd parity is used the parity bit is 0 if an odd number of 1's exist in the binary word. The parity generator shown in Fig. 1-52 is an even parity bit generator for a 4-bit word.

The parity generator shown in Fig. 1-52 produces a logical 1 (high-level) any time the data word contains an odd number.

■ **1-52** *4-bit-word even parity generator*

Exclusive NOR gate

The exclusive NOR gate functions similar to the exclusive OR gate except that the output is inverted. It is shown logically in Fig. 1-53. If exclusive NOR gates were used in the parity generator shown in Fig. 1-52, it would become a 4-bit word odd parity generator. Also, if exclusive NOR gates were used in Fig. 1-51 the functions would be reversed.

Counter (dividers)

A counter is a device that is capable of changing state in a specific sequence upon application of appropriate signals. Normally a counter will provide an output pulse (or combination of pulses) after receiving a specific number of input pulses.

■ **1-53** *Exclusive NOR gate logic symbol.*

AEPS-13206-0

There are four basic counters. These include ripple, synchronous, shift, and programmable.

Generally, a counter consists of flip-flops which are connected in series to produce a desired count-down or division of the inputs. From the operation of flip-flops we found that each requires two input signals to produce a complete cycle in the output. This is graphically shown in Fig. 1-54.

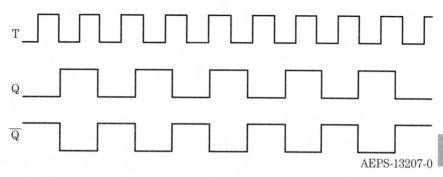

AEPS-13207-0

■ **1-54** *Toggle flip-flop waveforms.*

Shift counters

The shift counter is a clocked counter where the flip-flop only changes state once for each cycle. Figure 1-55 shows a three-stage shift counter together with timing waveforms. This type of circuit provides easily decoded outputs and does not require gating between the clocked flip-flops.

As shown in Fig. 1-55, the reset input clears the counter to where all Q outputs are low (Q are high). This means that a high is applied to the J input of the first flip-flop; therefore, Q1 goes high on the next clock. Q1 remains high until Q3 becomes high to produce a high at the input K of the first flip-flop. The first flip-flop then changes state on the next clock. The process then continues as shown in the timing diagram. The main advantage of this counter is that the output gating circuits require only two inputs. Only six two-input AND gates are required to provide the six different conditions. A three-stage synchronous counter would require six three-input AND gates to provide the six different conditions.

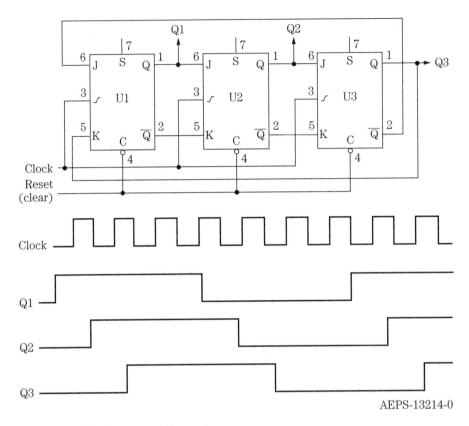

■ **1-55** *Synchronous shift counter.*

A programmable counter is one in which the divide-by ratio is selectable. To select a ratio, it is necessary to program a binary number into the counter which leaves only the desired divide-by ratio as a reminder. For example, if the counter must divide-by-145, start with a divide-by-256 counter. (Always select a counter that is a higher divide-by than actual division required; in this case 145 is between 128 and 256.) Then convert 145 to its binary equivalent which is 10010001 (LSB to the right). Complement this binary number to get 01101110 (LSB still to the right) and load the complement (decimal 110) into the counter programming inputs. The counter now requires 145 clock inputs to return the count to zero. This is equivalent to a divide-by-145. Figure 1-56 illustrates a programmable counter set-up in this way.

Note that when the entire counter produces all 1's in the output, full count gate U14 sets the reference flip-flop to clear the programmable counter back to the programmed count of 110. The counting process will start over once more.

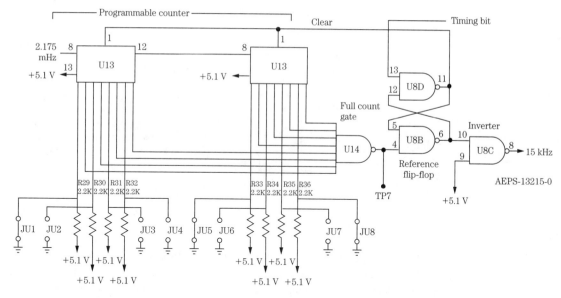

■ **1-56** *Divide-by-145 programmable counter.*

Register

A register is a device used to store a certain number of bits (usually a complete binary word). Two types of registers will be reviewed. These are shift and storage. In a shift register, data bits are moved either from left to right or right to left by synchronizing clock pulses. At the end of a timing cycle information with in the shift register can be "read-out" either by indicators or gates. A storage register can be used to store a data word (such as an address, ID number, etc.) which can then be used for a comparison check of the incoming data.

Shift register

One of the primary functions of a shift register is to convert serial data into parallel form or to convert parallel data into serial form. Figure 1-57 shows a basic shift register that is used to accept 4-bit serial words and then convert the word into parallel form.

Referring to Fig. 1-57, note that serial data is applied to the first stage of the register and is clocked into the register. Assume that the register is initially cleared, than all of the data lines (D0, D1, etc.) are 0. Also, now assume that the input is a BCD (Binary Coded Decimal) number representing the decimal number 5 (0101). In this case the LSB (a 1) is loaded into the first stage of the register

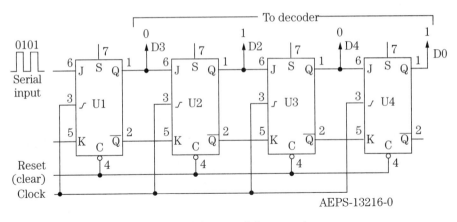

■ 1-57 *Basic shift register; serial-to-parallel conversion.*

by the first clock. The second clock then shifts the 1 to the second stage and loads a 0 into the first stage. After four clocks, the BCD 5 is loaded into the register and applied in parallel to the decoder. Upon receipt of a signal (Strobe, enable, etc.) the decoder decodes the BCD and then generates a reset to the shift register, clearing it for the next word.

Storage registers

Storage registers can be placed in two general categories; temporary and permanent. For example, if we wish to store binary information (word) while performing other logic functions then a temporary (or buffer) register can be used. However, if we wish to hold a specific binary number permanently, such as in an address register, then the permanent register would be used.

Three-state devices

A three-state IC device is one in which two of the states are conventional binary (1-0) states, and the third state is a high impedance state. These devices can operate logically in the same manner as other ICs, with one advantage; when not performing a function, the device output represents a high impedance to their respective output lines. This feature not only reduces power drain but it also allows access to the common bus lines by other devices. This device is extremely important with the advent of the low-powered mobile and portable microprocessor-type circuits. Because multiple circuits (MPUs, ROMs, RAMs, PIAs, flip-flops, buffers, multiplexers, demultiplexers, etc.) are continuously connected to the data bus or logic lines, it is important that all devices not actually performing a function be effectively disconnected from the data line. Each three-state device provides high output impedance to the data bus or logic lines at all times except when performing its function. The diagram in Fig. 1-58 shows one-half of an inverting octal line driver in which the three-state control is applied to E2. Note that E1 controls the other half.

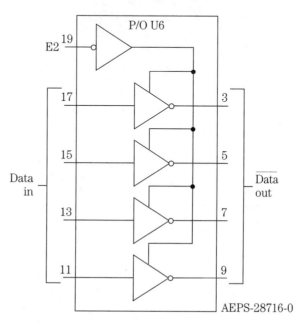

■ **1-58** *Three-state inverting line driver.*

Microprocessors

The chip pin-out in Fig. 1-59 is for a Motorola MC-6800 Family 48-bit Microprocessor Unit (MPU). This device contains 40 pins and is shown in the normal "data-book" configuration. When used on logic diagrams, the pin number sequence will vary to conform with the normal signal flow. For example, the address lines (A0–A15) might all appear on the right side and the data lines (D0–D7) might appear on the left side. In other logic diagrams, the rectangle might be horizontal instead of vertical with the output lines extending from the top or the bottom. In any case, to make the microprocessor easier to locate on the diagram, the rectangle outline will be heavier than the other integrated circuits.

Although the signal names may vary between different micro-processors, the functions will remain basically the same.

```
 1  | V_SS          Reset | 40
 2  | Halt            TSC | 39
 3  | 01            N.C.  | 38
 4  | IRQ             02  | 37
 5  | VMA            DBE  | 36
 6  | NMI           N.C.  | 35
 7  | BA            R/W   | 34
 8  | V_CC           D0   | 33
 9  | A0             D1   | 32
10  | A1     U8      D2   | 31
11  | A2     MPU     D3   | 30
12  | A3             D4   | 29
13  | A4             D5   | 28
14  | A5             D6   | 27
15  | A6             D7   | 26
16  | A7            A15   | 25
17  | A8            A14   | 24
18  | A9            A13   | 23
19  | A10           A12   | 22
20  | A11          V_SS   | 21
```

AEPS-28717-0

■ **1-59** *MC6800 series 8-bit microprocessor unit.*

Troubleshooting logic circuits

2

THIS CHAPTER REVIEWS THE DIGITAL SIGNAL AND ITS VARious states, shows and explains pulse signals, covers the operation of logic probe testers for checking out microprocessors and their associated logic circuits, and describes how to use the pulse generator probe to "jog" a pulse through various gates for "freeze time" digital logic circuit analysis. This includes pulse-"memory" and pulse-"stretcher" techniques.

Various clip-on logic monitor testers are discussed, to help you sharpen your microprocessor and digital logic circuit troubleshooting techniques and cut down on diagnosis time.

43

Digital circuits & signals

Modern digital ICs perform more complex functions than discrete circuitry can. Instead of observing simple characteristics, you must observe complex digital signals and decide if these signals are correct.

To solve these problems and to make digital circuit troubleshooting more efficient, you must take advantage of the digital nature of the signals involved. Tests and techniques designed to troubleshoot analog circuits do not take advantage of the digital signal and therefore are less effective when used to troubleshoot digital circuits.

TTL logic signal

Referring to the waveform in Fig. 2-1, you will find a typical TTL pulse signal. The scope displays these digital pulses of absolute voltage with respect to time. For digital pulses, however, absolute values are not important. A digital signal exists in three states—high, low, and an undefined or in-between level—each determined

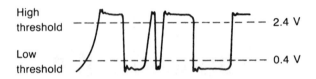

■ 2-1 *A typical TTL digital pulse.*

by a threshold voltage. It is the relative value of the signal voltage with respect to these thresholds that determines the state of the digital signal. And this digital state, not absolute levels, determines IC gate operation. Note that in Fig. 2-2 if the signal is more than 2.4 V, it is a high state. For a low state, the voltage must be below 0.8 V. It is not important what the absolute level is as long as it is below this threshold. Thus, when using the scope, you must always determine if the signal meets the threshold requirement for the desired digital state.

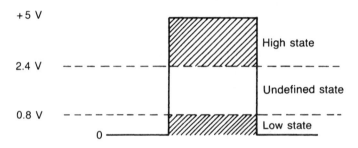

■ 2-2 *TTL logic levels diagram of a pulse.*

Each gate in a TTL logic family has a certain propagation delay time, rise time, and fall time. The effects of these timing circuit operations are considered by the design engineer. Timing parameters rarely degrade or become marginal, so scope checks of these timing parameters will contribute very little to the overall troubleshooting process.

The circuit in Fig. 2-3 illustrates a problem created by the TTL logic family and is often referred to as a totem pole device. In either the high state or the low state, it has a low impedance. In the low state, it appears as about 5 or 10 Ω to ground. This presents a problem for in-circuit stimulation. A device that injects a pulse at a node driven by a TTL output must have sufficient power to override the low-impedance output state. Many pulsers used for troubleshooting do not have this capability, and you either have to cut the printed circuit runs or pull IC leads to pulse the circuit under

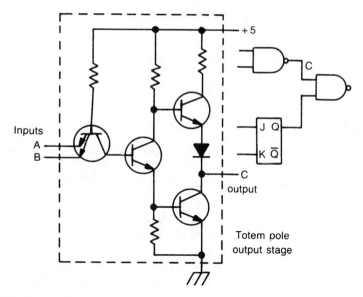

2-3 *To jog this gate, you must override the low-impedance totem pole output stage.*

test. These techniques are time-consuming and can damage other circuit components.

A scope and traditional signal sources are inefficient for this reason. Because modern electronic circuits are so complex, it makes good economic sense to find the most efficient solution to this problem. Therefore, you should use test instruments that take advantage of the digital nature of these signals when checking digital logic circuitry.

Normal IC failures

To troubleshoot ICs, you need to know what normal types of faults are found in these digital circuits. They can be put into two main classes: those caused by internal IC faults, and those caused by a circuit failure external to the IC chip.

The following failures can occur internally to an IC:

☐ An open bond on an input lead or an output lead
☐ A short between an input or output and V_{CC} or ground
☐ A short between two pins
☐ A failure in the internal circuitry (often called the steering circuitry) of the IC

The following failures can occur externally to an IC:

☐ A short between a node and V_{CC} or ground
☐ A short between two nodes
☐ An open signal path
☐ A failure of an analog component

Internal failures

For an open bond on the output (see Fig. 2-4), the inputs driven by that output are left to float. In TTL and DTL circuits, a floating input rises to about 1.4 to 1.5 V and usually has the same effect on circuit operation as a high logic level. Thus, an open output bond will cause all inputs driven by that output to float to a bad level, because 1.5 V is less than the high threshold level of 2.0 V and greater than the low threshold level of 0.4 V. In TTL and DTL, a floating input is seen as a high level. The effect will be that these inputs will respond to this level as though it were a static high signal.

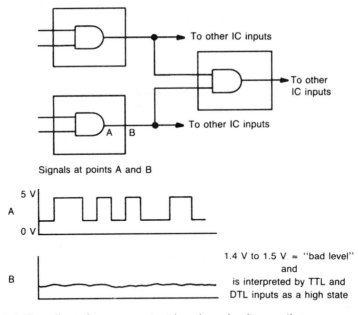

■ 2-4 *The effect of an open output bond on circuit operation.*

With an open input bond (see Fig. 2-5), the open circuit blocks the signal that drives the input from entering the IC chip. The input of the chip is thus allowed to float and will respond as though it were a static high signal. Note that because the open occurs on the input inside the IC, the digital signal driving this input will be unaf-

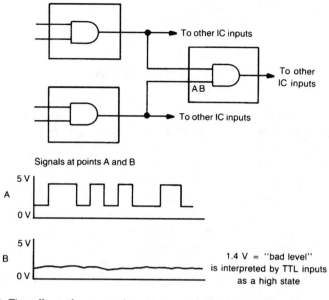

Signals at points A and B

1.4 V = "bad level" is interpreted by TTL inputs as a high state

■ **2-5** *The effect of an open input bond on circuit operation.*

fected by the open and will be detectable when looking at the input pin, such as at point A shown in Fig. 2-6. The effect will be to block this signal inside the IC, and the resulting IC operation will be as though the input were a static high.

47

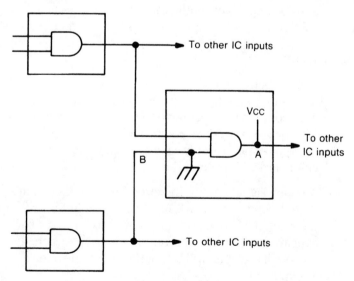

■ **2-6** *Short between input or output and V_{cc} or ground.*

A short between an input or output and V_{CC} or ground holds all signal lines connected to that input or output either high (in the case of a short to V_{CC}) or low (if shorted to ground), as illustrated in Fig. 2-7. In many cases, this will cause expected signal activity to disappear at points beyond the short, which is catastrophic in terms of circuit operation.

A short between two pins is not as easy to analyze as a short to V_{CC} or ground. When two pins are shorted, the outputs driving those pins oppose each other: one tries to pull the pins high while the other tries to pull them low, as shown in Fig. 2-8. In this situation, the output that is attempting to go high will feed through the upper saturated transistor of its totem pole output stage, and the output trying to go low will sink this current through the saturated lower transistor of its totem pole output stage. The net effect is that the short will be pulled to a low state by the saturated transistor to ground. Whenever both outputs attempt to go high or low simultaneously, the shorted pins will respond properly. Whenever one output attempts to go low, though, the short will be constrained to be low.

The fourth possible internal failure of an IC is in the steering circuitry within the IC (see Fig. 2-8). This always causes the upper transistor of the output totem pole to turn on—locking the output in the high state—or the lower transistor of the totem pole to turn on—locking the output in the low state. This failure blocks the signal flow and has a catastrophic effect upon circuit operation.

External failures

A short between a node and V_{CC} or ground external to the IC or a short internal to the IC will appear the same. Both make the signal lines connected to the node to be either always high (for shorts to V_{CC}) or always low (for shorts to ground). When you encounter this type of failure, only a very close eyeball examination of the circuit board will reveal if the short is external to the chip package.

An open signal path in the circuit has an effect similar to an open output bond driving the node, as shown in Fig. 2-9. All outputs to the right of the open will be allowed to float to a bad level and will appear as a static high level in circuit operation. Those inputs to the left of the open will be unaffected by the open and will respond as expected.

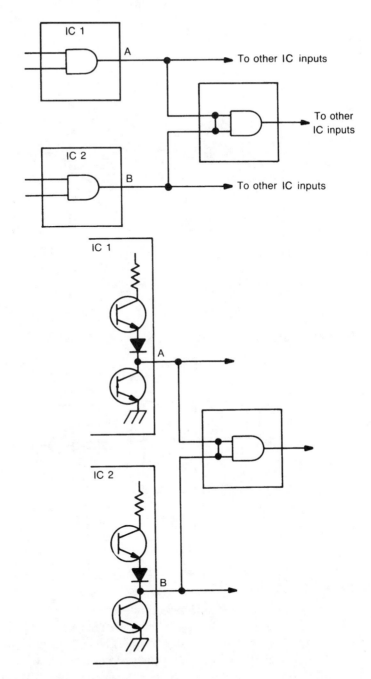

49

■ 2-7 *Effect of a short between two pins of an IC.*

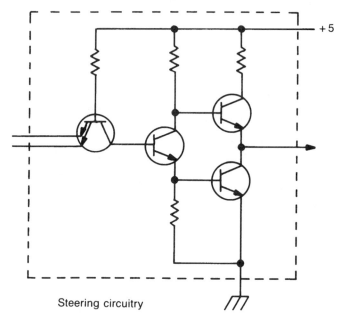

Steering circuitry

■ 2-8 *Failure of an internal steering circuit within an IC chip.*

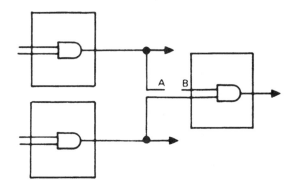

■ 2-9 *Effect of an open circuit external to an IC chip.*

The B & K logic probe

The model DP-50 B & K logic probe is designed for fast analysis of digital circuits and is compatible with TTL, DTL, RTL, CMOS, MOS, and other solid-state circuitry. Three LED indicators at the probe tip display pulse presence, high logic state (1), and low logic state (0). An incorrect logic level or an open pin is indicated by the absence of a lighted LED. Two switches allow you to select TTL or CMOS logic thresholds and pulse-stretch mode or memory modes. In the pulse-stretch mode, short-duration pulses are stretched for a clear visual

■ **2-10** *B & K DP-50 logic test probe.*

indication. In the memory mode, a single digital pulse causes an LED to remain lighted until reset. This permits you to freeze the display of digital action. The B & K logic probe is shown in Fig. 2-10.

Threshold level modes

Set the threshold switch to the TTL position to select the correct threshold level for TTL, DTL, and so on. Use the CMOS position for MOS and CMOS digital circuits.

Mode selection

The mode switch provides pulse detection to either pulse stretch (pulse position) or memory (MEM position) modes. In the pulse-stretch mode, the pulse indicator lights a minimum of 200 milliseconds (ms) in response to each single pulse of 20 ns or greater in duration. If the input pulse is short, it is stretched to 200 ms to ensure a high-visibility flash on the LED.

In the memory mode, the pulse indicator remains lighted after the first pulse or logic transition until you reset it by moving the mode switch to the pulse position. To use the memory mode, set the mode switch to the pulse position and then connect the probe tip to the point being checked. The initial contact will make the pulse indicator flash. After the initial flash, move the mode switch to the MEM position. The probe is now ready to operate in the memory mode.

Using the logic probe

The 1 (high) indicator will remain lighted only during the time period when logic level 1 is present at the probe tip. The 0 (low) indicator will remain lighted only during the time period when the logic level 0 is present at the probe tip. The pulse indicator will light as the result of a transition in logic levels. Thus, typical operating modes may be encountered as follows:

☐ With the probe tip touching symmetrical pulses, the 0 and 1 indicators will both be lighted at half brilliance, and the pulse indicator will be lighted at full brilliance.

☐ With the probe tip touching a positive-going, high-speed pulse of a short duty cycle, the 0 and pulse indicators will be lighted, and the 1 indicator will be partially lighted on duty cycles greater than 10 percent.

☐ With the probe tip touching negative-going, high-speed pulses of a short duty cycle, the 1 and pulse indicators will be lighted. The 0 indicator will be partially lighted on duty cycles that are greater than 10 percent.

☐ When only the pulse indicator is lighted, system noise or pulses above 50 megacycles (MHz) are indicated.

☐ With the probe touching an open pin or an incorrect logic level (a voltage within the dead band), the pulse indicator will then light.

Logic probes & logic monitors

With the increasing appearance of digital circuitry in today's electronics, it has become increasingly important that it be designed, serviced, and maintained in as fast and cost-effective a manner as possible. This section examines logic probes and monitors. The information given is provided courtesy of Global Specialties Corporation, one of the leading suppliers of IC troubleshooting tools.

How logic probes operate

Logic probes are portable, circuit-powered digital tools for diagnosing state-oriented logic. They compare the voltages of the pin, pad, path, or node at the probe tip to reference thresholds for the user-selected logic family, and light a high or a low LED, as appropriate. Certain voltage levels represent invalid logic states, and these light neither LED. Transitions between states, whether positive-going or negative-going, are stretched into visible blinks of a pulse LED.

The relative brightness of the high and low LEDs is an approximate indicator of duty cycle when a logic probe senses a pulse train. Also, the polarity of a narrow pulse can be judged by whether the high or low LED is lit while the pulse LED is flashing.

Because they rapidly diagnose logic states and sense and, optionally, store pulses, logic probes have become almost universally accepted as an effective diagnostic tool for all but the most complex digital service and troubleshooting problems. Logic probes offer speeds and storage capabilities equalled only by the very fastest oscilloscopes.

Logic probes can be used for digital troubleshooting tasks in much the same way as signal tracers are used in conventional analog amplifier circuits. This same technique may be used with a digital pulser, which is used in much the same way as a signal injector. Together, these two testers permit methodical stimulus-response evaluation of specific sections of a circuit. Because entire logic trees can be followed and predicted results compared with observations, you can quickly isolate and repair faults. Figure 2-11 illustrates the various logic probe LED response indications to pulse states and transitions.

The same simple process can be used for prototype and development circuits to correct problems or to identify actual circuit performance in circumstances that are not easily predictable. Logic probes also permit quick verification of circuit performance, which makes them well suited to inspection, testing, and quality control applications with production environments.

Checking out the chips

Integrated circuits are very private solid-state devices. When something goes wrong, they don't cough, turn red, or make a funny noise. They just don't work right. It's bad enough working on one IC when part or all of that IC goes bad. But, in most cases,

Interpreting the LEDs

LED states High	Low	Pulse	Input signal	
○	●	○	○———————	Logic "0" no pulse activity
●	○	○	○══════════	Logic "1" no pulse activity
○	○	○	———————	All LEDs off 1. Test point is in an open circuit. 2. Out-of-tolerance signal. 3. Probe not connected to power. 4. Node or circuit not powered.
●	●	*		The shared brightness of the high and low LEDs indicates a 50% duty cycle at the test point (1.5 MHz).
○	○	*		High-frequency square wave (1.5 MHz) at test node. As the high-frequency signals duty cycle shifts from a square wave to either a high or low duty cycle pulse train; either the low or high LED will become activated.
○	●	*		Logic "0" pulse activity present. Positive-going pulses because high LED not "on"; pulse train duty cycle is low re <15%. If the duty cycle were increased above 15%, high LED would start to turn on.
●	○	*		Logic "1" pulse activity present. Negative-going pulses because low LED not "on"; pulse train duty cycle is high re >85%. If the duty cycle were reduced to <85%, LED would start to turn on.

● LED on
○ LED off
* * Blinking LED

■ **2-11** *Logic test probe LED readouts.*

when an IC goes bad, a large, complex system will not operate the way it is supposed to.

Until the logic probe was developed, it was not easy to determine just what was happening at one point in a logic system. You could use a voltmeter (DMM) and translate these readings into logic states in your head, but it is a slow process.

Oscilloscopes are another way of trying to look inside the IC chips. Indeed, for certain complex timing measurements, they have no equal. However, scopes are large and expensive. And it can take a very long time to set up an oscilloscope to measure exactly the phenomenon you are looking for.

Combining logic monitors, whether clip-on or bench-top, with a digital pulser greatly simplifies the testing of sequential circuits. Entire ICs or logic trees can be simultaneously monitored while the circuit is operating. All output and input states are conveniently visible for immediate detection of proper operation.

The LP-3 logic probe

The LP-3 multifamily Global logic probe detects, memorizes, and displays logic levels, pulses, and voltage transients in mixed and single logic family systems. It detects out-of-tolerance logic signals, open-circuit nodes, and transient events down to 10 ns while providing the user with an instant, easily interpreted high-intensity LED readout. The Global LP-3 logic probe is shown in Fig. 2-12.

55

■ **2-12** *A global LP-3 logic test probe.*
Global Specialties Corp

Operating instructions

Connect the probe clip leads to the power supply of the circuit to be tested. Set the logic family switch to DTL/TTL or CMOS/HTL and the memory/pulse switch to the pulse position. Now, just touch the probe tip to the circuit node to be analyzed. The three display LEDs on the probe body will instantly provide a reading of the signal activity at the node.

When catching pulses faster than 10 ns, use the ground lead. The memory mode of the LP-3 is used to detect, store, and display low-repetition (rep)-rate or single-shot pulses as well as transient events even when you can't see them occur.

Memory/Pulse switch-memory position

The LP-3 probe contains a pulse-memory flip-flop that catches and holds (memorizes) level transitions or pulses as narrow as 10 ns. The memory is activated by either positive- or negative-level transitions.

To set the probe for catching and memorizing an event, touch the probe tip to the node under test and move the memory/pulse switch to the memory position. The next event that occurs at the node will activate the pulse LED and latch it on. To reset and rearm the memory, move the memory/pulse switch to the pulse position and then return it to the memory position.

Note: When arming the memory, the probe tip must be in contact with the node under test. If you arm the memory with the tip floating (unconnected), the memory will be activated when the tip is brought in contact with the test point and give a false readout.

Catching fast pulses

The LP-3 probe contains a unique and highly sensitive pulse-detecting system capable of catching pulses faster than 10 ns. This ensures the capture of glitches and spikes for all logic families of TTL, DTL, HTL (high-threshold logic) and CMOS.

The pulse-detector circuit consists of a level-sensitive broadband amplifier coupled to a high-speed, pulse-stretching, monostable multivibrator. This circuit is capable of firing on both positive and negative transitions. The pulse stretcher enables a 100-ms oscillator and LED driver circuit that produces a visual indication of a pulse catch. The oscillator can also be switched into a bistable mode in order to catch a pulse for "memory."

This technology allows you to catch and display hidden spikes and glitches that most scopes and logic probes will not indicate. When catching these fast pulses, you must use basic rf techniques.

Ground lead caution

The ground lines must be kept as short as possible. Connect the ground lead of the LP-3 probe as close as possible to the test point. For an IC, clip the ground lead directly to the ground pin of the chip. The ground lead can supply the signal return and negative power-line path for the probe and will help prevent ground loops. Figure 2-13 is a chart for interpreting the LEDs readouts.

The LP-4 logic probe

Checking emitter-coupled logic (ECL) chips

Emitter-coupled logic (ECL) IC chips have long been used in mainframe computers, where the fastest possible switching rates translate almost directly into system performance. More recently, ECL usage has expanded into a broader range of consumer and test equipment applications.

The Global model LP-4 is a full-featured ECL logic probe capable of handling the high speeds and narrow threshold differentials of circuits. Figure 2-14 shows the LP-4.

The LP-4 detects the indicates valid ECL logic levels, using LED indicators for high (logic 1) and low (logic 0) levels (positive true logic levels). A third LED, labeled "pulse," indicates single-shot or multiple pulses. It is capable of detecting a single-shot occurrence down to 3 ns in duration and pulse trains with repetition rates up to 100 MHz minimum (150 MHz is typical at 50 percent duty cycle). With the pulse LED flashing (pulse train), the high or low LEDs will indicate a positive or negative pulse polarity or duty cycle by their relative brightness. For these indications, refer to the chart in Fig. 2-15.

Valid ECL logic levels & waveforms

The LP-4 includes a two-position slide switch for the selection of pulse or memory (latch) modes. In the pulse position, the pulse LED will flash a single 0.3-s (stretched) pulse indication for a single pulse occurrence. With the presence of a pulse train, it will flash continuously at approximately a 3-Hz rate. With the switch in the memory position, a single-shot pulse will be stored and the

Interpreting the LEDs

LED states High Low Pulse	Input Signal	
○ ● ○	○———	Logic "0" no pulse activity
● ○ ○	○═══	Logic "1" no pulse activity
○ ○ ○	———	All LEDs off 1. Test point is in an open circuit. 2. Out-of-tolerance signal. 3. Probe not connected to power. 4. Node or circuit not powered.
● ● *	○⊓⊓⊓	The shared brightness of the high and low LEDs indicates a 50% duty cycle at the test point (1.5 MHz).
○ ○ *	○⊓⊓⊓⊓⊓	High-frequency square wave (1.5 MHz) at test node. As the high-frequency signals duty cycle shifts from a square wave to either a high or low duty cycle pulse train; either the low or high LED will become activated.
○ ● *	○⊓⊓⊓	Logic "0" pulse activity present. Positive-going pulses because high LED not "on"; pulse train duty cycle is low re <15%. If the duty cycle were increased above 15%, high LED would start to turn on.
● ○ *	○⊔⊔⊔	Logic "1" pulse activity present. Negative-going pulses, because low LED not "on"; pulse train duty cycle is high re >85%. If the duty cycle were reduced to <85%, then it would be low.

● LED on
○ LED off
* * Blinking LED

■ **2-13** *Interpreting the LED readouts.*

pulse LED will remain on until it is reset by toggling the switch. This feature is useful for detecting spurious glitches or transients.

This probe will also detect valid, static ECL, logic levels. A logic 1 = −0.810 to −1.100 Vdc; logic 0 = −1.50 to −1.850 Vdc. It will also

■ **2-14** *The ECL LP-4 probe.* Global Specialties Corp

detect the absence of pulses and a particular logic state (all LEDs off)—for example, when the input of an ECL line receiver is biased to V_{BB} (–1.30 V) with no input signal. With the probe input floating, all LED indicators will be off, because the probe input is biased at V_{BB} (–1.30 ± 0.05 Vdc), the nominal ECL reference level. The chart in Fig. 2-15 shows the various static and dynamic conditions displayed by the LED indicators.

Other features of the LP-4 logic probe include an input impedance greater than 10 kΩ to avoid circuit loading, input overload protection of ±100 Vdc continuous, ±220 Vdc transients, and 120 Vac for 30 s (to 1 kHz). Power requirements are –5.2 Vdc at 100 mA with supply overload protection of –12 to +200 Vdc.

Functional description

Briefly, the LP-4 probe is basically composed of eight functional blocks, as shown in Fig. 2-16: the input protection circuitry, input buffer, high-speed logic 1 and 0 detectors, valid pulse selector, trigger and latch circuitry, 3-Hz (0.3 s) astable, ± voltage reference, and power-supply protection circuit.

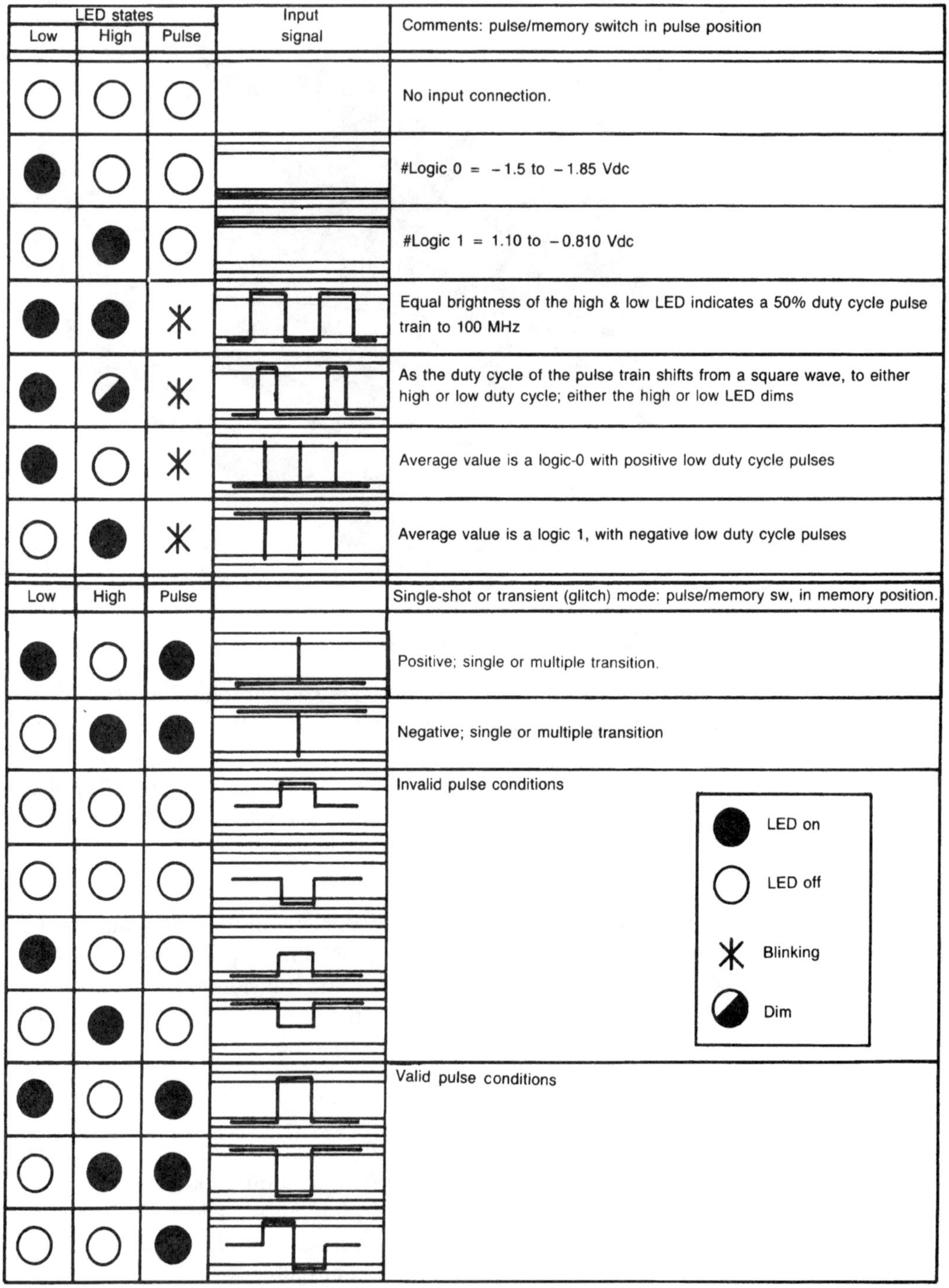

| LED states | | | Input signal | Comments: pulse/memory switch in pulse position |
Low	High	Pulse		
○	○	○		No input connection.
●	○	○		#Logic 0 = −1.5 to −1.85 Vdc
○	●	○		#Logic 1 = 1.10 to −0.810 Vdc
●	●	✳		Equal brightness of the high & low LED indicates a 50% duty cycle pulse train to 100 MHz
●	◑	✳		As the duty cycle of the pulse train shifts from a square wave, to either high or low duty cycle; either the high or low LED dims
●	○	✳		Average value is a logic-0 with positive low duty cycle pulses
○	●	✳		Average value is a logic 1, with negative low duty cycle pulses
Low	High	Pulse		Single-shot or transient (glitch) mode: pulse/memory sw, in memory position.
●	○	●		Positive; single or multiple transition.
○	●	●		Negative; single or multiple transition
○	○	○		Invalid pulse conditions
○	○	○		
●	○	○		
○	●	○		
●	○	●		Valid pulse conditions
○	●	●		
○	○	●		

Legend:
● LED on
○ LED off
✳ Blinking
◑ Dim

■ 2-15 *LED readouts chart for LP-4 ECL test probe.*

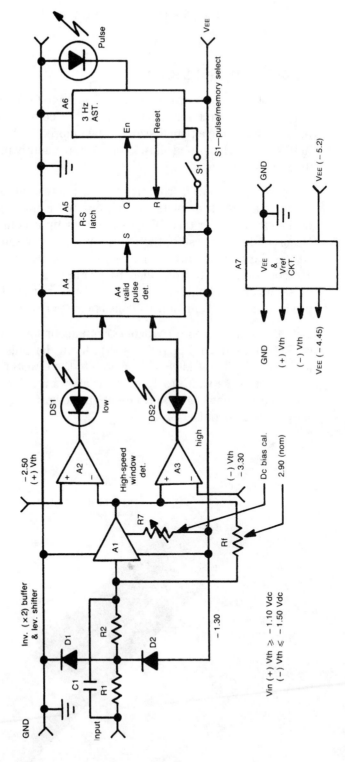

■ **2-16** Functional block diagram of ECL logic probe.

The LP-4 logic probe

Resistor R1 and diodes D1 and D2 protect the input from over-voltage conditions.

The DP-1 digital pulser probe

The DP-1 digital pulser probe was designed to fill a long-neglected need in the digital servicing field. It is a completely automatic pulse generator in a pencil-sized probe tailored for both bench and field service. This probe allows you to conveniently pulse any family of digital circuits.

By obtaining its power from the circuit it is testing, the DP-1 self-adjusts the amplitude of its output pulse to the input requirements of the circuit under test. When the pulser tip is connected to the circuit node to be tested, the DP-l's "autopolarity sensing system" selects the sink or source pulse required to activate the test point. Just depress the button once to produce a clean, bouncefree pulse. When you hold the pushbutton for more than 1 s, the probe produces a pulse train at a 100 pps (pulse per second) rep rate.

The DP-1 pulser probe is capable of sinking or sourcing 100-mA or 60-TTL loads at a 1.5-μs pulse width. If a wider pulse is required, just move the TTL/CMOS slide switch to the CMOS position to increase the pulse width to 10 μs. This allows reliable triggering of even the slowest CMOS devices at the lowest V_{CC}s. Figure 2-17 shows the DP-1 pulser probe.

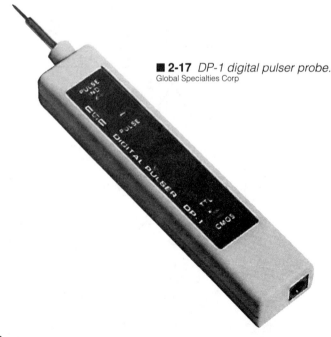

■ **2-17** *DP-1 digital pulser probe.*
Global Specialties Corp

The DP-1 has a "fail-safe" feature that permits an overvoltage condition up to 25 V. Further built-in protection withstands a reverse voltage to 50 V and allows the DP-1 to pulse continuously into a short circuit.

The pulser probe gives you all the versatility of a lab-quality pulse generator, without the need to set pulse levels or switch to complement the output pulse.

Autopolarity sensing

The probe contains a circuit that automatically selects the sink or source pulse required by the circuit under test. By comparing the test-point voltage (between pulses) to the center of the deadzone voltage for the family being tested, the probe senses whether a 0 level or a 1 level is present. If a 0 level, it outputs a 1 pulse; if a 1 level, it outputs a 0 pulse.

The autopolarity sensing level is checked after each pulse to allow for changes of state after a trigger pulse. This permits the pulser probe to trigger an RS flip-flop supplying alternate sink and source pulses to the cross-coupled junction to keep the flip-flop toggling. For these procedures, refer to Fig. 2-18. This feature allows you to jump from point to point on a circuit board without regard to the logic state of the test point.

Tri-state output

The DP-1 pulser probe has a tri-state output, which provides a minimum of 300 kΩ impedance when not being pulsed. This allows all logic families, including CMOS, to be unaffected by circuit loading between pulses.

Single-shot mode

By depressing and releasing the pushbutton, you produce a single, debounced pulse at the output. You can depress the pushbutton as rapidly as necessary to produce a controlled stream of single pulses (see Fig. 2-19). The pushbutton must be released within 1 s in order to remain in the single-shot mode. The LED flashes once for each single-shot pulse produced.

Continuous mode

When the pushbutton is depressed, a single pulse is instantly produced. If the pushbutton is held down more than 1 s, the output switches from single-shot to continuous mode and produces a

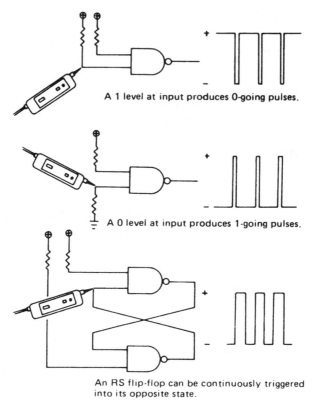

A 1 level at input produces 0-going pulses.

A 0 level at input produces 1-going pulses.

An RS flip-flop can be continuously triggered
into its opposite state.

■ **2-18** *The autosensing mode.*

■ **2-19** *Single-shot and
continuous modes.*

train of pulses at 100 pps rep rate. The LED stays lit during the
continuous mode.

TTL mode

When the slide switch is in the TTL position, the output pulse
width is 1.5 μs. The pulse rise time is less than 100 ns, with a maximum of 500 ns storage and fall times for a 1 TTL load. Storage and
fall times decrease as TTL loading increases. In the TTL mode the
output pulse can sink or source 100-mA or 60-TTL loads.

CMOS mode

When the slide switch is in the CMOS position, the output pulse
width is 10 μs. This allows ample time for the slowest CMOS de-

vices to be activated. The pulse rise time is less than 100 ns, with an 8-µs storage and fall times for a 100 kΩ load resistance. The output pulse can sink or source 50 mA to a logic 1 or a logic 0 level for any V_{CC} from +4 to +18 V.

Setting up the pulser probe

The DP-1's power cable not only supplies power to the unit, but it also acts as the return path for the output pulse.

To decrease common moding and ground loops, clip the power cable lead as close as possible to the pulsing point. When power is first applied to the pulser, the LED will light and stay on for approximately 1 s. After the LED has gone off, the pulser is ready to use.

The DP-1 comes complete with power cable and ground clip. In most cases, there is no need to use the ground clip; the pulser produces a crisp pulse under normal conditions. The ground lead, however, does help the pulser sink larger currents and can reduce the pulse storage time. If you use the ground clip lead, *do not hook up the black power lead*. Using both ground returns can cause common moding and ground loops, which may produce false triggering in the circuit under test.

Pulser applications

The DP-1 in combination with the LP-1 logic probe or the LM-1 logic monitor produces an extremely effective method of troubleshooting, in many cases more useful than using an oscilloscope. Figure 2-20 shows the hookup for checking out a 7490 decade counter with a pulser and a logic monitor.

The pulser CMOS/TTL slide switch is set to TTL and the pulser tip connected to the (0) set input of the 7490. The logic monitor is clamped onto the 7490 to display all the logic states of the counter simultaneously.

Depressing the DP-1 pushbutton once puts a 0 pulse into the 7490 and clears all the outputs to 0. The pulser can now be applied to the clock input to single-step or jog the 7490 through its decade cycle.

When the counter is pulsed, you can see all four outputs changing state while simultaneously monitoring the power-supply input, clock inputs, and clear lines. This technique shows you the advantage of the logic-monitor pulser approach over the oscilloscope, which can only monitor one or two points at a time.

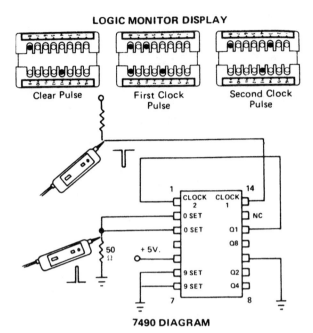

LOGIC MONITOR DISPLAY

Clear Pulse   First Clock   Second Clock
                   Pulse   Pulse

7490 DIAGRAM

■ **2-20** *Using the logic monitor and pulser probes.*

Troubleshooting gates

Although logic monitors work very well on counters, latches, and flip-flops, they are basically static devices and cannot display the DP-1's narrow output pulse. See Fig. 2-21 for the technique for troubleshooting gates.

When troubleshooting gates and decoders, use the LP-3 or LPK-1 logic probe. These probes incorporate pulse stretchers to aid in viewing even the fastest pulses put out by the DP-1. In addition, they can be used to indicate logic states and pulse polarity as well as estimate duty cycles.

In Fig. 2-21A, a two-gate circuit is being tested. G1's output is held high, causing G2's output to be low. Applying the pulser to the output of G1 makes the pulser override the output state of G1 and puts a train of 0 pulses into the gate of G2. The logic probe connected to the output of G2 has its low LED on, but now the pulse LED starts flashing. This shows the gate is passing the input pulses in proper polarity.

In Fig. 2-21B, the probe is moved to the output of G1 and the pulser is applied to the low gate input. The pulser now produces a

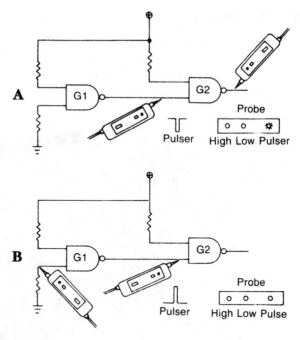

■ **2-21** *Troubleshooting gates with the logic probe.*

series of 1 pulses when the pushbutton is held. However, the probe pulse LED does not respond, indicating a defective gate.

Overriding a logic state

Because of its high fanout, the DP-1 has the unique ability to override the output level set by a gate, by feeding in the required input pulse to the circuitry under test. This sets the stage for system troubleshooting by using the jogging technique. You can deactivate a digital system by disconnecting the system clock and replacing it with the DP-1 pulser. The complete system may now be jogged through its cycle, and different points of interest in the system may be displayed with logic probes or logic monitors.

Several logic monitors may be used simultaneously to display the movement of a pulse from IC to IC or to show the response of several circuits to the same stimuli. The distinct advantage of this technique is quite evident after you try it a few times.

Global LM-1 logic monitor

The LM-1 logic monitor simultaneously displays the static and dynamic logic states of DTL, TTL, HTL, or CMOS 14-pin and 16-pin digital DIP (dual-inline package) ICs. Figure 2-22 shows the LM-1 logic monitor.

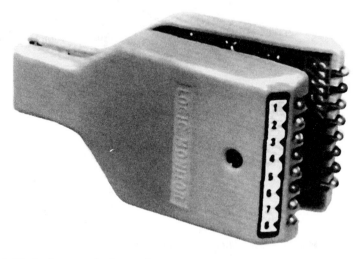

■ **2-22** *A clamp-on logic monitor.* Global Specialties Corp

The voltage at each IC lead is measured by one of 16 independent binary optical voltmeters. When one of the input voltages exceeds the 2-V threshold, the LED corresponding to the activated input pin is turned on. Inputs below the threshold or uncommitted (floating) do not activate their corresponding LEDs. A built-in, power-seeking gating network locates the most positive and negative voltages applied to the IC under test. It then feeds them to the internal buffered amplifiers and LED drivers.

To use the LM-1 monitor, just clip onto any digital IC up to 16 pins. Precision plastic guides and flexible web ensure positive connections between nickel silver contacts and IC leads. Static and dynamic logic levels appear on the 16 LEDs when the system is activated.

Operating information

To install, simply squeeze the top end of the logic monitor so that it will slip over the IC to be checked out, as shown in Fig. 2-23. Once in place, the logic monitor is ready for readout checks. The V_{CC} or the most positive IC terminal will be indicated by a continuously lighted LED. The least positive, uncommitted, and logic 0 IC terminals will appear as unlighted LEDs.

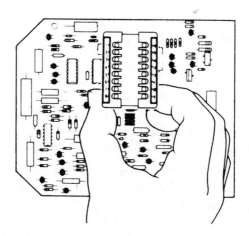

■ 2-23 *Using the clamp-on monitor.*

By reducing the system or IC input signal rate to 10 Hz or less, you will be able to see each logic state of the IC under test; however, troubleshooting with the logic monitor requires a knowledge of the IC logic pinouts. For example, consider a quad and gate configuration. If the output pin of one of the gates is constantly low (LED off) and the gate inputs are not simultaneously high, either the gate output is shorted to ground internally or a short exists on the lines fed by the gate output.

Note: Do not connect the LM-1 to any IC with more than 15 V across any two pins. The LM-1 is a two-level monitoring device. ICs with three supplies, −12 V, ground, and +5 V, are not compatible with the LM-1.

Some logic monitor applications

During the design, breadboarding, the testing phases of a new logic system the designer usually has full control of the system variables (clock, power supplies, input-output transducers, etc.) and can easily isolate ICs for detailed investigation with the logic monitor. When a logic block needs an additional gate, inverter, flip-flop, register, or other component, the designer can use the logic monitor to quickly "see" where unused logic elements are located within the system. Nonfunctioning components can easily be located and replaced. Long-term testing of individual modules can be implemented by merely clipping the LM-1 onto the questionable IC chip.

Because the entire IC can be monitored simultaneously, direct fast visual correlation of IC inputs and outputs simplifies and expedites signal-tracing data transfer and system fault-finding operations. System and IC reactions to power-supply changes, noise and limited temperature testing are other application areas that make the LM-1 an excellent design tool.

It uses mixed logic design DTL, TTL, HTL, CMOS, where you may want to take advantage of individual logic family chip characteristics. Thus, DTL input, CMOS signal processing, and TTL or HTL outputs are naturals for the LM-1 monitor.

With multiple printed circuit (PC) board systems, the LM-1 again displays its utility. One LM-1 on the inputs or outputs of the driving/receiving board and one on the board under test enable you to visually observe the results of any modification or stimulation on one board while giving full attention to the focal point of your investigation.

Global LM-2A logic monitor

The LM-2A logic monitor is a unique design and circuit testing tool that will simultaneously monitor and display the static and/or the dynamic states of up to 16 TTL- or CMOS-compatible circuit points. It also has a variable feature that lets you manually adjust the threshold settings. Figure 2-24 shows the LM-2A logic monitor.

The LM-2A will instantly and clearly display the logic states of any digital IC up to 16 pins or up to 16 independent circuit points when used with its standard, supplied connector cable terminated with a 16-pin IC test clip or the optional multipoint universal test cable, respectively.

The voltage at each input test point is measured by one of the 16 independent binary voltmeters within the LM-2A. If the voltage at any of the input points exceeds 2.3 V (TTL), 70 percent of V_{CC} (CMOS), or the manually adjusted threshold (variable), an LED corresponding to the activated input will be displayed on the LM-2A's readout. Any uncommitted (floating) inputs will not activate the display.

Setting up the LM-2A

See Fig. 2-25 for the setup of the LM-2A logic monitor. Plug the ac adapter or optional power cable into the jack provided on the side of the LM-2A. If the ac adapter is used, plug it into an ac power socket. If the optional cable (LDA-10) is used, feed a dc voltage (about 9 to 15 Vdc) to it—positive to the red alligator clip, nega-

2-24 *LM-2A logic monitor.* Global Specialties Corp

tive to the black alligator clip. The LM-2A is also protected against accidental reversal of these leads.

Each IC lead is connected to a logic state comparator contained in the LM-2A module. When an input voltage exceeds the preselected threshold, the LED corresponding to that input is turned on. Inputs below the threshold (or uncommitted floating IC leads) do not activate their corresponding LEDs.

Any IC lead connection to V_{CC} will read a constant logical 1 (LED on). A grounded IC lead will read a constant logical 0 (LED off). By reducing the IC input signal rate to 10 Hz or less, you can see each logic state of the IC under test.

When using the variable mode, monitor the test-point output with a voltmeter while adjusting the variable thumbwheel until the required threshold for the circuit under test is reached. An input voltage exceeding the preselected threshold turns on the LED corresponding to that input. Inputs below the threshold do not turn on their corresponding LEDs. For example, if the circuitry

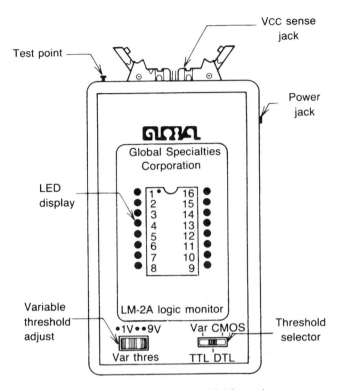

■ 2-25 *Front panel controls of the Global LM-2A monitor.* Global Specialties Corp

being tested contains DTL or RTL logic, then you should adjust the variable thumbwheel for a test-point voltage of 1.6 or 1.2 V, respectively. The variable mode is a unique feature of this second-generation LM-2 logic monitor, where you have the ability to test all logic families by adjusting the variable thumbwheel for the required threshold.

Some logic-monitor applications

You can use the LM-2A in many ways, as follows:

☐ To locate unused logic elements within an IC or system
☐ To monitor entire ICs or data buses simultaneously
☐ For direct, fast, visual correlation of IC (system) inputs and outputs
☐ For comparison testing of known "good" ICs and "questionable" components
☐ For mixed logic family design and testing.

The LM-2A is a 16-bit-input, logic state indicator that can be connected directly to an IC or to 16 physically independent logic nodes within a system. Input logic states are displayed by individual LEDs and provide a fast, direct method of checking the device's or mode's truth table.

When you are interested in logic states rather than exact voltage levels, the LM-2A is easier to use than either a scope or a voltmeter. Because you don't have to take your eyes off the circuit under test, the monitor will speed up the troubleshooting process.

Being free from these limitations, you can focus full attention on the input-output relationship of the LM-2A's LEDs, which indicate the flow of data "into" and "out of" the IC or logic nodes under observation.

The LM-2A, when used with other logic test tools, becomes a powerful test unit in the designing, testing, and troubleshooting phases of digital systems. Monitoring an entire IC by the LM-2A and injecting pulses into gates, flip-flops, registers, and so on, connected to the monitored device provides you with a fast, easy-to-implement, easy-to-interpret, digital signal-tracing and analysis technique unparalleled by conventional testing devices.

Whether used in field service or the circuit design lab, the LM-2A, 16-pin multifamily logic monitor is an indispensable diagnostic, design, and troubleshooting tool that provides rapid observations of digital logic states. The LM-2A has almost unlimited applications in all phases of logic testing and design work.

Global LM-3 40-channel triggerable monitor

The Global Specialties model LM-3 triggerable 40-channel logic monitor (see Fig. 2-26) is an innovative logic test instrument in one compact unit. It has 40 precision threshold, high-speed, high-impedance logic state indicators, combined with a unique and highly flexible triggerable latching circuit. The turn-on thresholds adjust for any logic family and supply voltage. Forty easy-clips connect to the IC pins, test points, or bus line combinations that you may select. The LM-3's 40-LED display then accurately follows the data or holds (freezes) the display in various ways.

In the retrig mode, the display follows the data until a rising or falling edge (switch-selected) appears at the trig input. This latches the display. The next selected edge updates latched displays each time it appears. Also, manual trig pushbutton permits manual triggering.

In the latch mode, display follows data and ignores trig input until you push the trig arm button and ready LED lights. At a trigger in-

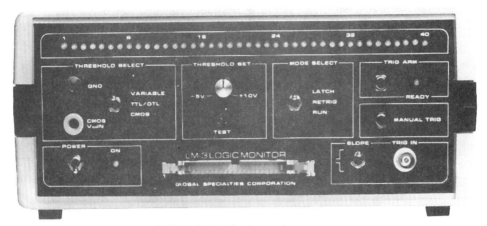

■ **2-26** *40-channel Global LM-3 logic monitor.* Global Specialties Corp

put, the display latches. Any further trigger inputs will not change the display until you push the trig arm button. The manual trig pushbutton also functions in this mode. In the run mode, display LEDs follow the input data.

Through its unique threshold selection scheme, the LM-3 is quite flexible and compatible with all logic families. It has three methods for determining logic threshold levels:

1. A fixed +2.2-Vdc threshold is provided for logic operation at standard TTL/DTL levels.

2. A variable threshold between –5 Vdc and +10 Vdc is controlled by a front panel adjustment.

3. A supply-dependent threshold, determined at 70 percent of the V_{CC} of the circuit under test, is sampled through two front panel, banana jack connectors.

A front panel test point permits precise monitoring of the logic threshold with a voltmeter regardless of which of the three methods you select.

Functional description

The LM-3 has 40 input channels that utilize an input attenuator that reduces the magnitude of the input signal going into the comparator. The comparator determines whether the data input exceeds the reference voltage. See Fig. 2-27. The output of the comparator is fed into a transparent latch that either transfers this input data to the display or stores it.

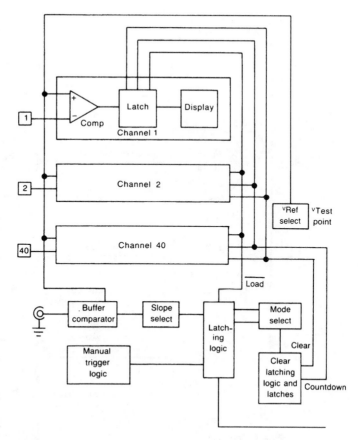

■ 2-27 *Block diagram of LM-3 logic monitor.*

In the latch or retrig modes the trig input and manual trig push-button are activated. When the trig input is used, the trigger signal enters an attenuator and a high-impedance buffer before going into the comparator. The output of the comparator is fed into a slope-selecting circuit that determines which edge triggers the latching logic.

The manual pushbutton triggers the latching logic at the output of the slope select circuit.

The mode select determines the operation of the latching logic. Any transitions of the mode select switch will clear both the latching logic and the displays while putting the input latches in the transparent mode. See Fig. 2-28.

Depending on which mode you select, the latching logic will freeze the display upon a trigger (manual) signal and stay in this state until you depress the arm pushbutton (latch mode), or it will up-

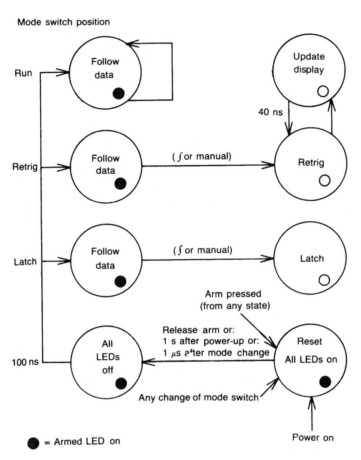

Mode switch position

● = Armed LED on

■ 2-28 *The LM-3 monitor state diagram.*

date with every occurrence of a trigger (manual) signal (retrig mode), or it will continuously hold the latches transparent letting the display follow the data inputs (run mode).

Applications for the LM-3 monitor

The LM-3 can perform some of the basic functions of a signature analyzer. You can do this by monitoring a known good board under a specific set of conditions and with recording data at different stages of the circuit. Compile the data in a troubleshooting book or on a schematic, giving the exact set of conditions when this data was recorded. When one of these boards fails, you can reconnect the LM-3 to the PC board at the data points indicated on the diagram, reproducing the conditions given on the schematic. You can then trace the circuit through and compare the new data with the old until you find a discrepancy in the new reading. This will

76

demonstrate that the previous stage was working, but this stage is defective.

You can use the LM-3 in this way as follows: If a master reset (clear) is available, then you should perform this operation to start the system at the same point every time. The data would be taken at strategic points of the circuit (e.g., input-output of flip-flops), borrow and carry outputs of counters, opposite ends of the same line to see if the data is being transmitted through connectors, state of gate packages. After the operation is performed, if the circuit times itself out, the LM-3 can be left in either the run mode or the latch mode and cause certain important transitions in the circuit to trigger the latching circuitry. In this case, take a series of data at different trigger input positions on the circuit, from which you can make a series of drawings showing the state of the display at different trigger inputs. You can give this data picture to the troubleshooting technician, who can use it to reproduce the test conditions to locate the problem.

When using the LM-3 to compare data points of a known good board with those of a defective board, set it up as follows (see Fig. 2-29).

If the data points are close together, then you can split the data input cable with odd easy-clips going to the good board and even easy-clips going to the defective board. Setting the easy-clips up in this way lets you start from the first display LED and, in groups of two, proceed to the right to find the data input that does not match the LED to the left of it. If the data points are not located close to each other, split the data input easy-clips in groups of 8 or split into two groups of 20. As a result, the ribbon cable takes less abuse and will be easier to use later.

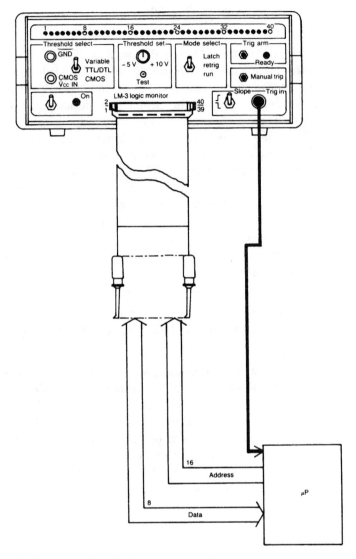

■ **2-29** *Diagram of the LM-3 setup information.* Global Specialties Corp

Microprocessor troubleshooting with an oscilloscope

3

THIS CHAPTER FEATURES THE NEW SENCORE SC61 OSCIL-loscope waveform analyzer for troubleshooting digital logic circuits and includes an in-depth look at this scope's unique circuitry, which has microcomputer-controlled auto tracking and direct readout (LCRs) for frequency and voltage signal measurements. It also looks at ways for using the delta bar for digital tests.

In addition, the chapter describes how to use the triggered-sweep scope to pinpoint faults in microprocessor systems and to check the clock pulse that must be present and correct for proper microoperation. It then looks at ways to capture glitches and spikes with a scope during digital circuit analysis and discusses various digital logic scope troubleshooting.

Sencore waveform analyzer

The Sencore SC61 represents the first improvement in waveform measuring techniques since the first scope was introduced more than 50 years ago. Until now, all oscilloscopes were analog devices. Every measurement of peak-to-peak amplitude, time, or frequency required matching the waveform to cathode ray tube (CRT) graticule markings, estimating parts of a CRT division or part of a cycle of the waveform, and multiplying the size of the waveform by the setting of the horizontal or vertical switches. These measurements were not very accurate, were time-consuming, and were subject to many errors.

The SC61 combines the waveform analyzing capability of a high-quality oscilloscope with the speed and accuracy of a computer. The instrument has a microcomputer that monitors the vertical and horizontal circuits at all times. You just push a button when you want to measure all or part of a waveform. The microcomputer determines the reading, automatically sets the decimal, and produces a direct digital readout of the value. Figure 3-1 shows the Sencore SC61.

■ **3-1** *Sencore SC61 waveform analyzer scope.*

The waveform analyzer CRT display section has a bandwidth of 60 MHz; it is usable up to 100 MHz to show the needed detail for analyzing digital signals. Specially designed sync circuits (using differential amplifiers and ECL states) provide rock-solid triggering with the fewest trigger adjustments possible. The input capabilities extend from 5 mV per division all the way to 2000 Vdc or 2000 Vac peak-to-peak.

Special video circuits simplify the analysis of composite video waveforms. Sync separators produce stable triggering on these complex signals. Additional stages eliminate the half-line shift on interlaced signals and the vertical sync from interfering with digital readings of signals displayed at the horizontal sweep rate. Video preset buttons allow pushbutton selection of vertical or horizontal scanning frequencies.

Two types of digital measurements are made through the probe used for the CRT display. The first three functions for each channel are called the *auto-tracking tests*. Auto tracking occurs when the microcomputer automatically tracks the CRT display at all times. The three auto-tracking functions are dc volts, peak-to-peak volts, and frequency. All three functions measure the entire waveform.

The second group of digital tests contains the delta (Δ) tests, which let you measure part of a waveform. These tests measure the peak-to-peak amplitude, time, or frequency of any part of the waveform shown on the CRT.

Both types of digital tests are unaffected by the vertical or horizontal verniers or position controls. Thus, you can make the CRT display any size you like, without affecting the accuracy of the digital readout. All tests are automatically ranged or directly interfaced to the input attenuators for direct readings.

One final test allows the frequency of the signal fed to channel A to be compared to the frequency of the signal fed to channel B. The digital display shows the ratio of the two frequencies to troubleshoot divider or multiplier stages.

General scope operation

Use the block diagram in Fig. 3-2 to follow the discussion of the overall waveform analyzer operation. Starting with the signal input on channel A (the analysis for channel B is the same), the signal first enters the input coupling stage where it is either dc or ac coupled to the vertical attenuator. Also, at this point the dc component of the signal is sampled and sent to the digital control board. In the vertical attenuator, the signal first goes through a course step attenuator. It is then split and goes through a variable-gain preamp, then on to the vertical amp through a fixed-gain preamp to the peak-to-peak circuit.

In the vertical amp, the signal is further amplified before going through a delay line to the vertical output on to the CRT. The vertical amp contains a switching circuit that selects the signal (A and/or B) to be displayed on the CRT. Before making this selection, the vertical amp takes a sampling from each channel and sends them to the trigger circuits.

In the trigger circuits, one of the signals (A, B, line, or external) is selected and processed to control the start of the sweep across the CRT. A sampling of that signal is also sent to the digital control. The sweep and trigger work hand-in-hand to generate a linear ramp that is amplified by the horizontal output and fed to the CRT to produce a left-to-right sweep. In the vector mode, the signal from

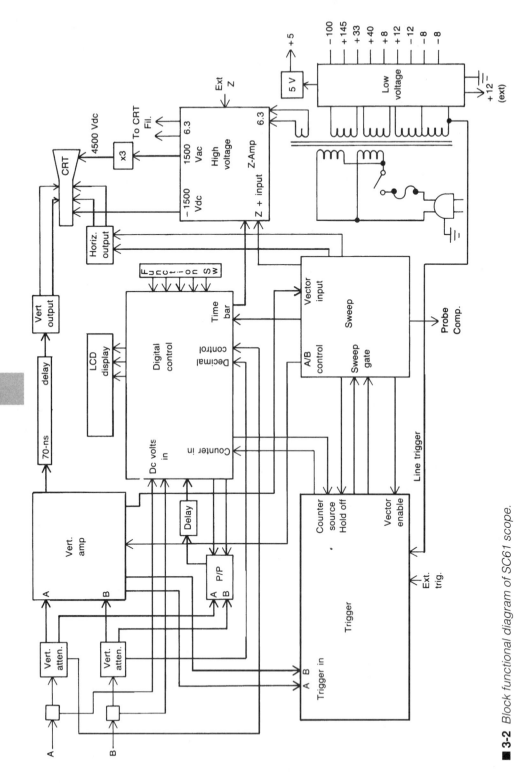

■ **3-2** *Block functional diagram of SC61 scope.*

duce a left-to-right sweep. In the vector mode, the signal from channel B replaces the ramp and controls horizontal deflection.

Another function of the sweep circuit is to generate a time bar signal. This signal is used to gate the intensity of the display on and off and is also used in the digital control block.

Operating voltages for the CRT are produced in the high-voltage and Z-amplifier block. The output is fed to the CRT cathode and to the X3 multiplier, where the second anode voltage is produced. Also in this block is the Z-amp, which produces a signal that is sent to the CRT grid to blank out the display during retrace time and chop transitions.

The low-voltage and 5-V blocks produce all dc voltages required to operate the scope. Many of these voltages are regulated.

The P/P, digital control, function switches, and LCD (liquid crystal display) blocks form the digital readout portion of the SC61. The three major functions performed by this group are frequency, P/P voltage, and dc voltage. These functions are selected by the function switches.

The frequency of a signal is determined by counting a signal coming from the trigger circuit. Because this signal is also used to trigger the sweep, it has been greatly amplified, allowing the SC61 to count very low level signals. A minor function performed by this circuit is Δ time. In this function, a 10-MHz clock is counted to measure the time of the time bar signal. The $1/\Delta$ time function is the software conversion of the Δ time function and is displayed as a frequency.

The P/P function measures the peak-to-peak amplitude of the display waveform by comparing a dc voltage generated by the digital control to the signal from the vertical attenuator in the P/P circuit. This function can be gated by the time bar signal to produce the Delta P/P function.

In the dc volt function, a dc voltage from the input coupling is converted to the equivalent digital signal and displayed on the LCD.

Microprocessor controller board

The heart of the digital functions of the SC61 is a microprocessor contained on the controller board. This analysis will not attempt to describe the software used by the microprocessor, but it will try to make clear what is being done and how the circuits go about doing it. You can follow the discussion of the circuit operation by referring to Fig. 3-3.

The microprocessor does not contain any of the software. IC15 is the memory in which the software is located. For the software to function as it should, it must be retrieved from IC15 (ROM) and read by the microchip. Eight lines called the *data bus* are used to do this. They come from the microchip at pins 12 through 19. When operating, the microprocessor addresses a specific memory location in ROM by first outputting the address on the data bus and then latching the address with the address latch (IC14). The latch pulse [address latch enable (ALE)] is on microchip pin 11. This pulse is inverted by IC13A and fed to the clock input on IC14, pin 11. When latched, the ROM outputs the data back onto the data bus to be read by the microprocessor. The microchip then does whatever it is instructed to do by the ROM (IC15).

Note that IC12 is an automatic reset that monitors the read pulses from the microchip and generates a reset pulse if the read pulses should disappear. The read pulses are fed to the base of transistor TR6, which acts as a switch to ground on one side of C23. This keeps the output high. If the read pulses stop, the circuit becomes a normal astable multivibrator and the output toggles. As soon as the output goes low, the microprocessor resets and the read pulses should reappear. This action is required to keep the microprocessor from hanging up in some sort of nondescribed loop.

Chip IC11 and associated circuitry make up a 6-MHz crystal oscillator. You can use capacitor C22 to adjust the frequency so that the counter reads correctly. The output of IC13B along with the data bus and the read line make up an 1/O port that is not used but is available for future use.

The function buffer (IC28) is used to provide a tri-state interface between the data bus and the function switches. The microprocessor interrogates this buffer when A0 is low and the RD (read) pulse is active. This information tells the microprocessor which function to be in. Buffer IC29 is used to provide a tri-state interface between the real-time counter and the data bus. It is also used to buffer the decimal point information that comes from the P/P board via the back wafer on the vertical attenuator switch. IC30A and B make up the real-time counter. IC30 divides the ALE signal by 4. This is used during the DVM function to keep track of actual time.

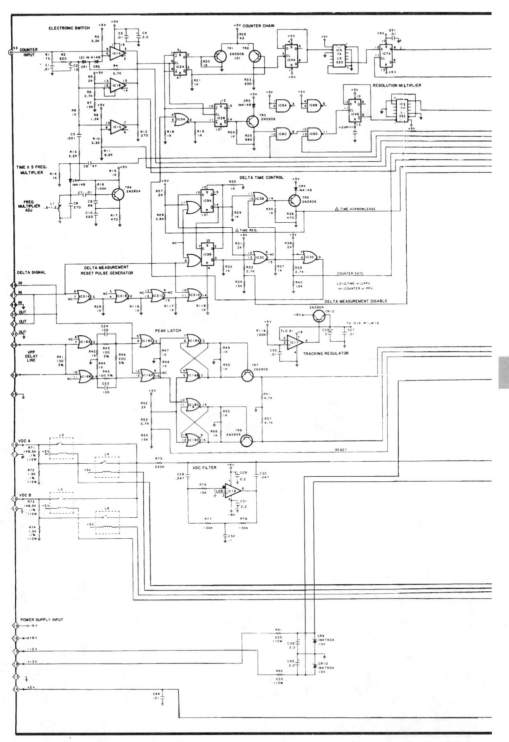

3-3 *Controller board schematic.*

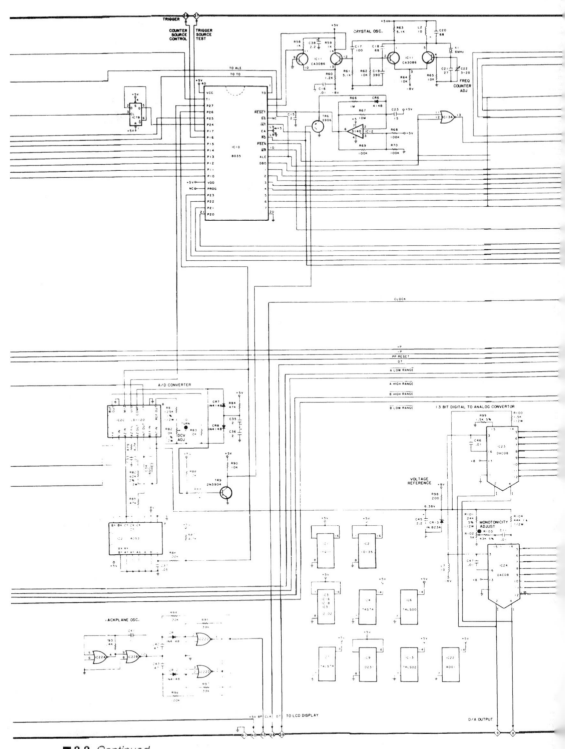

■ 3-3 *Continued.*

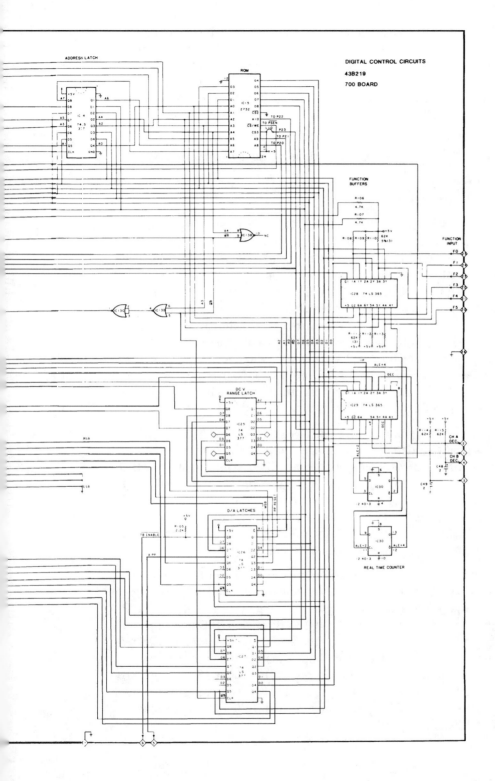

DIGITAL CONTROL CIRCUITS

43B219

700 BOARD

Microprocessor controller board

The range latch latches one of the four relays at the input to the DVM function A/D (analog-to-digital). It also has four unused outputs that are available as part of the aforementioned I/O port. The D/A (digital-to-analog) latch (IC26 and IC27) latches the digital word used by the 13-bit D/A (IC23 and IC24). This D/A converts 13 bits of digital information into an analog signal for use in the P/P function.

The next section describes functions of the data bus circuitry.

Peak-to-peak function

In the peak-to-peak (P/P) function, the microprocessor, ROM, D/A latches, and 13-bit D/A work with other circuitry to arrive at a value of the P/P voltage of the signal being viewed on the CRT. The signal comes from the vertical attenuator board via IC1C and IC1D and out on lines 5 and 6. Channel A comes into the P/P board on lines 4 and 5, channel B on lines 10 and 11. These signals are fed to a diode switch (CR1 through CR8). This switch is controlled by IC1, TR1, and TR2. The microprocessor controls IC1. A high on line 1 allows channel A to be measured, and a low allows channel B. Lines 2 and 3 go to the vertical attenuator boards to be switched to provide the microprocessor information on where to put the decimal point on the readout.

Transistors TR3 and TR4 are used as a comparator. They compare the signal to a dc current from the D/As on the controller board. The comparator acts as a class C amplifier. The signal from the D/A is the bias, and anything over the bias results in a signal being fed to IC2A. IC2A and IC2B further amplify the output of TR3 and TR4. Transistors TR5 and TR6 plus IC2C produce an output on lines 16 and 17 that is an ECL level. Lines 16 and 17 enter a 120-Ω delay line that is routed to the controller board.

The signal from the P/P board enters the controller board on lines 33 and 34. The IC16A and IC16B chips terminate the delay line and reshape the signal. The signal is then gated (used in Delta P/P function) by IC16C and IC16D. IC18A through IC18D make up two RS flip-flops (F/F), which latch the signal and are interrogated by the microprocessor. If they are high, the microprocessor increases the current out of the D/As and resets the F/F. IC18A and IC18B are for the positive peak measurement, IC18C and IC18D for the negative peak. TR7 and TR8 convert the RS F/F output to a single-ended signal.

The IC3 chip and TR7 transistor on the P/P board make up a tracking-voltage regulator. Five volts from the controller board enters on line 14. Then 8 V enters on line 9 and provides power to the board. IC3 and TR7 drop the 8 V to 5 V, which runs the ECL. This circuit is needed to make sure the voltage on the P/P board is exactly the same as the voltage on the controller board so that no errors are introduced in the measurement of P/P.

Also, IC17 and TR10 on the controller board set the 5 V for the ECL on that board. Both tracking regulators are referenced to the 5 V already on the controller board.

Digital voltmeter function

The DVM function is contained on the controller board. The voltage to be measured enters on line 10 for channel A and line 12 for channel B. Because channels A and B have the same operations, we look only at channel A.

In the DVM function, the microprocessor spends most of its time controlling the A/D converter (IC20). The A/D converter is controlled by two output lines and one input line from the microprocessor—pins 37, 38, and 6, respectively. The input line on pin 6 has been inverted and level shifted by TR9.

The output line (pin 37) switches the A/D from zero mode to convert mode. The other output line (pin 38) changes the polarity of the integrator so that it ramps either up or down. The input line (pin 6) comes from a comparator to tell if the integrator output is above or below ground. By measuring the amount of time that the integrator in the A/D ramps up and subtracting from this the amount of time the integrator ramps down, you can find the input voltage to the A/D. For example,

50 percent up = 0 V	25 percent = –1.0 V
75 percent up = 1.0 V	5 percent = –1.8 V
95 percent up = 1.8 V	

The 4½-digit A/D converter used in the SC61 is one-half of a set of chips developed by Siliconix. Only the A/D chip itself is used; the control chip functions are provided by the microprocessor. The operation of the A/D chip is involved and is not covered here.

When you make a dc voltage measurement, dc voltage at the scope's input jack is routed to the resistor divider R72 and R73 on the controller board. Dc voltage ranges are provided in the unit for 0 V, 20 V, and 2000 V. Voltage is picked off the top of the divider and fed to the A/D through relay L3 in the 20-V range. In the 2-kV range, voltage is picked off of the divider between R71 and R72 and fed through L4.

The low-pass filter (IC19) looks like a diagram error when you first see it on the schematic, because the input and output appear to be shorted together; but for this to be so, the signal would have to go through the filter, but it does not. What does happen is that a small change in level at the output of R12 couples through C8 to a high-gain inverting amplifier IC3. The output of IC3 couples right back to the starting point through C9. The input cannot change much before there is an immediate correction back through C9. Very low frequencies are attenuated by C8 and C9, so the correction will not be as great as for frequencies that readily pass through the coupling capacitors. This filter is very responsive from 2 Hz and up.

Dc feedback for IC3 is through R14 and R15. At low frequencies, the dc feedback is delayed slightly by C10, giving the effect of overcorrecting the output. This helps the filter to operate at the lowest possible frequencies.

Counter function

A rather unique feature of the SC61 is its ability to count very low level signals. If the scope can trigger on a signal, it can count it, because the scope actually counts its own trigger signal. This is accomplished as follows. On the trigger input board, the signal enters from channel A on lines 21 and 22 and from channel B on lines 19 and 20. Each signal then goes to a pair of identical common-base buffers. One buffer is for the trigger, and the other feeds the counter. These buffers can be turned on or off, so in use only one of each pair is on at any time. Line 15 comes from the controller board and is fed to IC1. IC1A controls the channel B counter, IC1B the channel A counter, IC1C the channel A trigger, and IC1D the channel B trigger. IC1A and IC1C have the same output as IC1B and IC1D. Thus, channel A counter and channel B trigger function together, as do channel A trigger and channel B counter. This allows the scope to display and trigger on one channel and count whatever is on the other channel.

The outputs of buffer TR1 and TR2 and buffer TR5 and TR6 are fed to the bases of TR13 and TR14, which make up a differential amplifier similar to others used in this instrument. The output of this amplifier is ac coupled to the bases of IC3A and IC3B. This chip functions as a zero-crossing detector to eliminate any false counting. It does this by storing a voltage on C10 and C12, which is then fed back to IC3A and IC3B to bias them into class C operation. The signal from IC3A and IC3B is amplified by IC4A, which then feeds the signal to IC4B to be squared to ECL levels. The output of IC4B is then applied to pin 10 of IC2 on the trigger logic board. IC1 and IC2 make up the counter source control. Under microprocessor control, IC1 selects one of IC2's gate and allows only one signal to pass. Present at IC2 are TVH, TVV, AUX signals, or the trigger signal. Count the trigger signal when viewing and counting one channel. Count the AUX signal when viewing on one channel and counting the other. Both signals are used in the ratio function.

The signal being counted is fed to the microprocessor board via a coax cable and applied to pin 5 of IC1. Chip IC1 functions as a switch and is under microprocessor control. The other signals on IC1 are 10 MHz (from the X5 multiplier) on pin 10 and a microprocessor signal (unload pulses) on pin 12. These signals are switched and fed to pin 9 of IC2. IC2, TR3, IC6, IC4, IC8, and IC7 compose the 1024 circuit (or resolution multiplier). That circuit is used to count the frequency as previously described.

Digital troubleshooting procedures

Clock or pulse generation

Microprocessor systems and many other digital logic devices require some type of clock (strobe) pulse to function and time the various operations. The clock (oscillator) accurately times pulses and may be crystal controlled. The logic systems are gated or enabled by these clock pulses. The faster the clock frequency, the more functions that can be performed in a given time, but this speed is limited by the response time of the chips used in the system. Clocks vary from simple local devices to diverse and complex systems.

The basic clock puts out equally spaced pulses. It should be as narrow as possible and still enable the gates. The reason for the narrow clock pulses is to discriminate against noise spikes or glitches. Some systems require a two-phase clock, such as the 8080A microprocessor chip.

Thus, the clock is the very heart of most digital systems. So the clock pulses should be one of the first items you check with the scope when troubleshooting these systems.

One note of caution when using a scope probe for viewing these clock pulses. If the shielded scope probe case is not properly grounded, erroneous clock pulse waveforms on the scope screen might trick you into seeing a distorted pulse that isn't there. The ground lead from the scope case must be connected to the equipment chassis ground under test, and the ground shield of the test probe must be connected to the ground pin of the clock IC you are testing. See the clock pulse in the bottom scope trace of Fig. 3-4, which the probe shield was not grounded. Note the ringing distortion on the pulse waveforms. A clean clock pulse is shown in the top trace with the probe shield properly grounded. Always use an ×10 attenuation scope probe for checking out clock and logic pulses. Remember that clock pulses can radiate, or transmit, very potent rf signals (if the complete unit is not properly shielded and I/O lines filtered) and can cause interference in other nearby electronic devices. Thus, if you have some strange-acting equipment problems, be on the alert for this type of rf spectrum pollution.

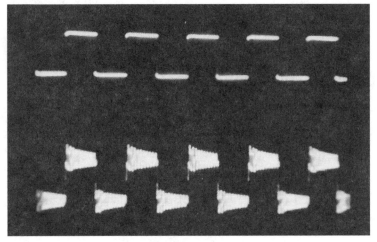

■ **3-4** *Pulse distortion when probe shield is not grounded.*

8080A chip clock inputs

An 8080A microprocessor chip requires a two-phase clock pulse input. A *clock* in digital logic jargon is a device that generates at least one clock pulse, or a timing device that provides a continuous series of timing pulses. A two-phase clock is a 2-input timing device that provides two continuous series of timing pulses that are synchronized together, with a single clock pulse from the second series always following a single clock pulse from the first series. The scope traces in Fig. 3-5 show the timing of these two clock pulses. The top trace is the phase 1 clock pulse, and the bottom trace is the phase 2 clock pulse.

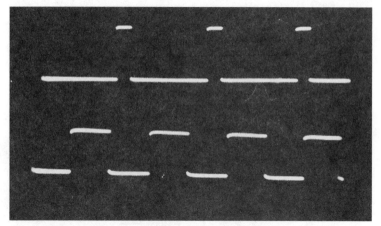

■ **3-5** *Timing of the 8080A two-phase clock pulses.*

In the 8080A specifications, the minimum pulse width for clock phase 1 is 60 ns, and the phase 2 clock pulse width is 220 ns. Figure 3-6 shows the key pinouts of the Intel 8080A microchip. These clock pulses can be generated with an Intel 8224 clock generator IC.

Checking the clock frequency

A frequency counter can be used for checking out digital logic, microprocessor, phase-locked loop (PLL), and other divider systems now found in many electronic devices. The first steps for isolating problems in a nonoperational logic system are to check for clock operation and correct clock frequency. The frequency counter or scope with built-in counter, such as the model SC61 Sencore, is used to check the output from the clock generator chip. When troubleshooting a system that uses the popular 8080A microprocessor, these two checkpoints would be pins 10 and 11 of the 8224 clock generator chip. Note block diagram for the 8224 in Fig. 3-7. The 8080A requires two-phase clock signals at pins 15 and 22. This clock generator IC also requires a crystal for accurate frequency generation and control.

Pickup loop measurements

In some situations you cannot make a direct connection to the clock input signal, or you may not want to because of circuit loading. The probe capacitance of the frequency counter could cause the frequency of the oscillator to change, or stop the clock oscillator from running in a worst-case condition. The pickup loop lets you pick up the signals without a direct probe connection. For this application, the inductive loop is used to pick off the frequency

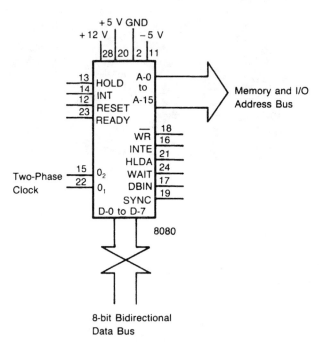

Sync (pin 19)
DBIN (pin 17)

■ **3-6** *Key pinouts of the 8080A microchip.*

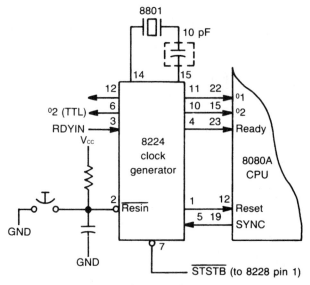

■ **3-7** *Block diagram of the 8284 Intel clock chip.*

Microprocessor troubleshooting with an oscilloscope

pulses quickly, without any direct connections. This action eliminates any interference with the measured circuit. You probably won't obtain an accurate count of the clock pulses because the input signal to the frequency counter from the pickup loop will be a sawtooth or sine-wave shape due to coil induction. You can connect the pickup loop to the input of the scope to take a quick look at various oscillator signals, but they will be distorted and of incorrect amplitude.

Inductive pickup loop applications

These tests use the Sencore model FC51 1-GHz frequency counter and rf pickup loop. First, select the desired input, read rate, and frequency range. Place the pickup loop near a capacitor or coil in the oscillator circuit to be tested. If an unstable count is obtained, reposition the pickup loop to stabilize the count. If no count is obtained, turn over the pickup loop (which reverses the polarity of the pickup loop coil), or select a different component in the clock circuit.

Although the pickup loop will work best when placed next to or around a coil, a high-sensitivity counter will let you pick up signals from capacitors, transistors, chips or even crystals in many circuits.

Most microsystems use a clock to keep the frequency pulses stable and accurate. Should the clock not operate or be off frequency, the crystal or chip would be the prime suspects. You can check the crystal quickly and accurately on the Sencore FC51 counter. Any crystal with a fundamental frequency of 1 to 20 MHz can be checked. Figure 3-8 shows a crystal being inserted in the front panel universal crystal socket to check for crystal activity. The crystal will be made to resonate at its fundamental operating frequency.

Crystal check procedure

Use the following procedure to test a crystal with the FC51 frequency counter. First, insert the crystal to be tested into the front panel, crystal-check socket. Select the desired read rate button. Depress the 20-kHz-to-100-kHz frequency range button. Now depress the crystal-check button. Read the fundamental crystal frequency on the digital LED readout of the counter.

The crystal check reads the approximate fundamental frequency of the crystal under test. Defective or inoperative crystals will be indicated by an intermittent or zero counter readout.

■ 3-8 *Frequency of crystal being checked on a counter.*

Microsystems power supplies

You need a correct and stable dc voltage power source for proper microprocessor system operations. All digital logic systems must have precise, regulated, well-filtered dc power supplies. Use your scope to check for a smooth dc output voltage from the power supply and check for correct regulated dc voltage levels to all logic circuits. Most of the microvoltage supplies are electronically regulated and filtered.

You can use the scope to monitor the dc supply lines to catch spikes in TTL systems as the gates function so you can locate open bypass and filter capacitors. Thus, you will need a very fast rise-time, wideband, triggered-sweep scope to detect these transient pulses.

When a TTL circuit is switched from a low to a high state, transients occur on the supply voltage line because of the TTL totem pole output action. Figure 3-9 shows a typical TTL gate circuit. When the logic level goes high, it briefly short-circuits the supply voltage.

If several gates switch on simultaneously, the current spike on the supply line increases linearly with the number of gates. These spikes or glitches, which are caused by insufficient dc supply-line filtering, can trigger on fast TTL gates and be quite fatal; that is, information stored in memory systems (PROMs, ROMs, RAMS, etc.) can be destroyed. Use the scope to check out the dc voltage power-supply lines for open filter or bypass capacitors.

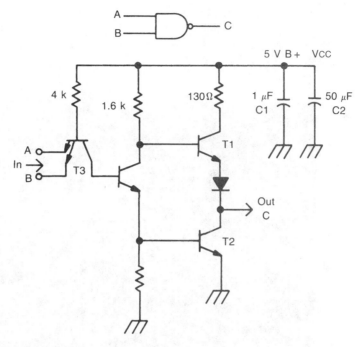

■ **3-9** *Typical TTL gate circuit.*

To track down these spikes or glitches in a microprocessor system, you must check the dc power-supply voltage output terminals and the various filter or bypass points throughout the system. Many filter and bypass capacitors are located throughout any logic device containing many gates. The logic-pulse scope trace in Fig. 3-10 is from a properly operating gate. If a filter or bypass capacitor be-

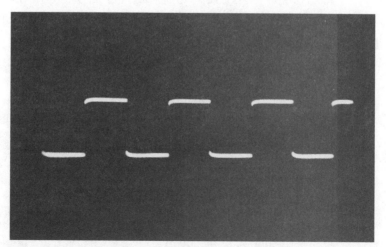

■ **3-10** *Pulse of a properly operating gate.*

comes open at this stage, you may see a scope pulse like that in Fig. 3-11. Note the small spikes as the pulse goes from a high to a low transition. The amplitude of these spikes will vary depending on which filter capacitor (C1 or C2 for the TTL gate circuit in Fig. 3-9) is defective.

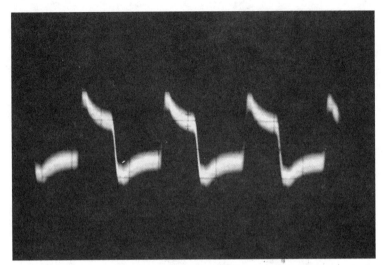

■ **3-11** *Distorted pulse caused by an open filter capacitor.*

If you use the scope to check the dc regulated voltage coming out of the microsystem power supply, you should observe a smooth, clean trace, such as in the top trace of Fig. 3-12. This is true even with a very high, vertical-gain control setting. If trouble occurs in the electronically regulated dc circuit or filter capacitors, some hash or spikes (bottom scope trace in Fig. 3-12) will show up.

Intermittent spike indicator

This technique, used with a triggered-sweep scope, can help you locate an intermittent spike or pulse that may be found riding on the regulated dc voltage lines in microsystems. For this technique, your scope must have a single-sweep mode or a one-shot sweep mode. These features will usually be found on scopes with a delaying time base or an A-delayed-by-B time-base generator.

This technique is used because these spikes are very narrow—usually only 10 or 20 ns—which makes them difficult to see even on a wideband (30 to 50 MHz) scope. Also, they are usually random in nature. With this setup, you can use the ready light, which shows the one-shot has been armed, even if you are not looking at

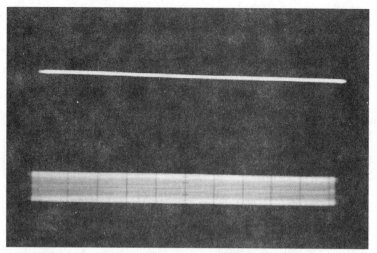

■ **3-12** *Hash on bottom trace indicates loss of filtering.*

the scope screen. Thus, the scope becomes an automatic glitch monitor.

To catch these intermittent spikes, which may occur on regulated B+ supply lines, set up the scope as follows. This technique cannot be used on circuit lines that normally carry pulse signals. To activate the one-shot mode, depress the single-sweep button, as shown in Fig. 3-13. When a spike is detected in the scope's vertical amplifier, the sweep will be triggered on for one single trace, and the ready light will go off. Punch the single-sweep button again, and

■ **3-13** *Scope in single-sweep or one-shot mode.*

the ready light will come back on, indicating that the sweep has been armed again. Hence, you are using the ready light as a visual indicator to determine when a spike has occurred in the circuit under test. Therefore, you need not constantly watch the scope screen but can do other work at the service bench. Although the spike may be so narrow that you cannot see it on the scope, there will be an indication of some action taking place that has fired the single-sweep mode.

You may have to try various time-base generator settings—negative or positive slope (sync) and vertical-amplifier gain levels—to obtain the spike that triggers on the single-sweep trace. Some scopes have a trigger level control, which you might have to adjust. You should also adjust the CRT intensity control level for a bright trace, because there will only be one sweep across the CRT. Thus, the one-shot sweep lets you know that a spike has occurred, even though you can't see it on the scope trace.

Delayed-sweep scope trace

Most triggered-sweep oscilloscopes that have a single-sweep feature (one-shot) also have delayed-sweep functions. The scope controls, shown in Fig. 3-14, include A and B time-base generator, a main sweep, A-intensified-by-B, B delayed-sweep, and delayed-time controls. The A and B delayed-sweep modes can be used to look at digital logic pulses and any other complex waveforms that you may want to observe in greater detail. This delayed sweep

■ **3-14** *Scope in the delayed-sweep mode.*

stretches out digital pulses and vertical interval test (VIT) signals located in the TV video vertical interval blanking bar much better than the ×10 sweep expander mode.

Now use some square-wave pulses to see how the delayed-sweep control settings operate. The scope trace in Fig. 3-15 is a normal pulse as you would see it using the A time-base generator. Now the trace in Fig. 3-16 was obtained by pushing the A-intensified-by-B time-base generator button. Note that the two pulses are much brighter than the other pulses. They are intensified. Rotate the delayed-time control, and the brightness portion will move smoothly

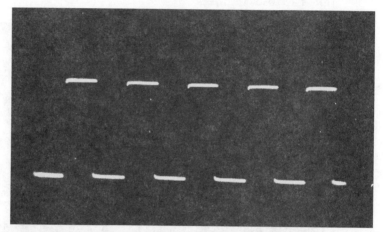

■ **3-15** *Pulses shown are for normal scope operation.*

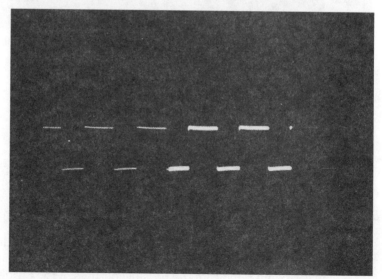

■ **3-16** *The brighter are A intensified.*

across the CRT display screen. The brightened portion represents the delayed sweep and occurs according to the SEC/DIV switch setting. The delayed sweep is independent of the main sweep speed and may be set to any speed equal to or faster than the main A time-base generator.

Now press the B delayed-sweep button and make sure that the intensified portion of the triggered waveform is now displayed across the entire scope screen as shown in the Fig. 3-17 scope traces. In the delayed-sweep mode, the trace has no jitter or bounce, which usually occurs when you use the ×10 expanded mode on single-time-base oscilloscopes.

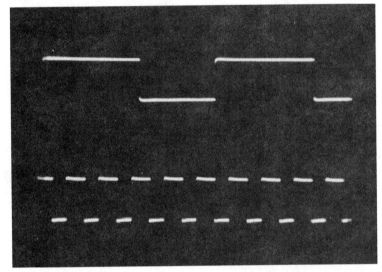

■ **3-17** *The top trace is produced when the B delayed-sweep button is depressed.*

More digital logic scope applications

A most useful function of a dual-trace scope is its capability for simultaneously viewing two waveforms that are frequency or phase related or that have a common synchronizing voltage, such as in digital circuitry. Simultaneous viewing of two related waveforms is an invaluable aid when you are troubleshooting digital circuits.

Frequency-divider systems

Figure 3-18 shows the basic waveforms involved in a divide-by-2 circuit. Waveform A indicates the reference or clock pulse train. Pulses B and C indicate the possible outputs of the divide-by-2 cir-

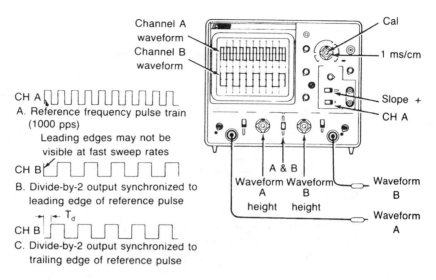

Channel A waveform
Channel B waveform

Cal
1 ms/cm
Slope +
CH A

CH A ⊓⊔⊓⊔⊓⊔⊓⊔⊓⊔⊓⊔⊓

A. Reference frequency pulse train (1000 pps)
   Leading edges may not be visible at fast sweep rates

CH B ⊓⊔⊓⊔⊓⊔⊓⊔⊓⊔⊓

B. Divide-by-2 output synchronized to leading edge of reference pulse

→| |← T_d

CH B ⊓⊔⊓⊔⊓⊔⊓⊔⊓⊔

C. Divide-by-2 output synchronized to trailing edge of reference pulse

A & B
Waveform A   Waveform B
height   height

Waveform B
Waveform A

■ **3-18** *Waveforms seen in a typical divide-by-2 circuit.*

cuitry. Figure 3-18 also shows the settings of specific scope controls for viewing these waveforms. In addition to these basic control settings, the trigger level control, as well as the channel A and channel B vertical position controls must be set to produce a suitable display. In Fig. 3-18, waveform levels of 2 cm are indicated. If you want the exact voltage amplitudes of the channel A and channel B waveforms, put the variable controls in the CAL position. Figure 3-18C shows the divide-by-2 output waveform for a case where the output circuitry responds to a negative-going waveform. In this case, the output waveform is shifted with respect to the leading edge of the reference frequency pulse by a time interval corresponding to the pulse width.

Divide-by-8 circuit waveforms

The pulses in Fig. 3-19 indicate relationships for a basic divide-by-8 circuit. Set the scope up as in Fig. 3-18. The reference frequency of Fig. 3-19 is fed to the channel A input, and the divide-by-8 output is applied to the channel B input. Wave pulse B indicates the ideal time relationship between the input pulses and the output pulse.

In an application where the logic circuitry is operating at or near its maximum design frequency, the accumulated rise-time effects of the consecutive stages produce a built-in time propagation delay that can be significant in a critical circuit and must be compensated for. The waveform in Fig. 3-19C indicates the possible

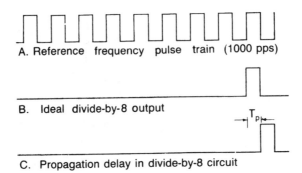

A. Reference frequency pulse train (1000 pps)

B. Ideal divide-by-8 output

C. Propagation delay in divide-by-8 circuit

■ **3-19** *Waveforms in a divide-by-8 circuit.* B & K Instrument Co.

time delay that may be introduced into a frequency-divider circuit. By using a dual-trace scope, you can superimpose the input and output waveforms to determine the exact amount of propagation delay that occurs.

Propagation time measurement

Propagation delay in a divide-by-8 circuit has already been discussed. Significant propagation delay may occur in any circuit with several consecutive stages. You can do this measurement on a dual-trace scope with vertical amplifiers that algebraically add and subtract. Figure 3-20 shows the waveforms produced when the dual-trace presentation is combined into a single-trace waveform by selecting the A+B or A–B position of the mode switch. In the A+B position, the two inputs are algebraically added in a single-trace display. Similarly, in the A–B position, the two inputs are algebraically subtracted. Either position provides a precise display of the propagation time (Tp). Using the procedures given for cali-

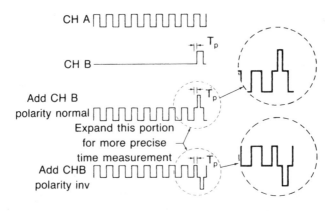

■ **3-20** *Using the add scope mode for propagation time measurements.*
B & K Instrument Co.

brated time measurement, you can calculate Tp. You can get an even more precise measurement by horizontally expanding the Tp portion of the waveform. You can do this by pulling the 5× or 10× expand control. It might also be possible to view the desired portion of the waveform at a faster sweep speed.

Digital circuit time relationships

A dual-trace scope is a must for troubleshooting digital equipment. This type of scope permits quick comparison of time relationships between two waveforms.

In microsystems, it is common for many circuits to be synchronized or to have a specific time relationship to each other. Most of the circuits are frequency dividers, but waveforms are often time related in numerous other combinations. In the dynamic state, some of the waveforms change, depending on the input or mode of operation. Figure 3-21 shows a typical digital circuit and identifies several points where you should take waveform scope checks. The pulse trains in Fig. 3-22 illustrate the normal waveforms to be expected at each of these points and their timing relationships. The individual waveforms have limited information unless their timing relationship to one or more of the other waveforms is known to be correct. The dual-trace oscilloscope lets you make this comparison with very little effort. For typical scope checks, waveform 3 would be displayed on channel A and waveforms 4 through 8 and 10 would be successively displayed on channel B, although other timing comparisons might be required. Waveforms 11 through 13 would probably be displayed on channel B in relation to waveform 8 or 4 on channel A.

In the family of time-related waveforms in Fig. 3-22, waveform 8 or 10 is an excellent sync source for viewing all of the waveforms, because there is only one trigger pulse per frame. For convenience, you might want external sync using waveform 8 or 10 as the sync source. With external sync, any of the waveforms may be displayed without readjustment of the sync controls. Don't use waveforms 4 through 7 as the sync source because they do not contain a triggering pulse at the start of the frame. You don't need to view the entire waveforms of Fig. 3-22 in all cases. Often a closer examination of a portion of the waveforms is appropriate. In such cases, it's a good idea to leave the sync unchanged and to use the sweep speed or 5×, 10× magnification to expand the waveform display.

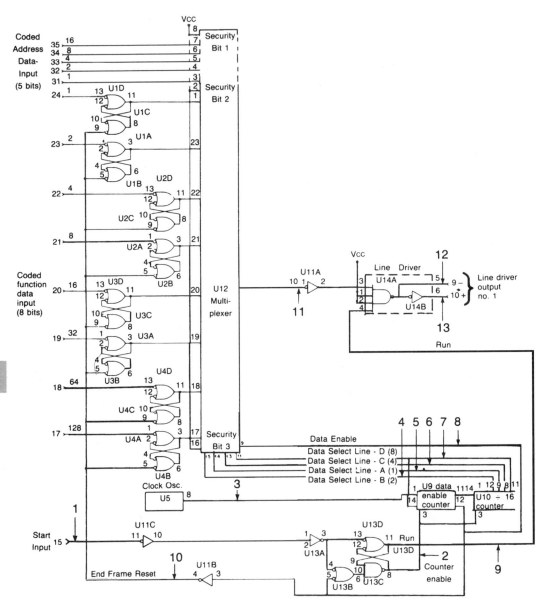

■ 3-21 *Typical digital circuit using several time-related scope waveforms.*
B & K Instrument Co.

Checking divider/multiplier stages

You can check very rapidly the countdown, divider, and multiplier digital circuits in microsystems, TV tuners, VCRs and servo circuits with the Sencore SC61 waveform analyzer in the A/B frequency ratio mode. Many digital frequency dividers are used in

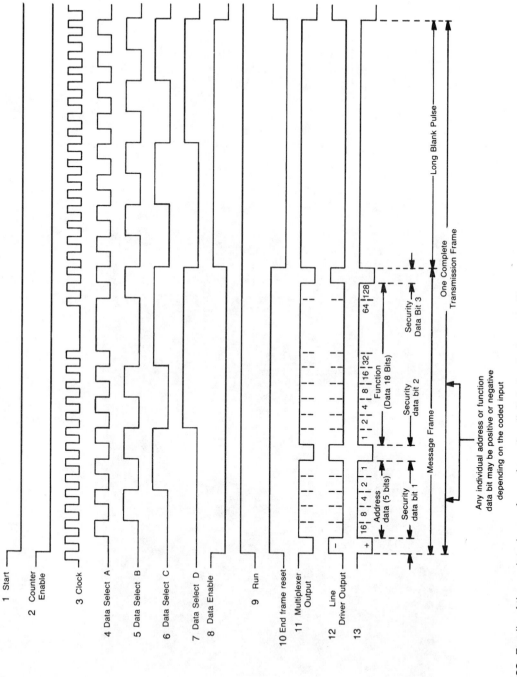

■ 3-22 Family of time-related waveforms from the digital circuit shown in Fig. 3-21.

microcircuits, which means several frequencies must be referenced to one master oscillator. To troubleshoot these circuits without an SC61, you would need a frequency counter to check and record the input and output frequencies of the stage. You may be able to figure out the ratio in your head with a divide-by-2 or divide-by-10 stage, but for higher ratios you need a calculator. For a programmable divider with lots of dividing ratios, the calculations could become quite difficult.

The SC61 automatically calculates the ratio of the frequency fed to channels A and B. You just push one button. The internal microcomputer calculates the ratio and displays it as a single number. Figure 3-23 illustrates how you can check a divide-by-77 stage in just seconds.

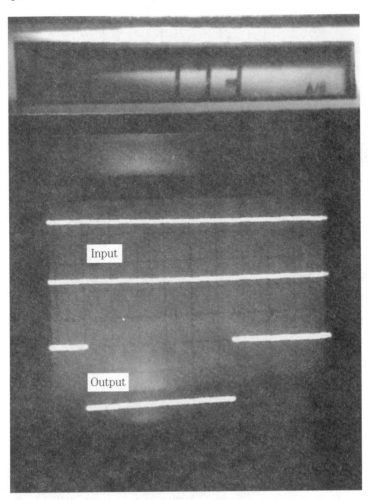

■ **3-23** *Waveforms found in a divide-by-77 stage.*

Tektronix DAS 9100 digital analysis system

The Tektronix DAS 9100 digital analysis system integrates high-performance, logic analysis functions, pattern generation, mass storage, and communication interfaces into a single system that opens up a new system of analysis and verification. The DAS 9100 enables you to interactively simulate and evaluate the response of a circuit or system under test before all hardware or firmware is completed.

You choose the DAS 9100 capabilities and features by plugging card modules into the system mainframe. You can add different modules at any time to change and/or upgrade the system's capabilities. Figure 3-24 shows the DAS 9100 system in operation. This system will save design time previously spent developing special test fixtures or system test codes to evaluate prototypes. The DAS 9100 was developed with design in mind, but you can use it for troubleshooting microsystems coming off the production line or plug-in units returned for repair.

■ **3-24** *Tektronix DAS 9100 in operation.*

The modular architecture of the system provides for up to 104 channels of data acquisition, synchronous and asynchronous sample rates to 330 MHz, resolution to 1.5 ns (660 MHz), and up to 80 channels of pattern generation at 25 MHz. Optional magnetic tape storage, RS-232C or GPIB interfaces for remote programmable control, and standard composite video are also available.

You can configure a combination of data-acquisition and pattern-generation modules along with mass storage and communication options to meet current requirements. The power supply is modular, allowing its capability to be increased as more modules are added to the system.

The color-coded functional keyboard and menus presented on the CRT combine to allow an easy-to-use system. By using the keyboard as prompted, you can access and display instrument setup menus. Variable parameters are highlighted in the menus.

With a single keystroke, you can run the data-acquisition and pattern-generator functions separately or combined, load the reference memory, run tests comparing acquired data against reference, and display data in state table or timing diagram format. Scroll keys permit examination of the entire 512-word acquisition memory. The user interface allows easy reformatting of the displayed data, magnification of the timing diagram format, and editing of the reference data.

Three data-acquisition modules are available to meet specific design requirements. The 32-channel module provides 40-ns resolution (25 MHz) both synchronously and asynchronously with a memory of 512 bits per channel and two clock qualifiers. The eight-channel module provides 10-ns resolution (100 MHz) both synchronously and asynchronously with a memory of 512 bits per channel, separate acquisition and glitch memories, and one clock qualifier. The four-channel module provides 3-ns resolution (330 MHz) both synchronously and asynchronously with a memory of 2048 bits per channel and a special high-resolution mode that provides 1.5-ns resolution (660 MHz) on two channels.

You can intermix these modules to support a variety of applications. Up to 96 channels of data acquisition are available at 25 MHz, up to 32 channels at 100 MHz, up to 16 channels at 330 MHz, and up to 8 channels at 1.5-ns resolution (660 MHz) to a maximum of 104 total channels of data acquisition.

A unique trigger-arming mode lets you trigger a high-speed, data-acquisition module monitoring hardware activity from lowerspeed

110

modules tracking software flow; acquired data is time aligned in both timing and state table displays.

The pattern-generator modules are provided for interactive design applications, such as stimulation of memory, I/O ports, and other hardware, or for simulation of microcode and hardware. A single card module provides 16 channels of pattern generation at 25 MHz with two independent programmable strobes. You can extend this to 48 or 80 channels of pattern generation with up to 10 programmable strobes by adding one or two 32-channel expander modules.

Using a limited memory depth, the pattern-generator's instruction set allows compression of output data and, with subrouting and looping, continuous output of patterns. You control the timing of the pattern generator by an external clock or by the internal program-selectable time base. The pattern generator also has an interrupt input and can even tri-state on the fly.

State table data can be formatted in hex, octal, binary, or userdefined mnemonics. The timing diagram allows label assignment and programmable channel designation. Timing magnification to 10,000×, a memory window, word search, and glitch highlight are also provided.

You can select programmable thresholds to accommodate TTL, MOS, or ECL for each card module. Triggering modes include word recognizer, event counter, glitches, clock qualifiers, and arming. You can use up to three external clocks, which lets you demultiplex bus information and/or analyze multiprocessor systems.

The optional DC-100 magnetic tape drive lets you load and store all the system's setup information, pattern-generator programs and tests, reference memory data, mnemonic tables, and more. The tape can be used for transfer of tests and evaluation routines to production test personnel and service technicians.

The optional communications package consists of an RS-232C port, GPIB interface, and standard video output. The RS-232C port and GPIB interface allow remote control/programmability of the instrument and transmission of acquired data to another DAS 9100 digital analysis system computer. Two DAS 9100s can be operated remotely in a master/slave configuration.

In the GPIB mode, the DAS 9100 can perform as a "listener," programming all keyboard functions and downloading programs and data, or as a "talker," transmitting test setups and data or performing service requests.

In addition to custom configuring a system, you can choose one of four system configurations.

Tektronix PMA 100 personality adapter

Figure 3-25 shows the PMA 100 personality module adapter, which brings extensive microprocessor support to the DAS 9100 system. It is the first test and measurement product available with either a color or black-and-white CRT display.

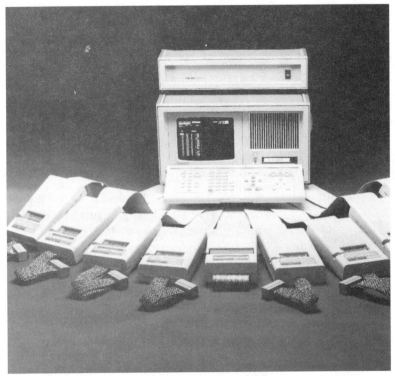

■ **3-25** *The Tektronix PMA 100 personality adapter.*

The PMA 100 allows the DAS to work in concert with the PM 100 series of personality modules. These modules support many popular 8-bit and 16-bit processors, including the Intel 8086, Motorola 68000 and 6809, and Zilog Z8000. In each case, the personality module performs all the necessary demultiplexing and control-line monitoring to acquire real-time microprocessor code execution. This information is subsequently disassembled and displayed by the DAS. The PMA provides one full word of data qualification and cuts setup time to a minimum through a single-system connection.

The PMA 100 acts as an interface between the DAS and the personality module in use. It connects to the DAS 91A32 data-acquisition modules, which feature multilevel triggering and synchronous/asynchronous operation to 25 MHz.

The preceding information concerning Tektronix equipment was supplied by courtesy of Tektronix, Inc.

Color video systems chips

THIS CHAPTER COVERS THEORY AND OPERATION OF SPECIAL
video processor chips used in color TVs and VCRs. These chips are
not microprocessor ICs but uniquely designed sophisticated circuits that process color video signals.

Luminance/chrominance chip

The luminance/chrominance (L/C) chip, in an RCA CTC-108 chassis, provides all the processing for the luminance and chroma signal information. Combining the two signal-processing systems
onto one chip allows color and contrast tracking to be built into
the IC. An internal block diagram of this IC is given in Fig. 4-1.

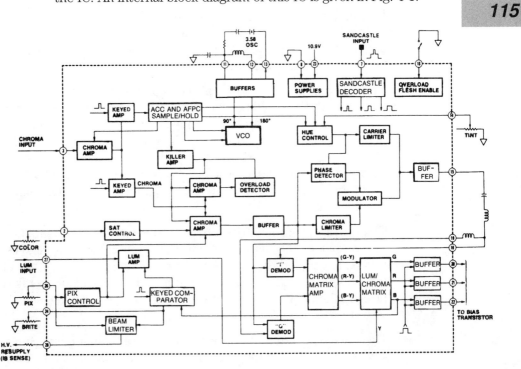

■ **4-1** *IC internal block diagram.* RCA Corp

IC operation theory

The chroma input signal is fed to pin 3 of the IC. The color level adjustment is input via a dc voltage to pin 2 of the IC. The 3.58-MHz local oscillator is controlled by pins 11, 12, and 13 of the IC. Pin 14 is the dc input for the tint control. Pins 18 and 19 are the inputs for the phase-shifted 3.58-MHz oscillator, which is used for the I and Q demodulation of the chrominance signals.

Luminance information is fed to the IC at pin 27. The signal is then amplified and applied to the L/C matrix amplifiers in the chip. The contrast or picture level is set by a dc voltage applied to pin 26 of the IC. The output of the picture control amplifier in the IC is fed to the luminance amplifier channel as well as the chrominance amplifier channel and provides color and contrast tracking. The picture control amplifier is also modulated by the beam limiting circuit to provide contrast tracking with beam limiting.

The beam limiter circuit is controlled by the high-voltage resupply line to the sweep transformer and the set's brightness control. Brightness is set by comparing the setting of the brightness control (pin 24) to the level of the blue output blanking signal. During horizontal retrace, the brightness dc voltage and the level of the blue output blanking signal are compared and a resultant voltage is developed that controls the brightness level of the luminance amplifier. This maintains consistent brightness ratios that depend on incoming blanking levels.

Brightness limiter operations is accomplished by sampling the dc current to the high-voltage windings of the horizontal sweep transformer by a resistor connected to pin 28 of the chip. With a picture of normal brightness being viewed, the voltage at pin 20 of the IC is clamped at 12 V. As the beam current increases, the voltage at pin 28 drops. As the voltage drops below 12 V, the beam limiter conducts, reducing the beam current by acting upon the luminance amplifier within the IC.

The L/C signals are matrixed together in the matrixing amplifier. The output of the matrix amplifier is three color video signals, which are coupled through blanker/buffer stages to the output of the IC at pins 20, 21, and 22. Horizontal and vertical blanking takes place in the blanker/buffer output stages before the video signals leave the IC.

The signals governing horizontal and vertical blanking and burst keying are applied to the IC through IC pin 7. The input waveform consists of a matrixed combination of horizontal and vertical blanking and burst-keying pulses. This input signal is called a *sandcas-tle* signal because of the unique shape of the waveform. The IC has an internal decoder network that decodes the three signals and feeds them to the proper circuitry in the chip.

Sandcastle circuit operation

The sandcastle input waveform is important for the operation of the L/C circuit. See Fig. 4-2 for the sandcastle generator circuit. If there is no sandcastle signal input at pin 7, there is no output from the L/C IC. The sandcastle signal is developed by transistors Q801 and Q702 and some other associated circuitry. Vertical-blanking information is coupled into the base of Q702, causing Q702 to turn on during vertical blanking. Hence, the CR 703 anode voltage increases during vertical blanking. This voltage is coupled through R711 to TP 806 at IC pin 7.

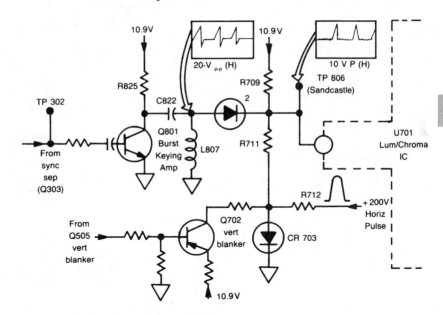

■ **4-2** *Sandcastle generator circuit.* RCA Corp

Horizontal blanking is done by feeding a positive-going horizontal pulse through R712 to the anode of CR 703. This positive-going horizontal pulse is also applied through R711 to TP 806 and IC pin 7. The color keying signal is developed from the horizontal sync by capacitively coupling the sync into the base of Q801. C822 and L807 in the collector of Q801 generate a ringing pulse when sync is applied to this circuit. Diode CR 702 couples the positive-going portion of the pulse to TP 806 and pin 7 of chip U701.

Luminance/chrominance chip

Servicing the combined color processing IC

The following are some symptoms for this combined processor circuit:

- ☐ No chroma, no video
- ☐ No chroma, video good
- ☐ Weak chroma
- ☐ Wrong color
- ☐ No tint or color control

Note: This set has a "hot" grounded (nonisolated) chassis. Use an isolation transformer, disconnect the line cord during all static checks, and use insulated tools or clip leads for dynamic checks. See Fig. 4-3 for scope waveforms and check points.

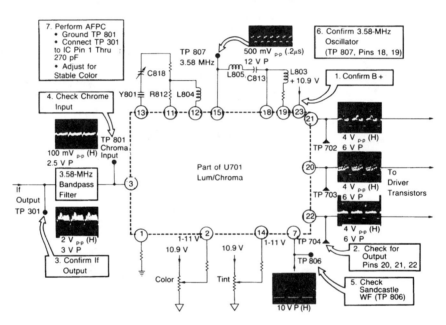

■ **4-3** *Combined luminance/chrominance circuit checks.*

No chroma, no video

1. Confirm proper B+ of 10.9 V at pin 23 of U701.

2. Check for correct output signals at TP 702, 703, and 704.

3. Check for presence of IF (intermediate frequency) output signal at TP 301.

4. Check for presence of chroma input signal at U701 at TP 801.

118

5. Verify correct sandcastle input waveform to pin 7 of U701 TP 806.

6. Confirm the 3.58-MHz oscillator operation at TP 807 and pins 18 and 19 of the chip.

7. Check color sync adjustment. Always check and, if required, readjust after servicing chroma circuitry. To adjust the color sync,
   a. Ground TP 801.
   b. Connect TP 301 to IC pin 1 by a 270-pF capacitor with very short leads.
   c. Adjust for stable color in picture.

Note: Check the color sync lock and readjust whenever you service the chroma circuitry.

No chroma, video good; Weak chroma

1. Check for chroma input to U701 at TP 801.

2. Verify correct sandcastle input waveform at TP 806 (U701-7).

3. Confirm 3.58-MHz oscillator operation at TP 807 and pins 18 and 19. Check and, if necessary, perform color sync adjustment.

Wrong Color

Short TP 801 to ground. If wrong color symptoms still remain, check picture tube setup adjustments.

No tint or color control

Check for correct voltages at pins 2 and 14 of U701 as color and tint controls are varied. Voltages should vary between 1 and 11 V.

Servicing the luminance section

The following are possible picture symptoms:

☐ No video or chroma
☐ No video, chroma good
☐ No picture or brightness control
☐ Weak or washed-out picture
☐ Color in B/W picture

Caution: Use an isolation transformer because of the "hot" chassis.

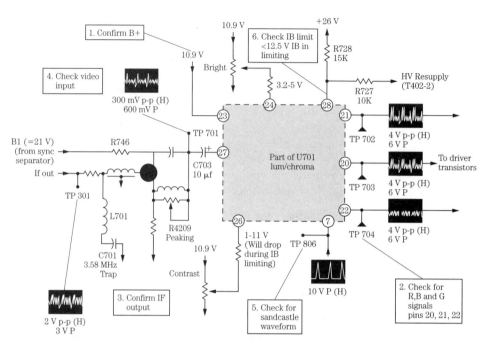

■ 4-4 *Steps for servicing luminance section of IC.* RCA Corp

Note: After servicing these circuit areas, always check the color sync adjustment. See Fig. 4-4 for scope waveforms and test points.

No video or chroma

1. Confirm B+ of 10.9 V at U701 chip pin 23.
2. Check for red, blue, and green output signals at TP 702, 703, and 704.
3. Confirm IF output signal at TP 301.
4. Check for video input at TP 701.
5. Check for sandcastle waveform at TP 806.
6. Check beam limiting operation. Voltage at pin 28 should be less than 11.5 V during limiting.

No video, chroma good

1. Check for video input at TP 701.
2. Confirm presence of correct sandcastle input waveform at TP 806.
3. Check operation of beam limiter. Voltage at pin 28 should be less than 11.5 V during limiting.

No picture or brightness control

Check control voltages at pin 26 for contrast and pin 24 for brightness. If voltage does not vary when appropriate control is varied, suspect a defect in the wiring at that point.

Weak or washed-out picture

Check brightness limiter circuitry action (pin 28). Voltage should be approximately 11.5 V or above with normal low-brightness picture.

Color in B/W picture

Short TP 801 to ground. If color remains, check setup of the CRT adjustments.

SAW filter IF circuit

The output of the SAW filter device, which is an IF signal that has the proper frequency response, is fed differentially to the IF chip. The signal is then passed through three stages of IF amplification in the IC in the RCA CTC-108. After being amplified by the IF amplifiers, the IF signal is then fed to a synchronous video detector. Synchronous detection provides the lowest possible distortion in the video output signal. See Fig. 4-5.

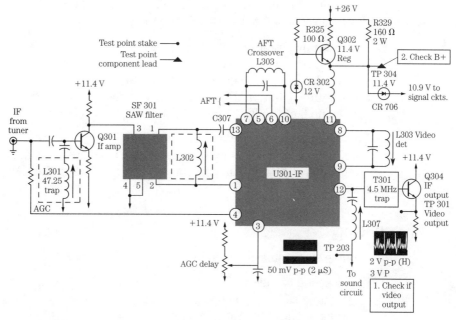

■ **4-5** *SAW filter and IF circuit checks.* RCA Corp

After being detected, the video is amplified, passed through a noise inverter, and coupled from the IC as a signal containing video, chrominance, and sound carrier information. The video output signal is passed through a 4.5-MHz trap (T301) to eliminate the sound carrier information from the L/C information being fed to the signal-processing circuitry. The output of pin 12 is also coupled through inductor L307 (a 4.5-MHz bandpass) and is used to feed the sound carrier information to the sound circuits at TP 203.

Intermediate frequency automatic gain control (AGC), which is developed in the IC, is used to vary the gain of the first, second, and third IF stages. The IF AGC is then used as a comparison against the setting of the rf AGC control to develop the rf AGC voltage. In this IF circuit the AGC voltage is no longer keyed by horizontal retrace. This feature allows the horizontal oscillator pull-in to be more effective due to elimination of phasing problems between the keying pulse and the transmitted horizontal sync. Noise-limiting circuits in the IC make it possible to eliminate keying for the AGC signal.

The IF signal from the tuner is amplified by Q301. A 47.25-MHz trap in the base circuit of Q301 eliminates the adjacent-channel sound carrier. The extra amplification is required to compensate for the large insertion loss of the SAW filter device. This loss results from the need to eliminate triple transient response and other spurious signals in the device. After passing through the SAW filter, the IF signal is applied to the IF amplifier stages in the chip.

The IF is powered from an external 11.2 V regulated source, which is developed by CR 302 and Q302. An external B+ regulator allows simpler design and lower power dissipation in the IF chip. The automatic fine tuning (AFT) voltage fed to the tuner is taken from pins 5 and 6 of the IC. Nominal AFT voltage is 6.4 V.

This chassis uses the synchronous detection techniques and the operation of the noise-limiting circuits. Therefore, you need to modify conventional IF alignment procedures to align the SAW filter IF section.

IF servicing

Trouble symptoms are as follows:

☐ No sound or video
☐ Picture drift
☐ Weak or snowy picture

Note: The SAW filter device (SF301) is rugged, but be careful when handling it and don't connect ohmmeter leads to any of the pins. Generally, failure of a SAW filter will produce degraded IF performance, such as some adjacent-channel interference. Again, refer to the block diagram in Fig. 4-5 for scope waveforms and test points.

No sound or video

1. Check for IF output waveform at TP 301.
2. If scope waveform is not found at TP 301, check U301 IC for waveform at pin 12.
3. Check for correct B+ supply of 11.4 V at TP 304 or IC U301 pin 11. If voltage other than 11.4 V is found, suspect a defective Q302 or faulty CR302.
4. Disconnect IF link cable and connect center conductor to U301 pin 16 through a 1000-pF capacitor. If picture appears (may be distorted), suspect Q301 or SF301. If no change, then suspect tuner or U301.

Picture drift

Monitor the AFT voltage at pins 5 and 6. Voltage should be approximately 6.4 V with no signal received. If not, suspect a defective U301.

Weak or snowy picture

1. Monitor the AGC voltage at U301 pin 14. It should be about 7 V with a strong signal and about 11 V with a weak signal. The voltage should go to 11 V when the IF link is unplugged. If not, suspect a defective U301 chip.
2. Now check voltage at U301 pin 4 (rf AGC). Voltage should be about 4 V with a strong signal and close to 11 V with a weak signal. With the IF link unplugged, the voltage at pin 4 should also read 11 V. If AGC voltages are correct, suspect a tuner module, Q301, or SF301.
3. Disconnect IF link cable and connect center conductor to U301 pin 16 through a 1000-pF capacitor. If picture now appears (even if poor quality), suspect Q301 or SF301. If no change, suspect a faulty tuner or U301.

The preceding information was supplied courtesy of RCA Corp.

VCR chrominance recording process

The simplified block diagram of the chrominance record process used in a Quasar VCR is shown in Fig. 4-6.

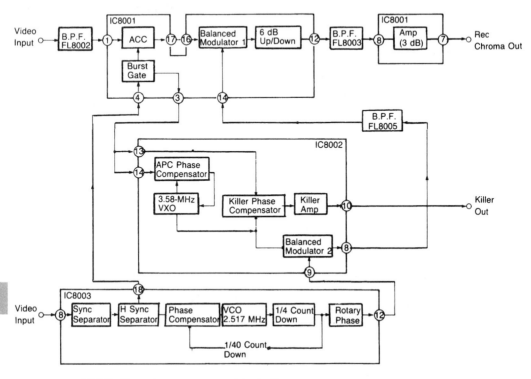

4-6 *Chrominance process block diagram.* Quasar Company

3.58-MHz bandpass filter

The incoming video signal is sent through a bandpass filter so that only the information centered around 3.58 MHz (color information) will remain.

Automatic Color Control (ACC) circuit

The ACC is performed on burst in the LP tape speed mode; however it is peak detected ACC in the SP/SLP mode. Two different ACC operations are used to improve the overall chroma signal-to-noise ratio (S/N) ratio during tape playback.

Because of the tape pattern, a horizontal line is aligned in the SP/SLP mode but not in the LP mode. If the picture quality is changed so that there is a very low light object, the incoming chroma level will drop slightly but the burst level will remain constant. In this case, when peak ACC is used, it increases the chroma gain corresponding to the incoming chroma. Hence, the noise components are also increased, which causes a poor overall S/N ratio during tape playback. It does not affect the SP/SLP mode, however, due to overlap cancellation. Thus, burst ACC is used in the LP mode.

Balanced Modulator 1

The balanced modulator inside IC8001 performs the necessary down-conversion and rotation of the chroma signal so that it can be recorded onto tape. One output to the balanced modulator is the chrominance signal itself, after ACC. In the SP/SLP mode, this signal has boosted color burst. The second input to the balanced modulator is a 4.2-MHz, phase-locked, rotational signal derived from another part of the chrominance board. The output of the balanced modulator is the difference between the two input signals, or 629 kHz, which is also phase-locked.

Boosted boost (6 dB up)

You can improve the overall color S/N ratio by increasing the level of the burst signal by 6 dB. The boost circuit is controlled by a burst gate pulse, which ensures that only the burst signal, and not the rest of the color signal, is boosted.

This boosting process is used in the SP/SLP mode only. In the LP mode, there is no horizontal alignment. If the boosting action were allowed here, it would have a negative effect. Thus, no burst gate pulse is passed by the boosting circuit in the LP mode, which then prohibits the boosting action.

Color killer

The color killer section of IC8001 either passes or blocks the signal coming out of balanced modulator 1. In the color mode, the signal is passed to the luminance section to be amplified and recorded. In the B/W mode, any output from balanced modulator 1 is blocked so that it does not contribute any noise to the recording.

AFT-rotary phase generator

To produce a 629-kHz signal whose phase changes by 90° every time the video signal progresses by one horizontal line, you need to phase lock the 629-kHz generator to the horizontal sync signal. This is the reason the AFC circuit and the rotary generator (IC8003) will work together.

The process starts with a 2.517-MHz voltage-controlled oscillator (VCO) inside of the IC8003 chip. This continuous-wave signal is sent to a divide-by-4 counter with four continuous outputs. These outputs are at 629 kHz and have phases of 0°, 90°, 180°, and 270°. Each output is used as one input to its own respective AND gate inside IC8003. These enabling circuit inputs are shown in Fig. 4-7.

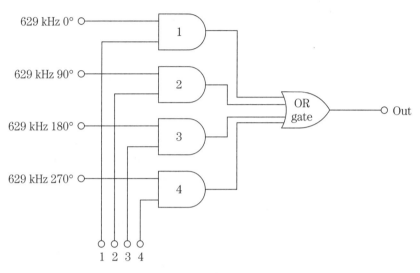

■ **4-7** *Block diagram of AND gate.*

Only one AND gate at a time is allowed to pass a signal. If the gates are fired in the proper order and change just at the time horizontal sync occurs, the phase rotation process will be accomplished. See Fig. 4-8.

The second input to the AND gates is the enabling signal, which allows the gate to pass its 629-kHz signal. Each gate receives a separate firing signal, as shown in Fig. 4-9.

All four of the 629-kHz signals are constant. It is the firing signal that turns on the successive gates. Therefore the four firing signals must be locked to the horizontal sync to perform the desired gating.

What you want is that for the first horizontal line of field 1 of the video information, gate 1 is on and gates 2, 3, and 4 are off. For the second line of field 1, gate 2 is on, and gates 3, 4, and 1 are off, and so forth.

Remember that the direction of phase rotation is different between video fields, so the firing order must be changed for field 2.

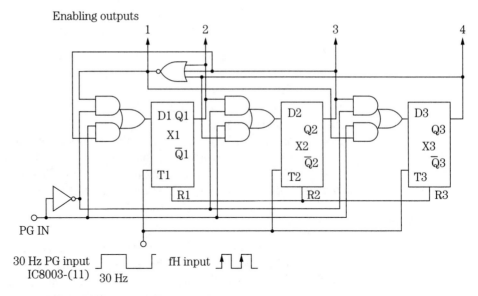

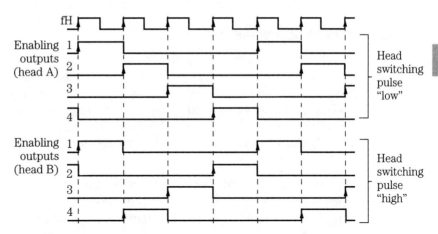

■ **4-8** *Ring counter diagram.* Quasar Company

■ **4-9** *Ring counter output.*

For line 1 of field 2, gate 1 is on and gates 2, 3, and 4 are off. For line 2 of field 2, gate 4 is on and gates 1, 2, and 3 are off. For line 3 of field 2, gate 3 is on and gates 4, 1, and 2 are off. For line 4 of field 2, gate 2 is on and gates 3, 4, and 1 are off.

Figure 4-8 shows that the 629-kHz signal is counted down by 40 to obtain a horizontal rate signal and is sent as one input to the switching pulse generator, which will produce firing signals to activate the gates in the proper order. Another input to the switching pulse generator is the head switching signal. This facilitates the reverse firing order by field 2, or the B video head.

The 629-kHz signal that is counted down by 40 is also sent as one input to the automatic frequency control (AFC) comparator circuit inside the IC8003. The other input to the AFC comparator is incoming horizontal sync. This forms a phase-locked loop (PLL). If the 629-kHz signal being generated is not perfectly phase locked to the incoming horizontal sync signal, the AFC comparator will detect this and deliver a dc error voltage back to the 2.517-MHz VCO to drive it in such a way that phase locking does occur. The output of each gate is OR-gated out of IC8003 into balanced modulator 2.

Balanced modulator 2

The 629-kHz rotary phase signal becomes one input to balance modulator 2 inside of IC8002. The other input is a 3.58-MHz sine-wave signal of the same phase as the incoming color burst signal. The output selected as the sum will be a 4.2-MHz signal, which is phase locked to the incoming burst and sync signal and is rotary phased.

Automatic Phase Control (APC) circuit

The 3.58-MHz sine-wave signal into balanced modulator 2 is obtained from a VXO (voltage-controlled crystal oscillator) in the APC loop of IC8002. The APC circuit is another PLL arrangement. One input to the APC comparator is the incoming burst signal as it is gated through the burst gate in IC8001. The APC circuit drives VXO (X8001) so that it produces the desired 3.58-MHz sine wave of the correct phase.

The output of the crystal oscillator in IC8004 is sent to the second input of the APC comparator. Thus, any deviation in the crystal's output is compared with the incoming burst signal in the APC comparator.

The comparator produces an error voltage to drive crystal oscillator X8001 and provide compensation. The 4.2-MHz, phase-locked rotational signal out of balanced modulator 2 is used in balanced modulator 1 to develop the final 629-kHz, phase-locked, rotational color signal.

The preceding information is supplied courtesy of the Quasar Company (Copyright 1981).

IF system gain block

Figure 4-10 shows the block diagram of the IF amplifier and detector system IC. The stages are connected internally in the IF/AGC processor chip (IC221-190). The block diagram consists of five amplification stages (all of the differential type). The first stage is a grounded-base stage to produce the low-impedance input. This stage, with a gain of 13 dB, has no AGC applied to it.

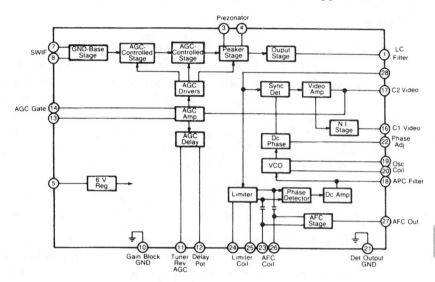

■ **4-10** *IF amplifier/detector block diagram.* Zenith Corp

The second and third stages are conventional differential amplifiers. They contain variable emitter degeneration to produce about 23 dB of gain reduction per stage. This variable emitter degeneration is brought about by controlling the forward bias on a diode that parallels the emitter resistor. These two stages have a gain of 17 dB per stage.

The fourth stage is the peaker stage. This stage contains a high-Q, series-tuned circuit in the form of a ceramic filter (called a *piezonator*) selectively placed across the emitter circuit. This selection is controlled by the AGC voltage acting on a forward biased diode, similar to previous AGC stages. When this high-Q circuit (which is tuned to the picture carrier) is placed across the emitter, it raises the gain of the stage to the picture carrier but leaves the gain of the rest of the IF band constant. The gain to the picture carrier is designed to increase 6 dB at maximum gain, placing the picture carrier at the top of the IF response curve. The rest of the response will remain the same during strong signal conditions.

VCR chrominance recording process

When the picture carrier changes 6 dB as a function of the AGC voltage, it amounts to 6 dB more gain reduction in the amplifier. This gain reduction, along with the 46 dB gain reduction of the two previous stages, adds to a total gain reduction of 52 dB.

The fifth stage is the output stage. Although the five stages in the gain block are operated differently, only one output is used in this stage.

Synchronous detector block

The signal received from the gain block is split two ways: one input goes to the synchronous detector stage, the other to the limiter stage. The limiter collector contains back-to-back diodes as the main limiting element. This signal from the limiter is sent onto the phase detector. In addition, a part of the limiter output is used to drive the AFC circuitry. The signal fed to the phase detector is multiplied by its other input, the reference oscillator signal. When these two signals are 90° out of phase, the output of the multiplier is zero. At any other phase condition, the output will produce a beat note accompanied by a dc component. This signal is filtered and amplified and used to control the reference oscillator, the VCO.

The VCO signal is fed to the synchronous detector stage through a voltage-controlled, phase-shift stage. This variable phase shift allows the sync detector modulation angle to be adjusted without affecting the limiter adjustment.

The video stage provides the correct levels for the C1 and C2 outputs. For the C1 output, the signal normally above zero carrier is inverted and fed to the output. This action takes place after it overcomes an offset voltage. You can adjust the zero carrier by varying the current in the C2 output emitter follower and dividing down the output signal using an internal resistor in the IC of the series element.

In addition to these stages, a 6-V regulator functions as a shunt regulator with a 5.3-V zener as the reference unit.

External IF circuitry

The external IF amplifier and detector circuitry on the 9-181 module is shown in Fig. 4-11. Note just two semiconductor devices: the 221-190 IC and the C1 emitter follower stage. The circuits also contain two ceramic devices, a piezonator, and the 4.5-MHz trap.

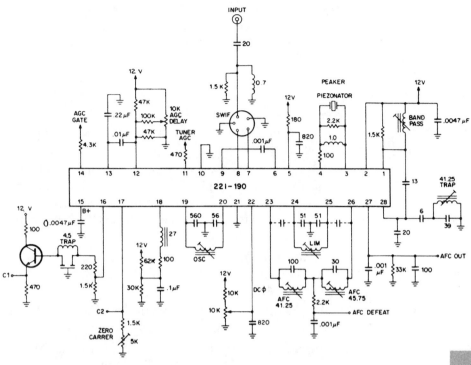

4-11 *External IF amplifier/detector circuitry.*

In operation, the signal from the tuner passes through a matching pad and then to the SWIF. Because the input impedance to the gain block is almost purely resistive, it is similar to having the output of the SWIF tuned. The result is that less power is lost in the interface between the SWIF and the gain block.

The output circuit is a simple capacitive-tap tuned circuit. A 41.25-MHz trap is included in the output circuit to lower the sound carrier from the picture carrier.

The 4.5-MHz trap circuit incorporates a ceramic filter. This trap circuit does not require any adjustment.

The limiter circuit is a single-tuned circuit tuned to approximately 45 MHz. The limiter coil is tuned to adjust the differential phase to ±2°, without regard to transient response. The dc phase control is then adjusted for best transient response.

A 5-kΩ control in the emitter circuit of the output emitter follower in the IC acts as the zero carrier adjustment. The control varies the current of the emitter follower, controlling the output voltage at C2.

IF circuit adjustments

The design of this IF system allows the 221-190 chip to be replaced in the field with little or no adjustments. If adjustment is required because of a change in a component on a near limit chip, you can align it as follows:

1. **Bandpass coil.** With a weak station signal (about 500 µV), finetune the set for best picture. Turn on the AFC or, for microprocessor tuning systems, operate in the normal mode. Adjust for maximum AGC voltage on the IF; then turn core counterclockwise one-half turn.

2. **41.25 trap coil.** Fine tune for the best picture. Turn on the AFC or normal mode. Connect scope to C2 and adjust for minimum 4.5 MHz.

3. **Oscillator coil.** Fine tune for best picture. Turn on AFC or normal mode. Adjust for 4.2 Vdc at APC test point.

4. **Limiter coil.** Fine tune for best picture and turn on AFC. Adjust for minimum buzz in the audio. After limiter adjustment, recheck the dc phase adjustment.

5. **Dc phase pot.** Fine tune for best picture and turn on AFC. Adjust for the best transients during large white-to-black excursions.

6. **AFC 45.75-MHz coil.** With AFC off, fine tune for best picture. Turn AFC on and off. Adjust AFC 45.75-MHz coil until picture looks the same with AFC on as with it off. For microprocessor tuning systems, operate in normal mode on low VHF channels (2–6) with voltmeter on AFC out test point. Adjust 45.75-MHz AFC coil for same dc reading as when connector 4L4 AFC defeat pin is shorted to ground.

7. **Zero carrier pot.** Pull out IF cable from tuner at IF end. Apply 6 V to IF AGC test point to cut off IF. Adjust pot for 7.0 V at C2.

8. **AGC delay pot.** Adjust for minimum snow in a strong signal, but also minimum channel 6 beat, if necessary.

AGC system

A color TV receiver should be able to operate in a fringe area as well as a strong signal area. Thus, to always ensure good reception, use an AGC circuit. The AGC maintains the picture carrier, at the input of the video detector, at a constant level and maintains the video sync at a predetermined level.

The AGC function is included in the 221-190 IC chip. The sync separator function is included with the HV processor 221-175 IC. Because of the separation of the sync/AGC into separate ICs, an external circuit is used to provide the function of AGC gate generation. See Fig. 4-12.

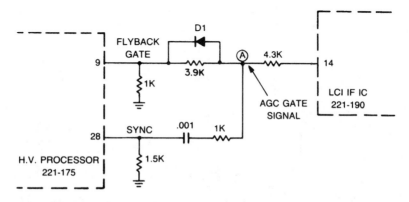

■ **4-12** *AGC gate generator circuit.*

Sync pulses from the sync output (pin 28 of IC221-175) are ac coupled to the flyback gate signal from pin 9 of IC221-175. When the sync and flyback gate signals are coincident, the AGC gate signal at point A is mainly sync. Now, when the sync pulses are absent the AGC gate signal is a reduced flyback gate signal. Diode D1 attenuates the noise during the nonflyback gate period.

The functions of the IF amplifier synchronous detector, AGC detector, AGC delay, IF AGC amplifier, and rf AGC amplifier are all incorporated into the 221-190 chip. The functions of the AGC detector and delay circuits are as follows:

AGC detector

The AGC detector samples the video during the sync period and charges or discharges the AGC filter capacitor to a voltage that represents the signal strength. The AGC filter voltage, via the AGC delay circuit, is fed to the IF and rf AGC amplifiers.

AGC delay

The AGC delay adjusts the minimum IF amplifier gain and determines the threshold below which only the IF amplifier's gain is adjusted, the rf amplifier remaining at maximum gain. Above this threshold, the rf amplifier's gain is adjusted, and the IF amplifier remains at the minimum gain. See Fig. 4-13 for the AGC system block diagram.

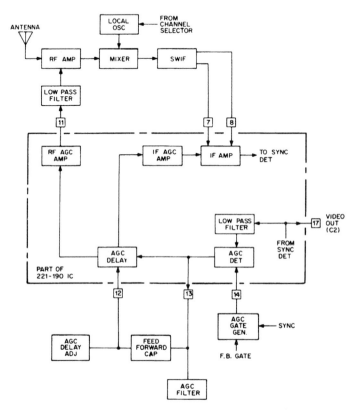

■ **4-13** *AGC system for Z chassis.* Zenith Corp

The feed-forward capacitor is connected between pins 12 and 13 of IC221-190. For abrupt changes in signal strengths above the AGC threshold, the feed-forward capacitor causes the IF amplifier to alter its gain and stabilize the video signal. During this transition, the rf amplifier's gain is not altered. After a time, the IF amplifier will return to its minimum gain, and the rf amplifier gain will adjust to a new level that will correspond to the new rf signal strength.

Luminance/chrominance processing (RCA)

The L/C system is used in an RCA CTC-110 color TV chassis. The composite video output signal from the SAW IF is first coupled to the CCD comb filter (U600). The comb filter has three major output signals (see Fig. 4-14). The first signal is the *combed* chroma information, which is sent to and processed by the L/C IC U700. The second is the *combed* luminance information, which is missing some low-frequency, vertical-detail information, which is characteristic of baseband comb filters. The third major output of the comb filter is the VDO (vertical detail output) signal. The VDO is amplified/buffered and then summed with the combed luminance information. Adding the VDO and combed luminance signal produces a "restored" luminance, which is then inverted and sent on to the autopeaker circuit.

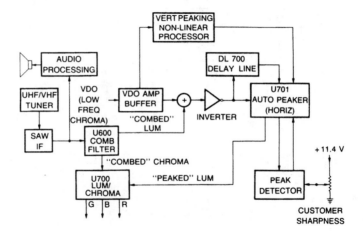

■ **4-14** *Signal-processing block diagram.*

Another input to the autopeaker is the vertical peaking signal. This peaked vertical information is obtained from the VDO amplifier/buffer stages previously mentioned and routed through the nonlinear processor (coring/circuit).

The peaked, restored luminance information is next coupled to the L/C IC where it is processed along with the chroma information. The peaked luminance signal is also coupled to a peak detector stage that processes and uses the luminance signal to generate a control signal that is looped back to the autopeaker (U701).

Chroma processor circuits (GE-EC Chassis)

The IC300 chroma processor is used in the EC chassis and several other General Electric color chassis. This chip features adjustable APC, fixed ACC, fixed killer, fixed chroma bandpass, and fixed individual (different) inputs to the demodulator. Tint, color, and color tracking are dc controlled circuits. The tint-control system has been moved to the chroma circuit because the APC system does not respond rapidly enough for the automatic color circuitry. The functional block diagram is shown in Fig. 4-15.

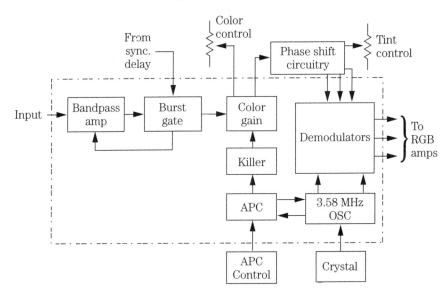

■ **4-15** *Simplified block diagram of IC300 chip.*

The 3.58-MHz color signal is extracted from the composite video by the filter placed between the module video input and the bandpass amplifier in IC300. The other signal required for color reproduction is the 3.58-MHz subcarrier applied to the color demodulators. This source of 3.58-MHz signal is supplied by the crystal and the oscillator circuit inside IC300. Between the points where the color IF enters the IC and where the R-Y, B-Y, and G-Y color signals emerge to drive the video outputs, various degrees of control are encountered. Because these control circuits are inside the chip, all of these functions will not be explained; but their necessity and something about their basic operation will be explained.

Burst gate

The burst gate is turned on by a pulse provided by the sync delay circuit. The pulse is delayed so that the burst gate is turned on only during color burst time, as shown in Fig. 4-16. From the burst gate circuit, color signals are fed to a color gain control block. This amplifier is controlled by the color control and the video differential amplifier. The differential amplifier output is regulated by the picture control. The picture control commands both video and color level so that picture color and contrast elements are correct for good viewing regardless of contrast settings. Thus, the color gain circuit is also controlled by the picture control through the differential amplifier. The color gain control is also controlled by the color killer circuit which prevents color snow on the screen when a B/W picture is received.

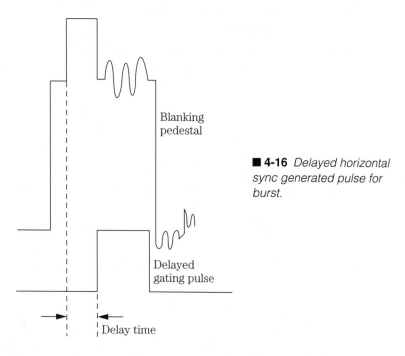

Blanking
pedestal

■ 4-16 *Delayed horizontal sync generated pulse for burst.*

Delayed
gating pulse

Delay time

Tint control

From the color gain amplifier, the color IF signal is fed outside the IC to the phase-shift/tint-control circuits, where the chroma IF phase can be changed by the tint control. The output of this phase-shift circuit is split into the three phases needed for reinsertion into the demodulator circuits for R-Y, G-Y, and B-Y recovery.

Oscillator stage

The demodulator inputs also include two 3.58-MHz oscillator inputs, which are kept in phase with the broadcast TV station color burst signal by the APC control circuit.

Color outputs

R-Y, G-Y, and B-Y signals exit the IC and are fed to the R, G, and B video outputs. Signals from this point are also coupled to the VIR (vertical interval reference) module for those sets that have this automatic color-adjustment feature. Video and color signals are combined (matrixed) in the R, G, and B output transistors and then fed onto the CRT cathodes for color picture reproduction on the screen.

For the following circuit explanation, refer to Fig. 4-17, which shows the signal circuit schematic.

Composite video is fed to terminal RL5 from the IF module via C220 to Q220, which amplifies the negative-going video signal, in-

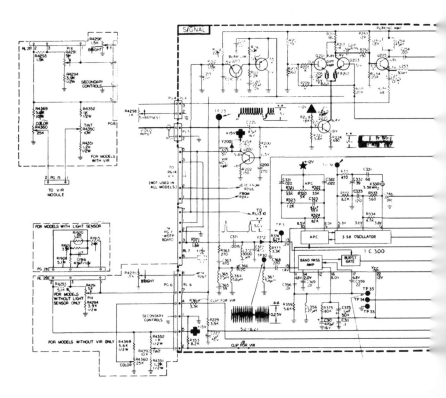

■ **4-17** *Chroma processor for Quazar TS-976 chassis.*

verts it, and drives the differential amplifier pair Q201 and Q203. In addition, Q200 is biased by the same network that biases Q220 and is fed partially integrated composite video. This video is amplified, inverted, and fed to the sweep (for sync) and to the VIR board.

Transistors Q201 and Q203 are a gain stage, controlled by dc voltage inputs from the picture control (R4291), the LDR (light-dependent resistor) (R1920), and the brightness limiter (Q210 and Q212). Picture control voltage is fed to the base of Q203 and to the chroma subcarrier gain (color control) block at pin 18 of IC300 to provide simultaneous video and color tracking. The picture control is connected between 15 V B+ and pin 7 of the RL6 connector.

Video is then fed to the common-emitter connection of Q201 and Q203 via the emitter-collector conduction of Q220. All current through Q201 and Q203 must pass through Q220, and it therefore passes its signal output on to this differential pair. Differential circuit current divides according to the input control voltage. If it tries to rise positive, more current flows in Q203 and less in Q201, thus

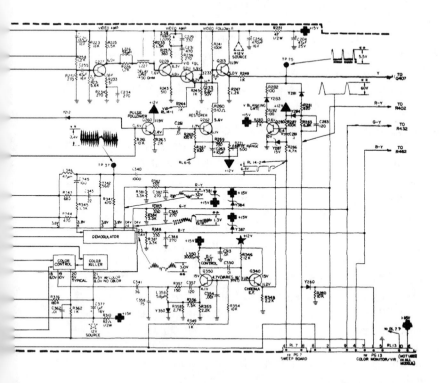

causing more video signal to appear across R213. If the control voltage goes negative more current flows in Q201 and less in Q203, bypassing, and thus causing more video signal across, R213. Resistor R211, in series with both transistors, causes a small amount of video to be present for the succeeding video stage even at minimum gain levels.

Video signal output at R213 is ac coupled to Q205 by C217. This stage splits the video into a high-frequency component and a low-frequency component. A sharpness control in the emitter circuit varies the current gain of the amplifier. Because of circuitry configuration, the low-frequency emitter circuitry is not greatly affected by the gain control. However, the high-frequency component in the collector circuit is gain controlled by R4298. When the sharpness control is at minimum resistance, the current gain is at maximum, and vice versa. The high- and low-frequency components are added at R257. The advantage of this type of peaking circuit is that preshoot and overshoot are controlled together to give an increased "apparent" peaking control range as viewed on the picture.

The signal from R257 is ac coupled by C255 to Q207, which amplifies and inverts it and feeds delay line L227. The delay line feeds Q209, another amplifier, which has a 3.58-MHz trap and some peaking in its emitter circuit. Transistor Q209 feeds positive-going video without the 3.58-MHz color signal, which has now been trapped out, to emitter follower Q211, which is ac coupled by C233 to emitter follower Q213.

From the base of Q213 to the CRT cathodes, the signal is dc coupled. The dc level on the CRT cathodes is actually controlled by the video itself. The black level of the video signal (without the burst signal, which was removed) is clamped during the back-porch time of the blanking pedestal at the base of emitter follower Q213 by clamping transistor Q262. The clamped level of Q262 is determined by the resistive setting of control R4296 and the brightness range centering control. Q262 is turned on by the horizontal sync pulse delayed and shaped by C371, L372, C372, and R373 and passed on by emitter follower Q260. During the time Q260 is turned on (back-porch, blanking pulse), it (in turn) biases Q262 on. Capacitor C263 will charge to a level determined by the brightness and brightness range control settings. Capacitor C233 charges during retrace via Q262 and maintains the same bias on Q213 during scan time. It is recharged during blanking and repeats the process, keeping the dc level constant. Resistor R241 tends to bias the base of Q213 more positive and works against the clamping circuit, which attempts to maintain the receiver's black level. Thus, as the brightness range control wants to allow a lower black level, R241 will pull Q213 to that level. Y212 is connected between the beam current limiter control (Q212 emitter) and the Q260 base. This allows the beam current limiter to be effective when full-field color information is transmitted and the chroma control is set high.

Video from Q213 is mixed with horizontal and vertical blanking pulses from Q280 and associated networks. The resultant signal is fed to Q407, which drives the emitters of the R, G, and B output transistors Q401, Q403, and Q405. Pulse origin is from the sweep module PG-7 pins 4 and 8.

The R, G, and B output transistors have dc biasing networks in their emitter legs for adjusting CRT cutoff. Note that the CRT has the G2 elements internally connected and that the G1 elements are internally connected and also near ground potential. This arrangement provides maximum arc protection for the signal circuits. CRT drive is adjusted with emitter circuit pots arranged to control the ac impedance. This is accomplished by connecting these controls in series between the emitters and the signal source.

Color processor circuitry

The input signal from the chroma bandpass or chroma IF amplifier comes from TP 23, the same origin as the video signal from the IF module. The path of the chroma signal is via various coils, capacitors, and resistors. These components make up the chroma IF tuned circuits. After the chroma bandwidth is restricted and tuned by input tuned circuits, color IF signals are fed to IC300 at pin 15 for processing. Color amplitude is regulated via a variable dc voltage on pin 20, which causes the IC to regulate chroma IF gain. Once amplified, the chroma IF exits the IC at pin 19, goes through a tint-control network, and is fed to pins 2, 3, and 4 into the demodulator circuits.

For tint control, the chroma IF signal is changed in phase with respect to the locally produced 3.58-MHz subcarrier. The chroma IF signal from pin 19 is fed to Q350. Then via a phase-shifting network, Y350 acts as a variable resistor to change the phase of the chroma in the network. Dc tint-control voltage from R4350 is fed to the base of Q350. The change in emitter dc voltage causes Y350 resistance to vary. The chroma sees Q350 as a common-base amplifier. The collector of Q350 then has chroma with variable phase. This signal is fed through emitter follower Q340 to the individual demodulator input phase-shift networks. These networks shift 0°, 12°, and 20° for B-Y, R-Y, and G-Y, respectively, because the 3.58-MHz oscillator produces approximately 90° vectors to the demodulators.

Burst separation

Burst separation is done by "gating." The negative-going sync pulses from the sync separator are applied to a tuned circuit consisting of L372 and C372. As these sync pulses are fed to the tuned circuit, it "rings," creating about four cycles of sine-wave signal. Because the original pulses are negative, diode Y372 keeps them from reaching pin 13 of IC30. However, as the tuned circuit rings, the first positive-going ringing pulse is allowed through Y372, which creates a positive-going, burst gate sync pulse. By means of this built-in "delay," the sync pulse arrives at the burst gate just as burst appears in the circuit. A 3.58-MHz burst signal now appears at pin 17 and, after phase shifting by C359, L356, and R359, is fed to pin 11 through C356 for APC circuit control.

3.58-MHz oscillator circuit

The color oscillator uses pins 6, 7, and 8 of IC300. Only one adjustment is available for the entire EM chassis chroma processor circuit. The APC adjustment and associated network are connected between IC pins 9 and 10. They determine the color oscillator free-running frequency. You might have to adjust the oscillator control circuit if any troubleshooting or components in the oscillator circuit need to be changed.

Demodulator outputs are at pins 1, 23, and 24, where the chroma and luminance signals are now matrixed to produce the color picture.

Quasar Color TV Chassis TS-976

All color processing stages for the Quasar TS-976 chassis are contained in the IC601 chip and its associated circuit components. Refer to Fig. 4-18 as you go through this color processor system.

Chroma section

The chroma sideband signal from the bandpass network is fed to pin 1, the first chroma amplifier and gate stage. The chroma signal is further amplified by the second chroma amplifier and exits the

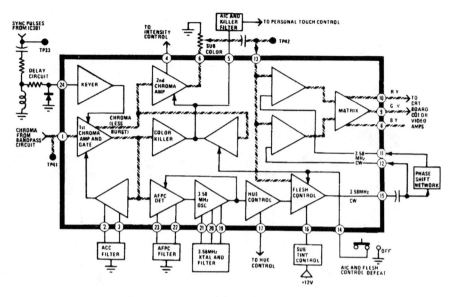

■ 4-18 *Block diagram of IC601 color chip.* Quasar Company

IC at pin 6. The gain of the second amplifier is controlled by a dc voltage fed from the intensity control at pin 4 and the personal-touch control at pin 5. Thus the personal-touch control varies both video and chroma gain to maintain a proper ratio as the control is adjusted. The chroma signal is capacity coupled from the sub color control to pin 13 of the IC and fed to pin I and pin Q demodulator circuits.

Keyer section

Negative-going horizontal sync pulses are differentiated by an RLC network. The diode conducts on the negative spike, thus clamping it to ground reference and producing a delayed positive pulse, which is fed to the keyer stage via pin 24. The keyer output pulse coincides with the first signal interval and is fed to the first chroma and gate amplifier. The pulses turn off the chroma amplifier and turn on the gate amplifier during burst time. Thus, the output of the chroma amplifier is chroma minus burst, and the output of the gate amplifier is burst only. The burst signal is applied to the color killer, ACC, and (automatic frequency phase-controlled) AFPC, detectors.

ACC detector & color killer

The ACC detector produces a dc voltage proportional to burst amplitude that varies the gain of the first chroma amplifier. During

B/W transmission, the color killer detects the absence of the burst signal, and its output turns off the second chroma amplifier. During B/W TV station signals, the voltage at pin 5 will be almost 0 V; during color reception, it will be 7 to 9 V depending on the setting of the personal-touch control and the amount of automatic intensity control (AIC) voltage (with Dynacolor switch on).

Automatic intensity control detector

Chroma sideband signals (minus burst) from the first chroma amplifier are fed to the AIC detector, which reacts to large areas of color or noise that may cause saturation. A dc output from the detector is fed to the second chroma amplifier for gain control independent of burst amplitude. One section of the Dynacolor switch grounds pin 14 (in the off position) and disables the AIC detector. AIC voltage can be measured at pin 5 by the difference in voltage with the Dynacolor switch on and off. The voltage decreases with AIC voltage (Dynacolor on).

Automatic Frequency Phase-Controlled (AFPC) detector

The AFPC detector compares the 3.58-MHz oscillator signal with burst from the burst gate amplifier. Any difference in the phase relationship between the two signals produces a voltage output proportional to the phase error. This control voltage is fed to the 3.58-MHz oscillator for phase correction.

3.58-MHz oscillator & hue control

The external components at pins 19, 20, and 21 provide filtering and tune the 3.58-MHz oscillator. After initial AFPC adjustment (C622) to set the oscillator free-running frequency, the PLL (oscillator and AFPC stage) functions independent of other external adjustments.

The 3.58-MHz oscillator CW (continuous wave) signal is phase adjustable, within preset limits, in the hue control stage by a dc-operated, customer hue control.

Tint (hue) control circuit

This stage corrects yellow/green or purple flesh tones that normally occur channel to channel or from different programs viewed on the same channel. Tint correction is accomplished by phase modulating the generated carrier (3.58-MHz signal) with minimum effect on the three primary colors (red, green, and blue).

The dynamic correction circuit includes a phase detector to compare the chroma and carrier signals. Its output controls a modulator that phase shifts the generated carrier proportional to the phase error and toward the flesh region. The greatest shift is in the yellow/green or magenta regions, and minimum correction occurs for errors in the vicinity of flesh colors. Maximum correction range is limited to ±20° so that color fidelity is maintained.

Carrier phase shifts beyond the correction range are prevented by a dc offset voltage which limits conduction of the modulator to the desired correction angles. The sub tint control centers the range of the customer hue control.

One section of the Dynacolor switch activates or defeats the tint correction circuit.

Demodulator & matrix

The 3.58-MHz CW signal from the tint-control stage exits the IC at pin 15 and is capacity coupled to pin 12, where it is fed to the I demodulator and through a phase-shift network to pin 11 and the Q demodulator. The demodulated color signals couple to the matrix stage, where R-Y, G-Y, and B-Y signals are developed. Filtering at each output removes any remaining high-frequency signals, and the color difference signals are coupled to the color amplifiers on the CRT board for matrixing with the video signal.

The preceding information is supplied courtesy of the Quasar Company.

5

TV electronic
tuner control systems

This chapter looks at TVs that use microprocessor and other digital logic chips for electronic tuner control systems. It covers operation, troubleshooting, and servicing, including circuit and block diagrams.

Zenith manual keyboard tuning system

The Zenith manual keyboard tuning system allows the customer to select CATV channels without the need for external converters. It has a tuning range of 112 channels, which are indicated by a two-digit LED readout. A scanning system cycles through all channels, upward or downward. Two buttons on the keyboard allow the viewer to select quickly and easily a program from any being telecast in the area.

Circuit description

Only two ICs are used in this tuning system. A 40-pin microprocessor IC is the heart of the system. It contains a 1-kilobyte (kb) ROM and a 256-bit volatile RAM. The PLL and LED decoder/driver circuits are in the IC. Timing for the microprocessor is derived from an internal oscillator and an external 7.16-MHz crystal.

The second IC (see block diagram in Fig. 5-1) performs the needed interface functions. This 18-pin device converts analog AFC and integrated vertical signals to digital data for use by the microprocessor. A 31-V regulator is used to regulate the tuning voltage supply. An operational amplifier with a field-effect transistor (FET) input is used as an active filter.

Two B+ and two bandswitching outputs are keyed by two binary inputs. A 5-V, three-terminal voltage regulator uses a +12-V TV set power source to provide system power.

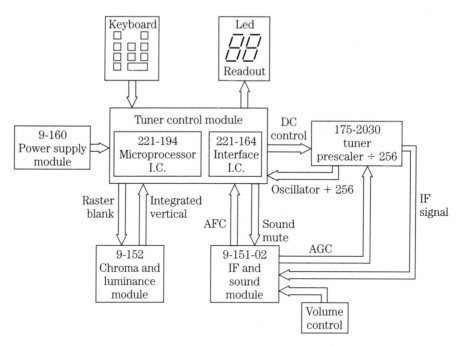

■ **5-1** *Zenith manual tuning system block diagram.*

Sound muting and raster blanking transistors are also mounted on the board, which has been reduced. Top and bottom shield covers over the circuits and help prevent static-discharge damage.

Control operations

When you turn on the TV, the tuning system searches upward from channel 2 at the rate of 3 channels per second and stops on the lowest active channel being received. The system stops at channel 14 if it finds no active VHF channel. The correct channel number is displayed by a two-digit LED readout on the front panel of the TV set. You can end the search by depressing any key.

You select channels in two ways. In the direct access mode, enter the number by using the number keys followed by the enter key. The tuning system then selects the requested channel. To select channel A-2, you must enter a single 0. You must enter a single 1 to select channel A-1. The scan mode allows the customer to scan through the channels to locate the active channels. After all of the available channels have been scanned, the system will return to the opposite end of the band and continue to scan in the other direction.

The AFC switch selects PLL operation in the normal position for exact tuning of TV channels. In the special mode, the AFC system is activated to permit proper tuning of signals on CATV systems with offset carrier frequencies.

When it is in the AIR position, the bandswitch allows normal reception of the VHF and UHF bands. When it is moved to the CATV position, CATV channels may be selected as shown in Table 5-1. An equivalent number for each channel is displayed on the LED channel readout of the TV set. The equivalents for each CATV channel are shown in the chart.

■ Table 5-1 A frequency chart of TV channels.

Channel	Band	Center freq.	Video carrier	Color carrier	Sound carrier	Osc. freq.
US TV frequencies including mid- and superband						
VHF lowband						
2	54–60	57	55.25	58.83	59.75	101
3	60–66	63	61.25	64.83	65.75	107
4	66–72	69	67.25	70.83	71.75	113
5	76–82	79	77.25	80.83	81.75	123
6	82–88	85	83.25	86.83	87.75	129
Midband						
A-2(00)	108–114	111	109.25	112.83	113.75	155
A-1(01)	114–120	117	115.25	118.83	119.75	161
A- (14)	120–126	123	121.25	124.83	125.75	167
B- (15)	126–132	129	127.25	130.83	131.75	173
C- (16)	132–138	135	133.25	136.83	137.75	179
D- (17)	138–144	141	139.25	142.83	143.75	185
E- (18)	144–150	147	145.25	148.83	149.75	191
F- (19)	150–156	153	151.25	154.83	155.75	197
G- (20)	156–162	159	157.25	160.83	161.75	203
H- (21)	162–168	165	163.25	166.83	167.75	209
I- (22)	168–174	171	169.25	172.83	173.75	215
VHF highband						
7	174–180	177	175.25	178.83	179.75	221
8	180–186	183	181.25	184.83	185.75	227
9	186–192	189	187.25	190.83	191.75	233
10	192–198	195	193.25	196.83	197.75	239
11	198–204	201	199.25	202.83	203.75	245
12	204–210	207	205.25	208.83	209.75	251
13	210–216	213	211.25	214.83	215.75	257
Superband						
J- (23)	216–222	219	217.25	220.83	221.75	263
K- (24)	222–228	225	223.25	226.83	227.75	269
L- (25)	228–234	231	229.25	232.83	233.75	275
M- (26)	234–240	237	235.25	238.83	239.75	281

US TV frequencies including mid- and superband

Channel	Band	Center freq.	Video carrier	Color carrier	Sound carrier	Osc. freq.
			Superband			
N- (27)	240–246	243	241.25	244.83	245.75	287
O- (28)	246–252	249	247.25	250.83	251.75	293
P- (29)	252–258	255	253.25	256.83	257.75	299
Q- (30)	258–264	261	259.25	262.83	263.75	305
R- (31)	264–270	267	265.25	268.83	269.75	311
S- (32)	270–276	273	271.25	274.83	275.75	317
T- (33)	276–282	279	277.25	280.83	281.75	323
U- (34)	282–288	285	283.25	286.83	287.75	329
V- (35)	288–294	291	289.25	292.83	293.75	335
W- (36)	294–300	297	295.25	298.83	299.75	341
			Hyperband			
AA-(37)	300–306	303	301.25	304.83	305.75	347
BB-(38)	306–312	309	307.25	310.83	311.75	353
CC-(39)	312–318	315	313.25	316.83	317.75	359
DD-(40)	318–324	321	319.25	322.83	323.75	365
EE-(41)	324–330	327	325.25	328.83	329.75	371
			UHF band			
14	470–476	473	471.25	474.83	475.75	517
15	476–482	479	477.25	480.83	481.75	523
16	482–488	485	483.25	486.83	487.75	529
17	488–494	491	489.25	492.83	493.75	535
18	494–500	497	495.25	498.83	499.75	541
19	500–506	503	501.25	504.83	505.75	547
20	506–512	509	507.25	510.83	511.75	553
21	512–518	515	513.25	516.83	517.75	559
22	518–524	521	519.25	522.83	523.75	565
23	524–530	527	525.25	528.83	529.75	571
24	530–536	533	531.25	534.83	535.75	577
25	536–542	539	537.25	540.83	541.75	583
26	542–548	545	543.25	546.83	547.75	589
27	548–554	551	549.25	542.83	553.75	595
28	554–560	557	555.25	558.83	559.75	601
29	560–566	563	561.25	564.83	565.75	607
30	566–572	569	567.25	570.83	571.75	613
31	572–578	575	573.25	576.83	577.75	619
32	578–584	581	579.25	582.83	583.75	625
33	584–590	587	585.25	588.83	589.75	631
34	590–596	593	591.25	594.83	595.75	637
35	596–602	599	597.25	600.83	601.75	643
36	602–608	605	603.25	606.83	607.75	649
37	608–614	611	609.25	612.83	613.75	655
38	614–620	617	615.25	618.83	619.75	661
39	620–626	623	621.25	624.83	625.75	667

Channel	Band	Center freq.	Video carrier	Color carrier	Sound carrier	Osc. freq.
			UHF band			
40	626–632	629	627.25	630.83	631.75	673
41	632–638	635	633.25	636.83	637.75	679
42	638–644	641	639.25	642.83	643.75	685
43	644–650	647	645.25	648.83	649.75	691
44	650–656	653	651.25	654.83	655.75	697
45	656–662	659	657.25	660.83	661.75	703
46	662–668	665	663.25	666.83	667.75	709
47	668–674	671	669.25	672.83	673.75	715
48	674–680	677	675.25	678.83	679.75	721
49	680–686	683	681.25	684.83	685.75	727
50	686–692	689	687.25	690.83	691.75	733
51	692–698	695	693.25	696.83	697.75	739
52	698–704	701	699.25	702.83	703.75	745
53	704–710	707	705.25	708.83	709.75	751
54	710–716	713	711.25	714.83	715.75	757
55	716–722	719	717.25	720.83	721.75	763
56	722–728	725	723.25	726.83	727.75	769
57	728–734	731	729.25	732.83	733.75	775
58	734–740	737	735.25	738.83	739.75	781
59	740–746	743	741.25	744.83	745.75	787
60	746–752	749	747.25	750.83	751.75	793
61	752–758	755	753.25	756.83	757.75	799
62	758–764	761	759.25	762.83	763.75	805
63	764–770	767	765.25	768.83	769.75	811
64	770–776	773	771.25	774.83	775.75	817
65	776–782	779	777.25	780.83	781.75	823
66	782–788	785	783.25	786.83	787.75	829
67	788–794	791	789.25	792.83	793.75	835
68	794–800	797	795.25	798.83	799.75	841
69	800–806	803	801.25	804.83	805.75	847
70	806–812	809	807.25	810.83	811.75	853
71	812–818	815	813.25	816.83	817.75	859
72	818–824	821	819.25	822.83	823.75	865
73	824–830	827	825.25	828.83	829.75	871
74	830–836	833	831.25	834.83	835.75	877
75	836–842	839	837.25	840.83	841.75	883
76	842–848	845	843.25	846.83	847.75	889
77	848–854	851	849.25	852.83	853.75	895
78	854–860	857	855.25	858.83	859.75	901
79	860–866	863	861.25	864.83	865.75	907
80	866–872	869	867.25	870.83	871.75	913
81	872–878	875	873.25	876.83	877.75	919
82	878–884	881	879.25	882.83	883.75	925
83	884–890	887	885.25	888.83	889.75	931

151

Circuit operation

Figure 5-1 is a block diagram of the manual tuning system. A type 175-2030 integral VHF-UHF-CATV varactor tuner with expanded tuning range and built-in prescaler is included in this tuning system. The IF output of the tuner is through a coax cable to the 9-151-02 module.

The oscillator output frequency from the VHF and UHF tuner sections is divided by 256 in the prescaler section. The prescaler output is fed to the PLL circuit on the tuning system control board. A 2-kHz, pulse-width-modulated output allows a "faster" filter circuit to be used. This also reduces ripple and increases interference rejection in the tuning-voltage circuit.

The pulse-width-modulated output from the microprocessor is fed to the amp in the interface IC. The input is a high-impedance FET. The op amp is used as an active filter, which gives a relatively smooth dc tuning voltage. It controls the frequency of the oscillator in the tuner, and the closed loop of the system is thus completed.

The tuning system control board is shown in Fig. 5-2. It contains two major system ICs and receives power from the 9-160 module in the TV set. The keyboard and the LED display plug into the control board. The control module also provides sound muting and raster blanking. These signals are sent to the 9-152 and the 9-151-02 modules. The 9-152 module provides the integrated vertical pulses used by the control circuit to determine the presence of a valid TV signal. The 9-151-02 module develops the AGC voltage needed by the 175-2030 tuner.

When a channel is selected, the microprocessor locates the code information in the ROM for the correct internal dividing ratio to be used in the PLL for tuning. It also locates the code information (2 bits) corresponding to the correct B+ and bandswitch information. The 2-bit code is decoded by the interface IC in Fig. 5-3. This IC generates UHF B+, VHF B+, bandswitching, and super-bandswitching voltages. The B+ voltages are fed directly to the tuner. The bandswitching voltages are buffered in external transistor switches.

There are seven signal output lines to drive the LED channel readout. Two additional outputs drive separate external transistors for digit drive and selection. The LED readout is multiplexed at a rate of 200 Hz.

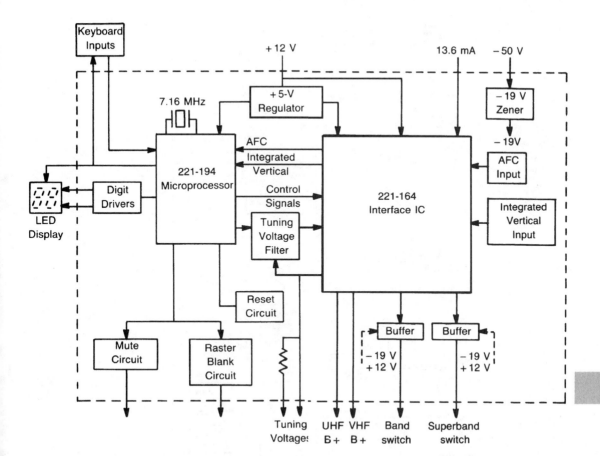

■ 5-2 *A manual control board block diagram.*

The microprocessor scans the keyboard for any key closures. When a key is closed, the microprocessor checks the keyboard twice more (to allow for contact bounce or noise) before a function is initiated. The states of the AFC and bandswitches are also constantly scanned.

Tuning voltage is limited to a preselected range on each band. If the tuning voltage goes too low, the tuner oscillator may stop. After a new channel is selected and the tuning voltage has had time to stabilize, the microprocessor checks the PLL for phase lock. If none is detected, the system reverses the slope of the tuning voltage, allows for a stabilization period, and tests again for phase lock. Phase locking is always attained by this method, and oscillator lockup is prevented. The complete circuit of the channel control unit is shown in Fig. 5-4.

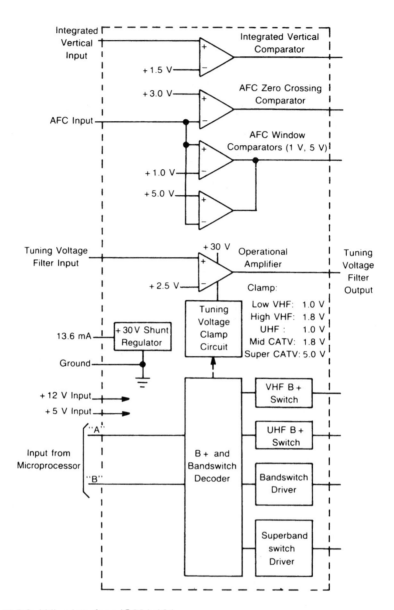

■ 5-3 *N line interface IC221-164.*

All adjustment controls and many discrete components have been eliminated from this tuning system. The number of ICs has been reduced from four to two. Reducing the number of modules has eliminated many interconnecting plugs and sockets and made the system more reliable.

Troubleshooting

Fewer modules in the system simplify servicing and locating a faulty module. When you find the defective module replace it because module repairs in the field are not recommended. If more than one symptom is present (e.g., nonoperating keyboard, no channel number displayed on the LED readout, no picture), there could be a problem in the control module or its associated power supplies; if not, check the tuner. A dc voltmeter can help locate the faulty module. If the correct dc voltages are present at the tuner plug, but there is no picture, the problem could be in the tuner. The tuner control module is probably faulty if the proper dc voltages are not present. You should check the power supplies for proper operation. It is a good idea to supply (with proper external test voltages) any missing control voltages to the tuner to verify that it will operate properly.

Electronic tuner & prescaler

A new tuner module has been designed for this system. Figure 5-5 shows the complete circuit for the 175-2030 tuner. The tuner is a single module that includes VHF, UHF, and CATV tuning and a prescaler for use with the N line tuning systems. It has expanded tuning range for CATV channels. Seven new channels are available. CATV channels A-2 and A-1 have been added below channel A in the CATV midband. Five new channels have been added above CATV superband channel W: the CATV hyperband channels AA, BB, CC, DD, and EE. Figure 5-6 shows the superboost circuit.

VHF tuner section

Extended CATV tuning capability is achieved by using new varactor diodes. The new glass-package diodes have a greater capacitance ratio which allows seven channels to be added without extra switching diodes. The matching between the diodes in the tuner is improved, which in turn provides a significant improvement in electrical alignment and tracking.

A new cross-package FET rf amplifier improves noise figure performance.

Modifications to the FM trap circuit optimize performance on the additional CATV channels. Cochannel pickup where strong signals are present has been reduced. Improved shielding design and construction has reduced the amount of local oscillator energy present at the antenna input.

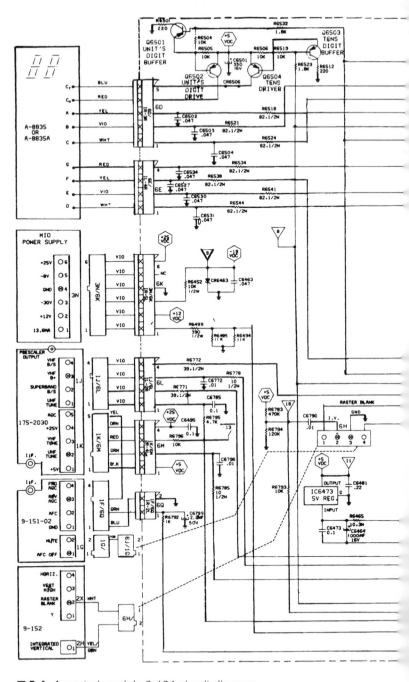

■ **5-4** *A control module 9-164 circuit diagram.*

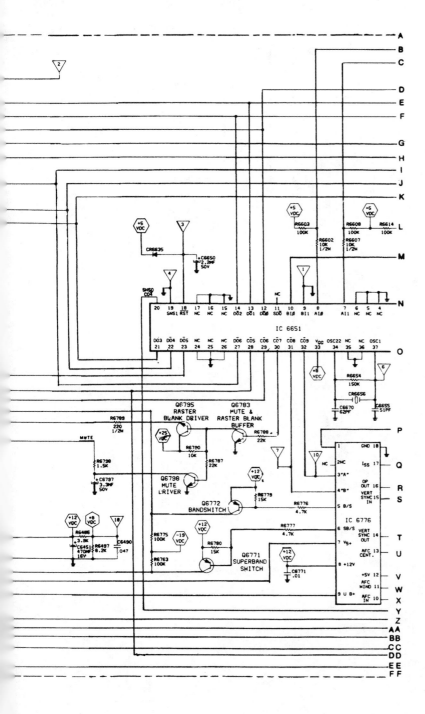

157

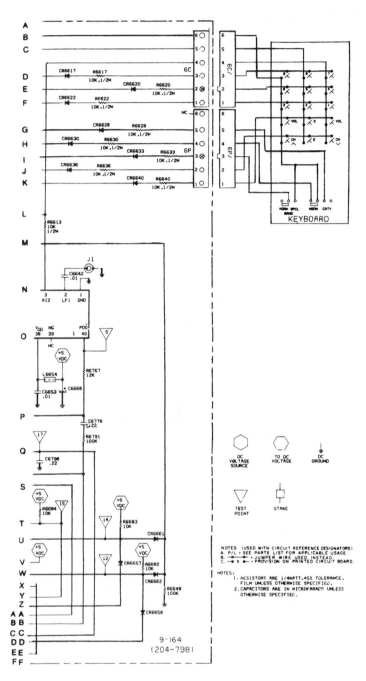

5-4 *Continued.*

A superband boost circuit enhances the performance of the extended range CATV channels. This special impedance-matching network is electronically switched into the circuit when the tuner is operating in the superband.

More trapezoidal capacitors are used instead of disc capacitors.

UHF tuner section

Due to improved shielding of the UHF circuits, interference of the 45-MHz range has been reduced by 16 dB. The amount of local oscillator energy present at the antenna input has also been dramatically lowered. The better UHF noise figure and cross-modulation performance due to the FET rf amplifier are also characteristic of the new tuner. The UHF oscillator sampling network for the prescaler circuit no longer needs adjustment, so a more uniform signal is output to the prescaler.

Prescaler

The prescaler is now included in the tuner module unit. A newly designed IC eliminates many of the discrete parts used in older models. External preamplifiers are no longer required because the new IC is 10 dB more sensitive. The S/N ratio has also not been degraded. The IC now contains the preamplifiers just mentioned along with circuits that divide the oscillator signals by 256. Separate VHF and UHF inputs to the prescaler are switched by the tuner switching voltages.

The shielding provides maximum isolation between the VHF and UHF oscillator sections of the tuner. Because of the improved heat conductivity of the IC package and fewer circuit parts, the prescaler is more reliable.

RCA tuning system—CTC-108 chassis

The RCA CTC-108 chassis uses the keyboard channelock frequency synthesis (FS) tuning system. This keyboard system has last-channel recall and an LED channel indicator and can receive midband CATV cable TV frequencies. A block diagram of this system is given in Fig. 5-7.

You can choose midband cable TV channels A-2 through I by placing the cable/normal switch, located in back of the set, into the cable position. You can then view these channels on UHF channels 31 through 71, as shown in Table 5-2. All VHF stations can still be

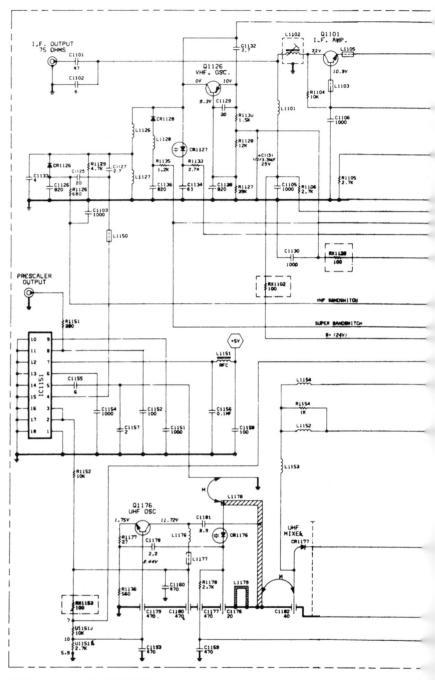

■ **5-5** *A circuit for 175-2030 tuner system.*

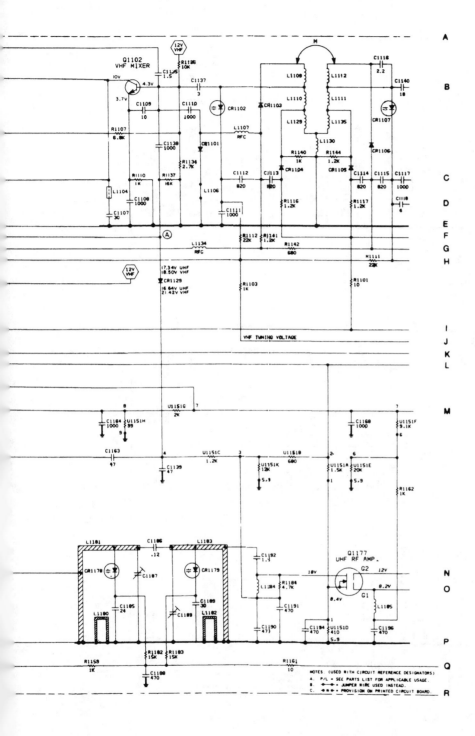

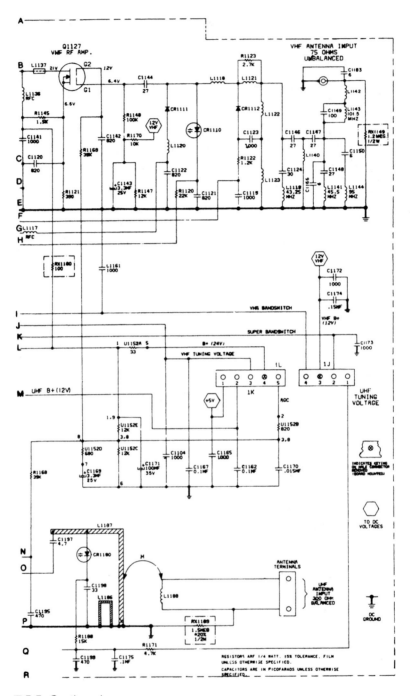

■ **5-5** *Continued.*

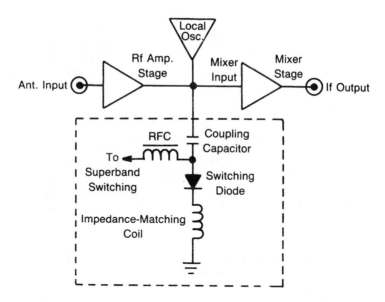

■ 5-6 *Superband boost circuit.*

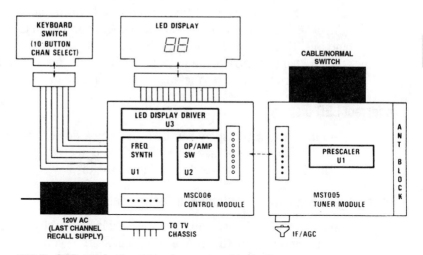

■ 5-7 *CTC-108 keyboard tuning system block diagram.* RCA Corp

tuned in normally. The tuner must be in the normal position to tune in UHF stations.

The following malfunctions are possible:

☐ Incorrect LED display
☐ Wrong channel tuned
☐ No channel selection capability
☐ Picture drift

**■ Table 5-2 Midband
cable channel selection guide.**

Cable-channel number	Displayed on channel number
A-2	31
A-1	35
A	39
B	43
C	47
D	51
E	55
F	59
G	63
H	67
I	71

Place cable/normal switch in cable (C) position

Note: This set has a "hot" grounded (nonisolated) chassis. Use an isolation transformer, disconnect the line cord during all static checks, and use insulated tools or clip leads for dynamic checks. Check all interface connections and wiring to and from the control module. Be sure the channel number entered is a valid entry. Each time a channel entry is made, note the display. This visual indication can prove useful in tracking down the problem.

Incorrect LED display

An incorrect LED display can be caused by a defective display or a faulty control module. Also check for defective interconnect wiring between the control module and the display.

Wrong channel tuned or no channel selection capability

Channel selection problems are most likely caused by a defective control module. If the problem remains after you substitute a known good module, suspect the MST 005 tuner module.

Frequency synthesis (RCA tuner control system)

Late-model RCA color sets include several models with an FS electronic tuning system. There are three systems: FS scan, FS scan remote, and FS keyboard. The keyboard is the simplest. You choose channels by pressing the right buttons to key the channel numbers you want.

Features of the FS scan system include up and down channel selection of the VHF/UHF channels that are programmed by the customer to stop only on selected channels. Scan remote units have manual control buttons to program channel selection for up or down.

Each system has a varactor tuner module, an FS tuner control module, and one or two channel display systems. The keyboard and scan versions feature a digital LED channel number display. Scan remote units also display time and channel on the screen.

A service problem with the tuning and/or remote system might seem complicated at first; but it need not be if you observe a few principles of operation and troubleshooting.

All units and modules that make up the FS system can be removed without unsoldering. Because all functions are performed by modularized circuits, solving the specific problem becomes, for the most part, an act of defining the defective function, identifying the associated module, and replacing that module. The exceptions occur when the defect involves module contacts or system-associated switches and controls. Because module connections and interconnecting plugs and jacks are used, a defect can be the result of poor connections.

Keyboard system control module

The MSC 001 FS control module (see Fig. 5-8) uses three LSI chips. Chip U1 accepts channel program commands and uses the

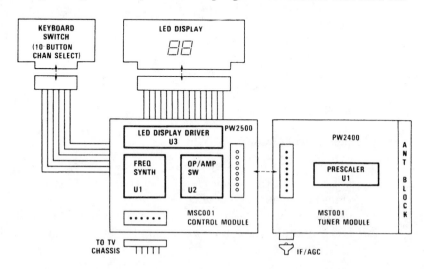

■ **5-8** *FS keyboard.* RCA Corp

decoded tuning information to properly tune the local oscillators in the tuner module through op amp switch U2. In addition, U1 feeds information to the LED driver LSI (chip U3) for processing channel indicator display; U3 also receives commands directly from the keyboard assembly.

Operational voltage for the system is developed on the MSC module from a 60-V horizontal pulse derived from the main TV chassis. AFT for the system is also an input to the MSC module and is derived from the circuits on the TV chassis.

Scan system control module

The MSC 002 frequency control module (see Fig. 5-9) uses the same three LSI chips as does the MCS 001 control module. A channel up and channel down command assembly replaces the keyboard channel select function. A fourth chip (U4) performs the duty of electronic tuning memory. A switch assembly is added to permit channel programming of the electronic tuning memory chip.

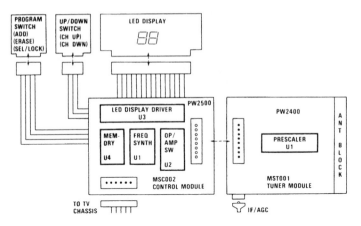

■ **5-9** *FS scan.* RCA Corp

Remote scan system control module

The MSC 003 frequency control module (see Fig. 5-10) has four LSI chips (U1 through U4). Chip U3 is a different type IC and provides on-screen display of channel and time information. The programming switches and time-set switches interface with U4 and U3. The remote receiver MCR 003 provides several inputs to the MSC 003 module.

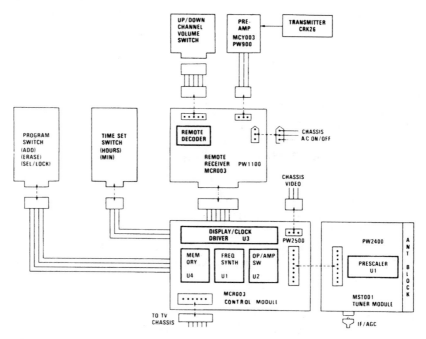

■ 5-10 *FS remote block diagram.*

As for the MSC 001 and MSC 002 control modules, operating voltages and signals are derived from the main chassis. Video information from the remote scan system module is routed to the set's video stages for screen readout information.

Synthesis tuner module

Inputs to the MST tuner module include a choice of a 75-Ω jack or 300-Ω terminals for VHF and UHF antenna terminals. Control voltages (bandswitching, tuning, and bias) are derived from the MSC control module. Outputs include a nominal 50-Ω impedance to match the IF input circuit of the TV chassis and a prescaler to the FS control module (MSC). The prescaler chip produces a signal that is fed into the MSC control module to aid it in its synthesizing process.

Remote receiver

The MCR 003 remote receiver for the FS remote scan tuning system can be addressed from two sources: remote hand unit or the manual control buttons on the TV receiver. The remote receiver accepts channel up/down commands and volume up/down information (on-off control operates in conjunction with the volume control system).

The remote receiver commands are processed by an LSI circuit located on the MCR 003 module. The IC contains a frequency counter and decoder that converts input ultrasonic frequencies (via MYC 003 preamp) into a binary code, which generates the correct function command signals.

Remote scan operation

The volume-up and volume-down buttons along with the channel-up and channel-down buttons provide the same functions, whether pressed at the receiver or on the remote transmitter. Time-channel screen display is accomplished whenever a channel and/or volume button is depressed; the display can be recalled by momentarily pressing either volume button. Note the front panel control locations in Fig. 5-11.

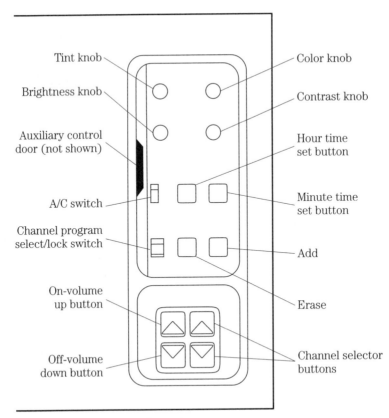

Tint knob

Color knob

Brightness knob

Contrast knob

Auxiliary control door (not shown)

Hour time set button

A/C switch

Minute time set button

Channel program select/lock switch

Add

On-volume up button

Erase

Off-volume down button

Channel selector buttons

■ **5-11** *RCA remote control panel.*

The receiver is turned on by depressing and holding the volume-up button. After initial receiver turn-on, the picture appears with an on-screen display of time and channel number. After about 30 seconds, the on-screen time-channel display disappears. If ac power line voltage was interrupted, the on-screen time display will appear as "−+−", indicating the clock needs to be reset.

Clock setting can be done with the set hours and set minutes pushbuttons. When you press either button, the time display appears on the screen and either hours or minutes is advanced at a 2 step s rate as long as the button is held down. Holding both buttons down stops and holds the clock for setting to a time tone standard.

Adjusting the volume or changing channels recalls the display to the screen. The display remains on screen for 5 s after the button is released.

Turn off the TV receiver by pressing and holding the volume-down button; the sound will step to a low level, at which time the TV set will go off.

Basic PLL theory

The basic FS system uses a PLL principle in conjunction with a digital frequency programmer to generate discrete frequencies. This section reviews basic PLL system operation. Refer to the block diagram in Fig. 5-12.

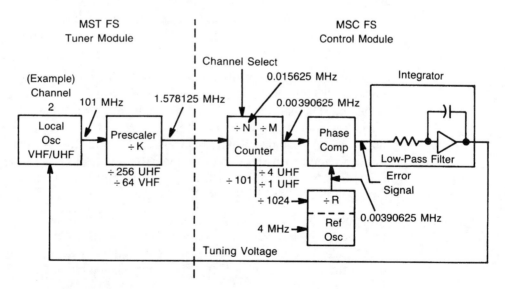

■ **5-12** *Basic PLL operation.*

Phase-locked loops have been used in FM stereo decoding, demodulation of FM signals, CB radios, and TV and FM receiver tuners. Phase locking is actually a technique of forcing the phase of an oscillator signal to exactly follow the phase of a reference signal. The PLL automatically locks onto and tracks a signal, even though its frequency changes. The PLL does all this with the help of its phase comparator and a VCO. The phase comparator samples the frequency of an input signal with that of a reference oscillator and produces an error voltage directly proportional to the difference between the two. The error voltage serves two purposes: it is fed back to the VCO and changes its frequency to match that of the input signal. This feedback enables the PLL to lock onto and track it continually over a given range.

Basic PLL operation

The FS tuning system for the TV receiver includes a PLL for synthesizing local VHF/UHF oscillator signals. When the rf input receives standard television frequency carriers, the mixer combines them with local oscillator signals to form IF signals with a picture carrier equal to the nominal IF picture carrier frequency (45.75 MHz). As shown in Fig. 5-12, the PLL configuration includes a local oscillator, a divide-by-K prescaler, a divide-by-N unit, and a divide-by-M unit, operating in conjunction with a comparator, a reference oscillator, a reference divider, and a low-pass filter.

The local oscillator, located in the MST tuner module (a voltage-controlled type) generates a signal whose frequency is determined by the dc voltage applied to it from the low-pass filter located in the tuner control module.

The output of the local oscillator is coupled to the divide-by-K prescaler, which divides the frequency of the high-frequency local oscillator. This step is necessary to produce signals whose frequency is compatible with the operating frequency range of the portions of the tuning system following it. The factor K is switched in accordance with the band in which the selected channel resides; for channels in the UHF range, for example, K is equal to 256, whereas in the VHF range, K is 64.

The output of the divide-by-K prescaler is coupled to the divide-by-N unit, which divides the frequency of the output signal of the K prescaler by a number (N) equal to the frequency necessary to derive the correct local oscillator signal for the wanted channel.

The factor N is controlled in accordance with the channel a viewer selects via the channel selection unit. The channel selection unit might have, for example, a calculator-type keyboard that is used to select the two decimal digits for the channel number. The channel selection unit converts the selected two-digit decimal number into binary signals arranged in a binary-coded decimal (BCD) format. The binary signals are partitioned into a group of 4 bits (binary digits) for the most significant digit (MSD) and another group of 4 bits for the least significant digit (LSD). The binary signals are coupled to the divide-by-N unit and to a display unit that provides the viewer with a visual indication of the channel selected.

A band decoder (part of the divide-by-N unit) determines the frequency band in which the selected channel resides. A band identification signal, indicating that the selected channel is in the VHF or UHF range, is coupled to the divide-by-K prescaler from the bandswitch stage to control the factor K (64 or 256). Thus, the bandswitch couples either a VL (VHF low), VH (VHF high), or a U (UHF) band signal to the local oscillator, indicating that the selected channel is in the correct band. The tuner module interprets these commands to control which of its varactor diodes are energized, thus controlling its frequency range.

The output of the divide-by-N unit is coupled to a divide-by-M stage that divides the frequency of the output signal of the divide-by-N unit by 1 for UHF channels and by 4 for VHF channels, in accordance with the state of the signal coupled to it from the band decoder. The output of the divide-by-M unit is coupled to the phase comparator, which provides an output signal comprising a series of pulses whose polarity and duty cycle represent the phase and/or frequency deviation between the output signal of the divide-by-M unit and the output signal of the reference divider R.

The output of the phase comparator is coupled to an active lowpass filter that integrates the output signal of the phase comparator to form a dc signal that controls the frequency of the local oscillator.

The loop just described is arranged so that the low-pass filter couples a dc tuner control voltage to the local oscillator, which tends to minimize the frequency and phase differences between the output signals of the divide-by-M unit and the reference divider.

Automatic offset tuning

The offset signals sometimes encountered with CATV converters, MATV systems, home video games, and video (VCR) recorders fall in a range of ±2 MHz around the FCC assigned VHF broadcast channel frequencies. These signals must be tuned by the receiver.

The following explanation gives the sequence of events involved with FS automatic offset tuning. First, the customer selects a VHF channel. The synthesis system (PLL) tunes the FCC assigned frequency for that channel. When a phase lock has been completed, the system switches to an AFT mode for signal searching within the AFT pull-in range. At this time, if a TV station carrier is within AFT range, the system stays in the AFT mode and remains on channel. If a station carrier is *not* detected, with the oscillator tuned to this center synthesis frequency to produce 45.75 MHz (or within the AFT range of ±1.25 of 45.75 MHz), the synthesis system is again activated. Now, however, the system automatically offsets the local oscillator plus 1 MHz above the nominal FCC frequency, and the AFT search mode is reactivated. If lock occurs, the system stabilizes in AFT mode, holding the offset carrier frequency. If lock does not occur, the system will again go to the synthesis mode; but this time it tunes the local oscillator to a frequency 1 MHz below the FCC nominal oscillator for the channel. AFT search is again activated and seeks a station carrier within ±1.25 MHz of this new, synthesized oscillator frequency.

If a carrier is available, AFT lock is established; otherwise, synthesis again retunes the oscillator to its nominal FCC channel frequency. The system will continue to perform alternate cycles of synthesis (PLL) and AFT in search of a station signal in the sequence as just described.

The choice of ±1.25 MHz for the AFT control limit prevents the possibility of AFT lockout to the lower adjacent sound carrier (−1.5 MHz) during dropout of the desired station's signal.

Summation

☐ A channel is selected and synthesis occurs, which tunes the local oscillator to the FCC nominal frequency to receive that channel.

☐ The AFT search mode is activated. If a station signal carrier is within ±1.25 MHz, AFT lock-up is established and the system stabilizes in the AFT mode.

☐ If no carrier is available during AFT search, synthesis is reengaged, shifting the local oscillator 1 MHz high; AFT search is activated and seeks a station carrier. If a station is available, AFT lock-up occurs and the system stabilizes.

- [ ] If lock-up is not achieved, the system now tunes the oscillator 1 MHz lower than nominal; AFT search is set up in the same sequence as the previous high offset mode in the above step.
- [ ] A third failure to get an AFT lock will return the system to the FCC nominal frequency, at which it will alternate between synthesis (PLL) and AFT in search of a signal, but with no further stepping. If AFT lock is accomplished for 3 s, further stepping is prevented.

DC tuning voltage & prescaler frequency

A dc tuning voltage and prescaler chart for VHF, VH and UHF is shown in Table 5-3. The dc tuning voltage is connected to the MST 001 tuner module. Tuning voltage is developed on the MSC control module, which is part of the synthesis tuning loop.

■ **Table 5-3   Prescaler frequency chart and dc tuning voltage.**

	Channel	Tuning voltage (typical)	Prescaler freq. (MHz)
V	2	1.8	1.58
H	3	3.3	1.67
F	4	5.4	1.76
	5	11.4	1.92
L	6	16.0	2.01
O			
W			
V	7	8.5	3.45
H	8	9.6	3.54
F	9	11.0	3.65
	10	12.6	3.73
H	11	14.6	3.84
I	12	17.5	3.92
G	13	22.0	4.01
H			
U	14	1.8	2.02
H	24	3.8	2.25
F	34	6.3	2.48
	43	8.4	2.69
	53	10.5	2.93
	63	13.4	3.16
	73	17.0	3.40
	83	24.0	3.63

If a tuning voltage problem exists, remove the power and check with an ohmmeter at point J1-MSC-5 to see if the tuning voltage is shorted out. If not, substitute a battery or power supply to serve as a test tuning-voltage source and to check tuner operation. Also check for correct bandswitch voltage. Now you can tune in the desired station by adjusting the test voltage to the desired tuning voltage, as shown in Table 5-3. You can now check the prescaler frequency with a frequency counter. If the tuner module checks out okay, the probable fault is a defective MSC control module.

Bandswitching

Because of the limited tuning range of varactor diodes, bandswitching capability is necessary to select low-band VHF channels (2 through 6), high-band VHF channels (7 through 13), and UHF channels (14 through 83). Bandswitching is achieved by applying +19 V to the appropriate bandswitching terminal.

LED display

The LED display decoder/driver IC is used to drive a two-digit, seven-segment LED channel indicator. Eight lines of BCD information are supplied to the IC located as part of the MSC 001-002 control module to allow continuous, nonmultiplexed operation. The code relating to the input and output states is the standard BCD-to-seven-segment code, which activates the appropriate segments of the display.

FS keyboard servicing

The FS keyboard system has a frequency synthesizer chip (U1), op amp chip (U2), and LED driver chip (U3), which make up the MSC 001 tuner control module—the heart of the complete control system. Because the MSC is a module, the isolation techniques will primarily look at the inputs and outputs of the MSC module and other key voltages located on the module. The following servicing tips should help you in locating defective modules, connectors, wiring, or other input/output problems to the MSC module.

For these checks, assume the MST 001 tuner module is operating normally and the IF link cable is not defective. The following symptoms are possible:

□ Channel selection problems in a certain band
□ Channel selection lost on all channels
□ Channel selecting OK—LED display incorrect
□ Improper or no volume mute
□ No tuning voltages to MST 001 tuner
□ Channel selecting OK—tuning system hunts

Make preliminary checks of all interface connections and wiring to and from the MSC control module. Make sure the channel number entered is a valid entry. Each time a channel entry is made, note the display readout. This visual indication can be a useful aid in tracking down a problem.

Channel selecting problems in a certain band

Channel selection problems usually indicate a defect in either the MSC or MST modules. Check bandswitch voltages on the MSC module. If voltages are correct, sub in an MST 001 module. Check that the proper keyboard data lines go to logic low when buttons are depressed on the keyboard. A logic low condition means voltage goes low, to about 0.2 V or lower.

Channel selection lost on all channels

First check that all dc operating voltages are present. Almost all dc voltages for the MSC 001 are derived from the negative 60-V horizontal pulses. These pulses are scan derived from the set's deflection system and can be checked with an oscilloscope at J2-MSC-5. Next, check keyboard data lines; if ground is not available to the keyboard assembly, channel selection capability is lost.

Channel selecting OK—LED display incorrect

When tuner responds to correct commands and display does not, check for proper output from the MSC board. Replace MSC 001 module if incorrect logic conditions are found on the MSC module. If correct logic conditions are found on the MSC module, then channel display assembly may be defective.

Improper or no volume/mute

Check volume/mute line at J2-MSC-6; check for a momentary "dip" toward a logic low condition when a channel change is initiated. If not, check plug connections and then try a new MSC module. Voltage ar J2-MSC-6 should be about +2 V during normal station reception.

No tuning voltages to MST 001 tuner

Replace MSC 001 tuner control module or sub in a variable power supply in place of the tuning voltage. The proper bandwidth voltage must be present to perform this check.

Channel selecting OK—Tuning system hunts

A channel selecting problem where the tuning system hunts usually indicates trouble in the AFT. Tuning capability is not lost, but the picture will drop in and out rapidly or hunt. Check AFT voltage at J2-MSC-1 on the MSC module. Dc voltage should measure approximately +6 V and should be stable with a strong station tuned in. The problem could be related to IF/AFT on the main chassis or MST control module.

FS scan servicing

The FS scan uses most of the same circuitry as the keyboard system with the exception of the scan memory IC (U4), memory program switch, and scan channel switch. Most of the circuitry is similar to that of the keyboard system, so this servicing technique only deals with those aspects that differ from the keyboard system. If problems occur in this system that were covered in the keyboard procedure, refer back to those isolation techniques. The following symptoms are possible:

☐ No or improper channel-up/channel-down action
☐ No or improper add or erase of scan memory
☐ No or improper channel change or skip

Check all interface connections and wiring to and from the MSC control module. Each time a channel is changed, note the display readout; this visual indication can be a help in tracking down a problem.

No or improper channel-up/channel-down action

Scanning up and down channel information requires that the frequency synthesizer chip (U1) receive proper logic conditions to pins 16 and 17 (from the scan channel switch). First, confirm good ground connection at terminal S on MSC 002 module and to up/down switch assembly. If the ground connection is open, scan capability will be lost. If either up or down action is lost, check the appropriate terminal on the MSC 002 module for a logic low condition when the button is pressed.

No or improper add or erase of scan memory

Confirm proper logic conditions at terminals T and U on the MSC 002 control module. Make sure the select/lock switch is in the select position and that there is a good ground connection at terminal S on the MSC board. The appropriate add or erase line must go to a logic low condition to indicate an add or erase function to the scan memory IC (U4). When add or erase functions are not activated, add and erase lines should be idle at logic high (+5 Vdc).

No or improper channel change or skip

Channel change or skip problems are usually associated with the MSC module; replace control module MSC 002.

The preceding information is supplied courtesy of RCA Consumer Electronics.

Electronic tuning systems (GE)

The KMP112 tuning system is the basic electronic tuning system from which other General Electric systems are derived. See Fig. 5-13. Most of the IC technology is carried over from the KMP91 tuning system to the present 112-channel system. Chip technology allows the many functions of the electronic tuning systems to be consolidated into a relatively small, single tuner control system.

IC601 microprocessor

The microprocessor (IC601) chip is the heart of all 112-channel tuning systems, as shown in Fig. 5-14. It receives commands from the user via the control panel keyboard or the remote transmitter. The microprocessor then acts on these commands, producing ac power control for the receiver, audio control voltages, tuning and bandswitching voltages, LED display data for channel

5-13 An electronic tuning system block diagram. General Electric

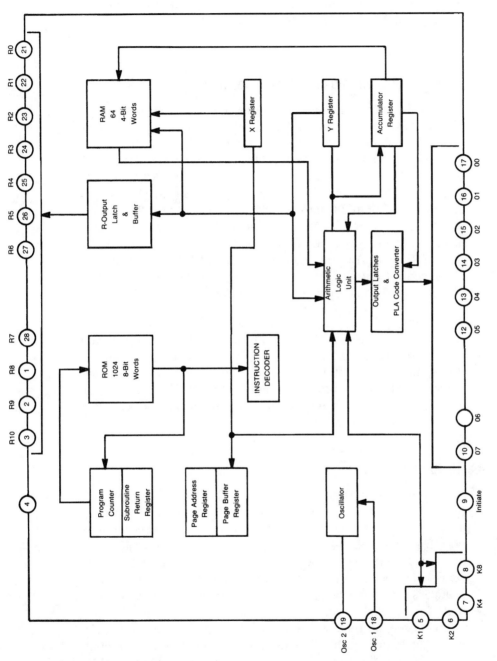

■ **5-14** *A microprocessor (IC601) block diagram.* General Electric

Electronic tuning systems (GE)

indication, frequency data for PLL operation, and storage of favorite and last channels in a nonvolatile memory (IC800). It also monitors AFC through a simple comparator for the AFT frequency search process and channel blockout on the KMP112 system.

Microprocessor (IC601) and I/O chip (IC600) operation

Keyboard inputs to the microprocessor include six keyboard lines plus an AFC detector line and a remote receiver signal line. Keyboard inputs are debounced and multiplexed into the microprocessor through the I/O chip (IC600). Pins 3 to 5 and 7 to 11 (A1 to B8) of IC600 are multiplexed to K1, K2, K4, and K8 (pins 5, 6, 7, and 8) of IC601 chip. A data stream from R8 (pin 1) of IC601, clocked by R7 (pin 28) into the I/O chip (IC600, pins 27 and 30) selects first A then B inputs to the microprocessor K inputs. After all data is sent, it is latched with an enable pulse from the R9 output (IC601, pin 2) to the I/O chip (IC600, pin 29). The LED and tuner control outputs on IC600 are also controlled by the data stream from the microprocessor R8 output.

The I/O chip (IC600) is a 44-pin flat-pack IC that contains an input shift register, pulse-width D/A converter (DAC) keyboard data multiplexer, LED display driver (2), reset counter, bandswitch driver, and its own internal RC clock. The clock drives the reset counter for the microprocessor and DAC for the volume control. The remaining circuits are controlled by the microprocessor data and clock output lines.

AFT search operation

When you press the enter button, the AFC detector is sampled after a 160-ms delay. If the AFC input is positive, a plus 250-kHz offset is loaded into the PLL chip (IC500). If the AFC input is negative, a minus 250-kHz offset is loaded. The detector is subsequently detected every 30 ms at 250 kHz/step until a change (crossover) occurs in the AFC detector output. After the first change is detected, the step size of the frequency offset is reduced to 31.25 kHz. The search reverses direction and looks for the AFC change a second time at the 31.25 kHz/step. After detecting the AFC change the second time, the search again reverses direction to detect the AFC change. Four successive crossovers at 31.25 kHz/step with only one step in the same direction terminate the search. The PLL then locks onto the correct channel frequency within 31.25 kHz.

The limits of AFT search are +2 MHz and −1.3 MHz away from the nominal oscillating frequency for the selected channel. Maximum time for the first crossover after initial keyboard entry is 400 ms, with the subsequent four crossovers requiring between 120 and 360 ms additional time. If the program frequency drifts and offsets nominal frequency, pressing the enter button will reinstitute AFT search and pull the selected channel back within 31.25 kHz of nominal frequency. The system does not automatically monitor subsequent AFC changes after locating the selected channel frequency.

Detailed tuning circuit analysis

The microprocessor and 1/0 chip have internal clocks whose frequencies are determined by external resistors and capacitors. The nominal clock frequencies range from approximately 300 to 400 kHz.

On power-up, C613 and R649 on IC600 produce an initialization pulse to IC600 pin 31 (all clear), which resets all counters (LED display is blank) and sets IC600 pin 39 (init out) to initialize the microprocessor (IC601) and drive all K input lines low. See Fig. 5-15.

The microprocessor will read the EAROM (IC800) nonvolatile memory for favorite channel and last channel information only when a power failure or CRT arc occurs or if the set is unplugged. These three actions will cause the microprocessor to reset. The EAROM (electrically alterable read-only memory) is only read after the receiver is switched on for the first time, after a reset of the microprocessor. Channels can be programmed into the EAROM so that only favorite channels will appear during the scan operation. Programming can be accomplished only at the transmitter unit and in the single step mode. All 112 channels can be stored in a favorite channel scan. The EAROM is programmed to store the last channel viewed after 1.2 s of viewing in order to enable the set to return to the same channel in case of power failure.

EAROM circuit analysis

Data input and output are from pin 12 of IC800. Pins D1, D2, and D3 are mode control pins; a 111 code means standby. This code is used to prevent loss of the favorite channel memory in IC800 (EAROM) when IC601 is "talking" to IC600 (I/O chip). When the EAROM is talking to IC601, the load data and address lines of IC500 (PLL) are held inactive. When the data and clock lines are used to talk to the EAROM, IC600 (I/O chip) data enable is held inactive. The preceding actions serve to isolate IC500, IC600, and IC800 during processing of data by the microprocessor (IC601).

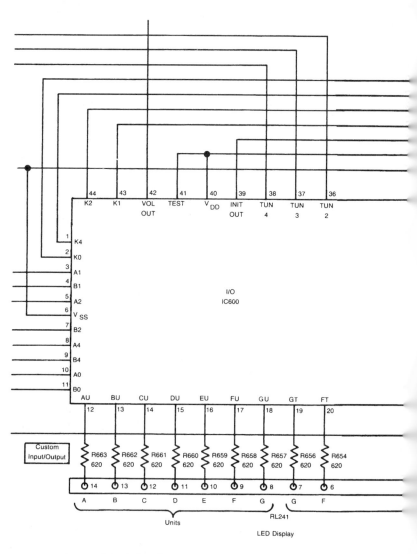

■ **5-15** *A microprocessor and associated circuitry.*

The following sequence occurs as the microprocessor reads the EAROM when the receiver is first switched on. First, select A and B bits for IC600 are set to 0, freeing the inputs. Then D1, D2 and D3 of IC800 are given the address accept code, and the address is clocked into IC600 (I/O chip). Pins D1, D2, and D3 are then given the read code, and data is clocked out to K1 of the microprocessor (IC601).

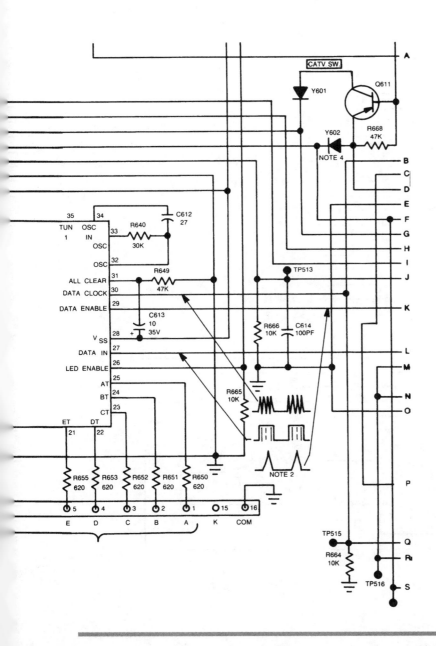

183

Q800 and Q801 are output buffers to IC601. Y800 provides CRT arc protection and prevents pin 12 of IC800 from floating to a negative voltage when data is being read out.

Finally, power to the EAROM (IC800) is supplied with +9 V (pin 1) and –25 V (pin 2). Also, an "option bit" is available (MP112 only) for reduced volume at turn-on. If the volume option bit is marked

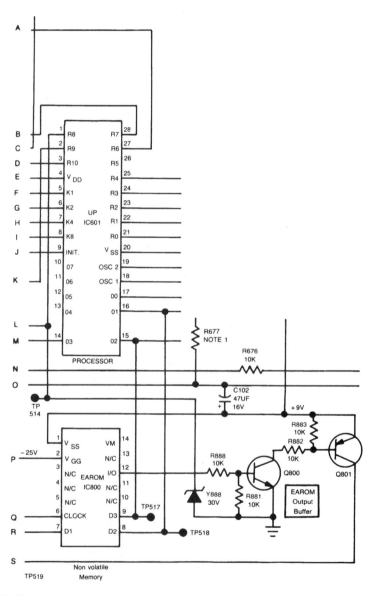

■ **5-15** *Continued.*

in the EAROM, the volume output of IC600 is reduced to a 12 percent duty cycle thereafter. This feature is inactive as long as stand-by power is applied.

KMP model microprocessor

On KMP models, the microprocessor looks at all six keyboard lines to determine if the set has been turned on. See Fig. 5-16. All six keyboard lines and B4 are normally high when the receiver is switched on. If any keyboard lines or B4 are low, the microprocessor will interpret it as the receiver being switched off. When the microprocessor determines that the set is on, a 270-ms delay is inserted into the program to allow time for the power supplies to rise, and audio is muted for 500 ms. The 9-V keyboard power source is fed through 10-Ω resistors from the receiver's main chassis power supply. Channel entry sequence is as follows:

1. A digit button is depressed, resulting in immediate LED display. If no other button is depressed within 5 s the display automatically changes back to the previously viewed channel.

2. If a second digit button is depressed within 5 s it will immediately be displayed in the "units" position, and the first digit will be shifted from the "units" position to the "tens" position.

3. Next, depress the enter button which gives program reception of the channel indicated on the LED readout display.

LMP model sets

On these models, the microprocessor looks at eight inputs, but only four at a time. Because inputs can be either remote or keyboard, the microprocessor is programmed to continually switch back and forth and examine the keyboard inputs and remote inputs. Inputs that are common to both the keyboard and the remote will respond in a single response regardless of origin. For example, a channel-up command at the remote unit does the same thing as a channel-up command at the keyboard. Also, the keyboard channel-up and channel-down are in the same mode as the remote transmitter. If the remote transmitter is single step, the keyboard is single step. If the remote is in favorite channel, the keyboard is also. If the keyboard is in favorite channel, it will remain in favorite channel, even during a power failure.

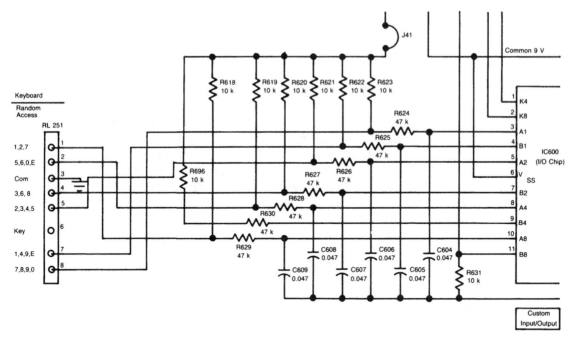

■ 5-16 *KMP112 keyboard input circuitry.*

When you press the on/off button, the microprocessor determines whether to turn the set on or off. Audio is unmuted at turn-on, and the on-off relay is energized through Q614 (relay driver) and closed. A 270-ms delay in any further action permits time for power supplies to stabilize.

MP model sets

The MP models operate like LMP models except for the additions of random access of channels at the remote hand unit, random access or five-button keyboard at the receiver front panel, and a channel blockout feature. The random-access channel entry operates as on the KMP models. Removing diode Y602 on the tuner control module readies the microprocessor for five-button keyboard operation. At reset, pin 3 (R10) of IC601 goes high and drives pin 5 (K1) high through Y602 if it is not removed. This sets up the microprocessor for random-access keyboard operation.

The PW (printed wiring) chassis uses only the five-button scan keyboard type with random access at the hand remote transmitter. The special blockout feature prevents viewing selected channels by a special blockout code determined by the user.

The preceding information is supplied courtesy of General Electric Company, Consumer Division.

Zenith Y LINE manual tuning system

The Zenith Y line manual microprocessor-controlled tuning system has been designed to receive up to 125 total channels which also include 55 CATV channels. Most Zenith Y line tuning systems have the keyboard and the control module separated. For a home service call, you should change the tuner control module, not the complete channel selector. The modules use the Molex interconnecting cable system.

Basically there are two manual tuning systems. One system uses the 9-164 tuner control module with the following features:

☐ Direct access of all channels
☐ Power-on search for first active channel lock-on
☐ 112-channel tuning capability

This manual tuning system incorporates the 9-164 tune control module interfacing with the 9-181 Z chassis. See the tuning system block diagram in Fig. 5-17.

The other manual tuning system is the deluxe version with the following features:

☐ Direct access of all channels
☐ Up/down scan channel selector
☐ Power-on search for numerically lowest active channel
☐ 125-channel tuning capacity

This system (see Fig. 5-18) consists of the 9-209 tuning control module interfacing with the system 3 chassis and the 175-2033 tuner.

To provide these added features, researchers developed the type 221-206-01 microprocessor chip. This chip can be used for both manual and remote tuning systems. It has a power control output

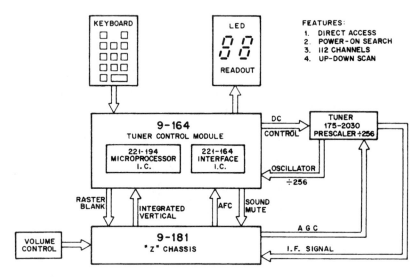

■ **5-17** *Block diagram of manual tuning system.*

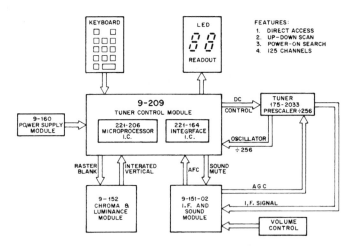

■ **5-18** *Block diagram of deluxe manual tuning system.*

to control a power relay and internal hardware to decode IR pulses.

In addition, the microprocessor program allows the customer to select the new CATV cable channels. The microprocessor uses a diode located in the keyboard matrix to determine if the IC is being used in a manual or a remote tuning system.

The 9-209 tuning control module will interface with the 175-2033 tuner. See the tuner circuit in Fig. 5-19. The dc control voltages required to activate this tuner are very similar to the 175-2030 tuner, but with one exception: The tuning voltage has a greater range. This was done by lowering the interface chip (IC 221-164) high-band clamp voltage to 1.5 V. In addition, the antilock program in the microprocessor prevents system lock-up due to tuner oscillator stalling.

Zenith remote tuning systems

The Zenith Y line remote tuning systems are capable of receiving up to 125 channels. Some also have programmed on and off TV set operation features. The remote space command 2400 series incorporates the following features:

- ☐ Direct access of all channels
- ☐ Up/down channel scan
- ☐ Power-on search for numerically lowest active channel
- ☐ 112-channel tuning capability
- ☐ Two-digit green LED channel readout.

189

The system (see Fig. 5-20) uses the 9-190 tuner control module interfacing with the 175-2030 tuner and the Z chassis by means of the Molex connector system. Volume control is a function of the on-board DAC, which also activates the mute function. The control module also incorporates the 221-164 interface IC chip.

This remote tuning system uses only two main ICs: the microprocessor and the interface chips. There is no memory IC because there is no channel programming. But there is last channel memory because the system remains powered when the receiver is off.

The heart of this remote tuning system is the 221-206-01 microprocessor. This unit has circuits to decode IR pulses and a power control output to control a power relay. The IC can drive the LED channel display directly, with external transistors, to provide the relatively high-digit drive current. Because this device controls the TV power, it must remain in operation while the receiver is off. The power for this IC is derived from a separate transformer, which supplies the higher current required by the LED driver circuitry.

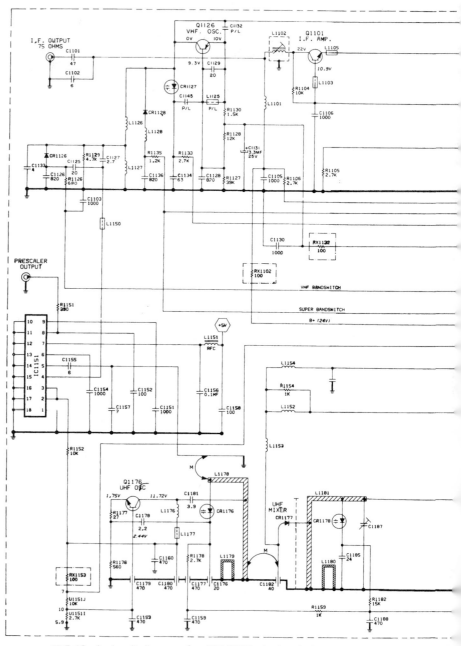

■ **5-19** *A circuit diagram for 175-2030 electronic tuner.*

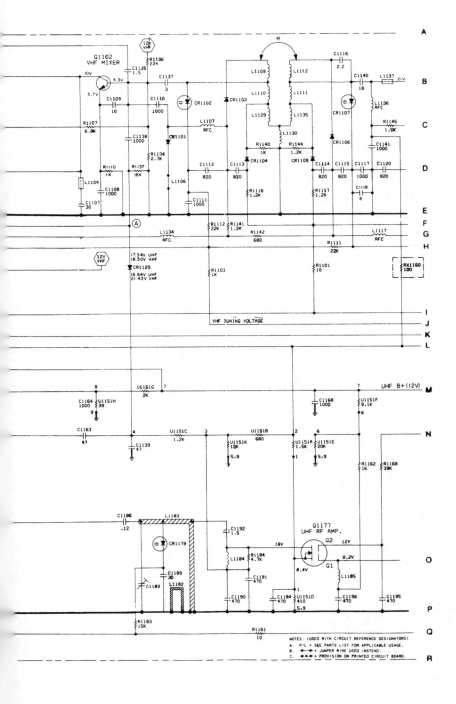

191

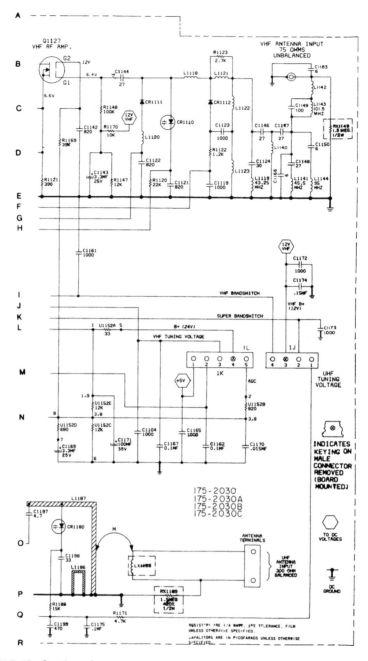

■ 5-19 *Continued.*

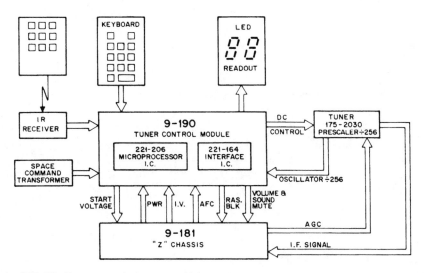

■ 5-20 *Remote tuning system (SC2400) block diagram.*

The only on-board power supplies are a single 5-V regulator, a 12-V regulator, and a low-current, 8-V bias supply. All other voltages are derived from the main TV chassis.

Zenith microprocessor tuning system

The microcomputer chip IC301 (221-216-01) function as a central processor for transmitting and executing instructions. Efficient operation of the tuning system (see Fig. 5-21) depends mainly on this small-scale computer. Various functions of the microcomputer chip are to:

☐ constantly scan the digital keyboard for a contact closure
☐ control the operation of the LED channel display through an LED driver
☐ provide B+ switching
☐ control the operation of the PLL IC303

This microcomputer is not capable of performing a single task, but is programmed to respond to input data and to recognize, arrange, and execute these instructions as the program specifies.

Microcomputer operation

The microcomputer is a low-end 4-bit device that operates from a single 5-V power supply. It has 16 I/0 lines and is available in a 20-pin package. One 8-bit port drives the LED channel display

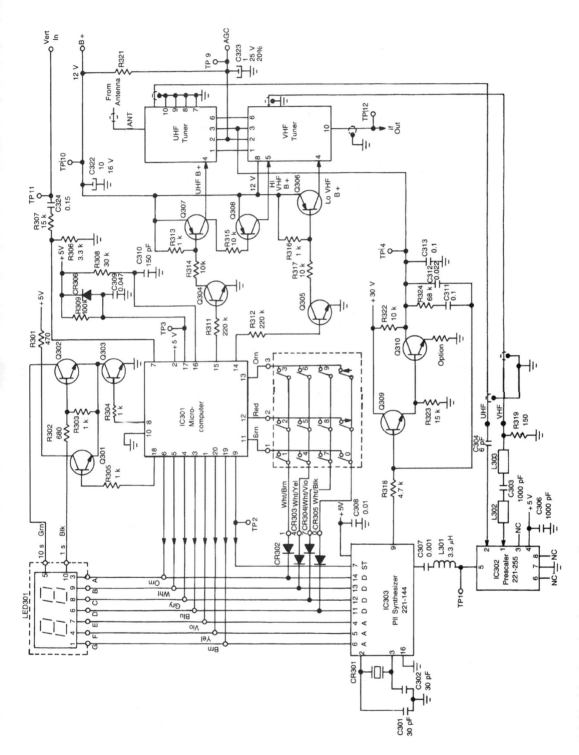

■ **5-21** *A keyboard tuning system diagram.*

TV electronic tuner control systems

segments, strobes the keyboard, and outputs the address and data information to the PLL IC (all in sequential order). The other lines read the keyboard, output the band information, give the data valid signal (strobe) to the PLL chip, and synchronize the entire system to the vertical retrace period.

The problem of noise being radiated into the TV chassis from logic and LED displays is eliminated by turning the LED display off and on during the approximately 1ms vertical retrace period. You can do this by connecting a serial input from a suitable point in the vertical circuit.

This line is low except during the vertical retrace pulse period. A brief software loop is written into the system to complement the serial output and escape from this loop when the vertical line goes high for at least two repetitions of this short loop. During each vertical retrace period, the keyboard is scanned for any key closure, the next 4-bit nibble is sent to the PLL IC, and, finally, the alternate digit is turned on. This allows most of the noisy switching to occur during the time that the screen is blanked. The continuous updating of the PLL IC ensures that a transient from picture tube arcs, which could alter the data in the PLL IC registers, is corrected immediately. This system has proven to be free of logic noise, and therefore no filtering or shielding of the microcomputer is required.

The most effective troubleshooting approach for the microcomputer is to use an oscilloscope for signal tracing. The microcomputer random-access tuning is an extremely reliable and maintenance-free tuning system. The varactor tuners do not have mechanical parts that wear, thus eliminating one problem area. Most operations performed by the system are done with ICs that simplify service. Noting the signal flow and the presence or absence of signals at appropriate points aids in locating trouble areas. When you use the scope signal-tracing approach, you can pinpoint faults very quickly.

Power-supply circuit

The power supply (see Fig. 5-22) uses a pulse coupled from pin 3 of the horizontal scan transformer through T301 to produce 30 V for the tuning voltage. This voltage, derived from a half-wave rectifier through CR309, is unregulated. The 5 V for logic and channel display is also developed through CR310 and is regulated by a simple shunt regulator (Q311 and CR307) to keep a constant load on the scan circuitry.

The microprocessor pinouts are shown in Fig. 5-23.

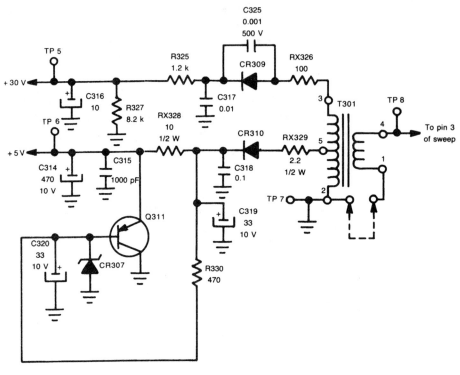

■ **5-22** *Tuning system power supply.*

Troubleshooting charts

The troubleshooting charts in Table 5-4 are a good service aid for quickly repairing the microcomputer process board unit. The charts contain 12 possible symptoms and associated measurements that should be made with the tuning system. To obtain the best results, locate the symptoms in the chart that best describe the problem and follow the steps listed under "Procedure" until you have located the defect.

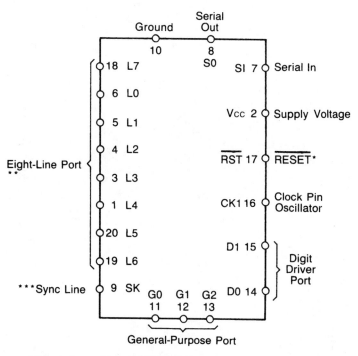

Ground

Serial
Out

10

8
SO

SI 7 ◯ Serial In

18 L7

6 L0

5 L1

Vcc 2 ◯ Supply Voltage

4 L2

Eight-Line Port
**

3 L3

$\overline{RST}$ 17 ◯ $\overline{RESET}$*

1 L4

CK1 16 ◯ Clock Pin
Oscillator

20 L5

D1 15 ◯

Digit
Driver
Port

19 L6

***Sync Line 9 SK

G0 G1 G2
11 12 13

D0 14 ◯

General-Purpose Port

*Reset: Low - Reset, High - Active

**Eight-Line Port: Output ports that drive LED segments
(Pins 18, 6, 5, 4, 3, 1, 20, and 19)

***Sync Line: Tells PLL when valid information is available

■ **5-23** *Microcomputer pinouts.*

197

■ **Table 5-4 A microprocessor random-access tuning troubleshooting chart.**

Symptom	Procedure	Result	Comments
No channel number or no keyboard response	Checkpoint designation #5	5 V	The horizontal pulse is applied to a small transformer that makes 5 V for the logic and display and approximately 30 V for the tuning voltage. The 5-V supply should be between 4.7 and 5.5 V. The vertical sync pulse synchronizes the switching of the microcomputer during the vertical retrace.
	Check vertical input	Vertical sync pulse	
	Check pin 16 of microcomputers	Occurrence of oscillations	
	Check reset pin 17 of microcomputer	Power going high	
	Check pin 8 of microcomputer	A display blanking pulse should appear in sync with vertical blanking pulse	
	Ground pin 17 of microcomputer	Square waves should appear on pin 19 of microcomputer. When released, the set should go to channel 2	
Various unpredictable errors in operation of readout, keyboard, channel selection	Check pins 1, 3, 4, 5, 6, 18, 19, and 20 of microcomputer	Grounds, solder bridges, or shorts	Pins 1, 3, 4, 5, 6, 18, 19, and 20 on the microcomputer are one eight-line port that connect to the display, keyboard and PLL IC at various times in the cycle of the computer. Any grounds, solder bridges, or shorts on these lines can cause various unpredictable errors in the operation of the readout, keyboard, and channel selection.

Symptom	Check	Reading	Comments
Two segments always Light	Check pins 1, 3, 4, 5, 6, 18, 19, and 20 of microcomputer	Lead dress shorts from circuit	(See above comments)
Flickering in display or erratic keyboard operation	Check pin 7 of microcomputer	Vertical retrace pulse	The display is scanned. One digit is on at a time. Switching between digits occurs at the vertical rate controlled by the vertical retrace pulse. An erratic vertical rate will cause flickering in the display and perhaps erratic keyboard operation.
Set stays on channel 2 when a channel from 2–6 is selected	Check tuning voltage supply and amplifier	20–35 V depending on channel selected	
Possible PLL failure	Check for proper operation of channel display & keyboard	Assume PLL is receiving the proper data	When proper data is presented to the PLL, pin 9 goes high briefly to enable the PLL IC. Grounding pin 9 therefore prevents the PLL from receiving data in 4-bit words during the vertical retrace period. A sequence of six words conveys channel frequency, fine tuning, and one null work in sequence. Seeing this information in a useful way is almost impossible in a service shop. Therefore, you should infer that if the channel display and keyboard operate properly and pulses are seen on pin 9 of the microcomputer, the PLL is receiving the proper data.
	Check pin 9 of microcomputer	Pulses should be seen	
	Check pin 8 of IC303	Pin 8 should read 195.3125007 Hz when fine tuning is in the middle of its range (a counter is recommended)	The PLL is connected to a quartz crystal oscillating at 3.5810547 MHz (desired). **Do not try to use either a color subcarrier crystal or a color tuning crystal for this part.** This frequency is divided by 18335 when the fine tune is in the middle of its range. This output appears on pin 8 of IC303. This represents a frequency of

■ **Table 5-4 Continued.**

Symptom	Procedure	Result	Comments
Prescaler failure	Open the loop: remove Q310 and R322 and supply the tuning voltage from an adjustable power supply of 0–30 V	Oscillator output: @50 MV magnitude with a frequency between 101 and 931 MHz	195.3125007 Hz if the PLL is properly receiving data. This frequency will change slightly as the fine tuning is exercised (checking with a counter is recommended).
	Select proper band (2–6, 7–13, 14–83) by key entry. Adjust the power supply	Check if the tuners tune properly, @50 MV magnitude with a frequency between 101 and 931 MHz	Note: Failure of the voltage supply will probably effect the prescaler first. If the prescaler goes out, it is recommended to check the line voltage supply.
	Note: If suitable voltmeter is available: check pin 5 of prescaler to judge adequacy of oscillator sample voltage	Pin 5 of prescaler should have a frequency of @394 kHz for channel 2, @3.636 MHz for channel 83	The prescaler will oscillate on its own at a frequency of 4 MHz or above if it has inadequate input. This frequency will be unstable and will not change in response to changes of the tuning voltage in a systematic way.
Correct prescaled output	Check output of PLL IC	Check for exact tuning point	
	Pin 5 of IC303	Check for variance around proper tuning point	It will probably be difficult to see the exact tuning point. It should be sufficient to see that the output changes as the output varies around the proper tuning point. This can be seen on pin 9 of IC303.

Symptom	Action	Possible cause	Notes
Set tunes but horizontal bars are present	Check for oscillations on tuning voltage	Tuning voltage should look very clean with only a slight noise on VHF (less than 5 MV)	Make sure scope leads do not pick up horizontal interference. on VHF (less than 5 MV)
Oscillators or an ac signal superimposed on the tuning voltage	Check for defective transistors in the tuning voltage amplifier	Possible transistor defect	If the problem has been corrected, proper tuning can be verified by measuring the prescaled output on pin 9 of IC302. This is the local oscillator frequency divided by 256. It is specified to be within 100 kHz at channel 83 and the error will decrease to the 10-kHz region at channel 2. It is important to remember that this tuning accuracy is completely independent of any received signal or lack of signal.
	Check for wrong time constants in the filter around the tuning voltage amplifier	Oscillations—locate defective part or wrong value associated with Q309 and Q310	
Beats or sound in picture	Resolve by IF alignment or other correction to the source of problem		Appearance of beats or sound in the picture cannot be corrected in the tuning system. These must be resolved by IF alignment or other correction to the source of problem.

Video recorder & color TV remote control systems

6

This chapter explains how video recorder and color TV remote control systems operate and how to troubleshoot the microprocessor chips used in these products. Information is also included for IR remote control hand units. Techniques to check out direct address and channel scan remote control systems and some real-world troubles and solutions are given.

RCA VFT650 VCR remote control unit

Infrared remote control circuit operation

The receiver for the infrared (IR) remote system is mounted directly behind the VCR front panel above the function buttons. A cleared opening in the front panel allows IR light from the remote hand transmitter to pass through the cabinet and fall on the photoconductive diode mounted on the remote receiver board. The pulse signal of IR light from the remote hand unit causes the photoconductive diode to turn off and on, thus feeding an input signal to pin 1 of IC6801 on the remote receiver board. Refer to Fig. 6-1 for circuit diagram. This pulse information is amplified and exits the IC chip at pin 7 and is then coupled to the slow/still board via P6706-3. On the slow/still board, Q6856 amplifies the signal and drives transformer T6851. The output from T6851 is then reapplied back to the remote receiver board into a shaper amplifier inside IC6801. After being shaped, the pulse code information is amplified, exits the IC at pin 4, and is fed to the remote input to microprocessor IC6851.

Remote microprocessor IC6851 operates from a clock signal of 500 kHz that is fed to pin 40 of the IC chip. It is responsible for decoding the pulse-coded information coming into the remote input of the microprocessor. When a pulse code train is present at pin 29, pin 11 of the microprocessor is pulled logic high. This signal is in-

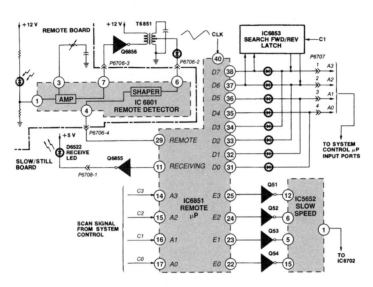

■ 6-1 *Infrared remote control circuit.* RCA Corp

verted by Q5855 and then makes receiving LED D6522 turn on. This lights up an LED on the front panel of the VCR when a remote code is being received.

The four C scanning pulses from the system control microprocessor (C0, C1, C2, and C3) are fed to the A input ports of remote microprocessor IC6851, which decodes the incoming pulse code information applied to pin 29 and activates the appropriate output port (D0 through D7) to generate the correct C scanning pulse on the correct output port to provide the function represented by the input code.

Because of the way the signal is decoded and because the clock in the remote microprocessor is not synchronized with the clock in the system control microprocessor, you must matrix together two of the D output ports to generate the four input signal lines to the system control microprocessor. For example, D0 and D4 output lines are ORed together by diodes to generate the A0 input to the system control microprocessor. Ports D1 and D5 are matrixed together to generate the A1 input. Therefore, the D0 or D4 output from the remote microprocessor is needed to generate the signal to the A0 input port of the system control microprocessor.

The remote hand transmitter sends codes in groups of two except during search forward and search reverse, and slow-speed up and slow-speed down operation. See the remote code chart in Fig. 6-2. In these cases, the code is generated continuously. During search,

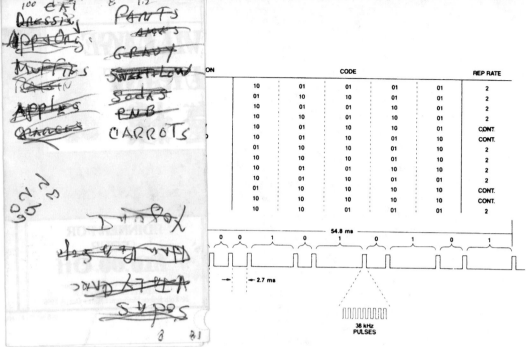

ON	CODE					REP RATE
10	01	01	01	01		2
01	10	10	01	01		2
10	01	01	10	01		2
10	10	01	10	01		2
10	01	10	10	01		CONT.
10	01	10	01	10		CONT.
01	10	10	01	10		2
10	10	10	01	10		2
10	01	01	10	10		2
10	01	10	01	01		2
01	10	10	10	10		CONT.
10	10	10	10	10		CONT.
10	10	01	01	01		2

0 0 1 0 1 0 1 0 1

54.8 ms

2.7 ms

38 kHz PULSES

■ **6-2** *Infrared remote code chart.* RCA Corp

you must latch the A3 and A2 output ports to prevent the system control microprocessor from dropping out of the search mode when the code from the remote hand unit is reset to generate the new code. The remote hand unit generates a new code every 54ms; thus, the search latch IC6853 must hold the output commands from the D7 and D6 ports for that period of time to ensure that the system control does not drop out of the search modes during the recycle time of the remote hand unit code system.

Slow-speed playback is controlled by output ports E0, E1, E2, and E3. When the slow-speed button on the remote hand unit is pressed, ports E0 through E3 generate output signals that are decoded by slow-speed decoder IC6852. This causes the capstan to play back the tape at the slowest possible speed, about $\frac{1}{32}$ of normal.

When the slow-speed up button is depressed, the output levels at ports E0 through E3 will begin changing at a 300ms rate. These changing levels at the output ports will be decoded by the slow-speed decoder IC6852, causing the slow-speed playback to increase in steps to the fastest possible speed, which is $\frac{1}{4}$ normal speed.

The following malfunctions are possible:

☐ No or improper remote control operation
☐ Intermittent remote operation
☐ Intermittent search operation

No or improper remote control operation

Use a known good remote hand unit directed at the opening on the front of the machine, and press a continuous output button, such as the search buttons or the slow-speed up/down buttons. Check for illumination of the receiving LED on the front panel of the VCR. If this diode is not glowing, the problem is in the slow/still or receiver boards. If the receiving LED is active, then the problem will probably be in the remote control microprocessor or the connection to the system control microprocessor.

If the receiving LED does not light up, use a scope to check for a pulse code signal at P6706-4. Refer to Fig. 6-3 for this scope trace. If no signal is present, check the output of transformer T6851 (P6706-2) for a sawtooth waveform corresponding to the IR pulse code information input. If this information is not there, check for the output of the rf amplifier at P6706-3. If no signal is there, you will find the problem in the remote receiver board receiver LED, which means you should replace the receiver board.

If the remote receiver LED does not light up, confirm that the C scan pulses are being applied to input ports A0 through A3. Also confirm that the correct C scan pulses appear at output ports A0 through A3 when you press the appropriate remote function button. If they don't, it means the remote microprocessor is defective.

Intermittent search operation

Confirm the generation of the correct C scan output pulse at the D6 and D7 output ports of the remote microprocessor IC6851. Confirm that the C scan output pulse is maintained at the A2 and A3 output ports during the time that the remote hand unit is recycling to regenerate the remote code again. If there is a pulse at D6 and if the pulse disappears at the cathode of the matrix diodes, search latch IC6853 may be defective.

RCA VGP170/TGP1500 VCR infrared remote control system

Infrared hand unit

The remote hand unit for the VGP170/TGP1500 generates a serial 16-bit digital code by a microprocessor chip during any operator request. When the hand unit is not activated, the hand unit microprocessor is in standby mode to conserve battery power. A logic low at pin 13, the halt input, provides this standby mode capabil-

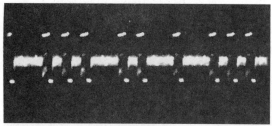

P6706-3

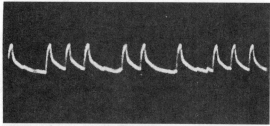

P6706-2

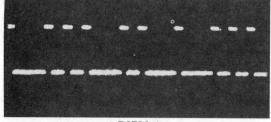

P6706-4

■ **6-3** *IR remote control waveforms.* RCA Corp

ity. The logic low is created by applying the normally high output of the G output ports of the microprocessor and the signal of the operation output to the 5-input NAND gate of the chip. The output of the NAND gate is only low during the time that all inputs are high. This chip turns on the microprocessor during an operator request and keeps the microprocessor turned on until the complete 16-bit code has been transmitted. When a key press is received, one of the G ports of the microprocessor is momentarily pulled low. This causes the output of IC02 to go high and allows full operation of the microprocessor. Pin 3 of the microprocessor then goes logic high and remains high during the time the microprocessor is generating the 16-bit code. The 16-bit code is output at pin 4 and passed to IC03 to be modulated on a 100-kHz carrier. The modulated carrier is passed to output driver transistors Q01 and

Q02. The driver circuit then develops enough power to drive the infrared LEDs.

To service a faulty remote hand unit, check the 200-kHz signal at pin 12 of microprocessor IC01. Then confirm that the halt line input goes high when you press a key. The final step is to check for the appearance of the correct 16-bit serial coded signal at pin 4 of the microprocessor. If there is no signal, the microprocessor chip is defective.

Remote decoder inputs & direct outputs

To simplify the explanation of the remote decoder, we have divided the IR decoder circuitry into four separate circuits. The circuit in Fig. 6-4 shows the operation of the preamp and decoder circuitry during the remote functions of power-on/power-off and channel up.

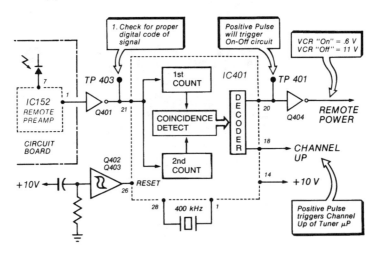

■ **6-4** *Remote decoder inputs and direct outputs.* RCA Corp

The remote receiver circuitry consists primarily of IC152 and a few discrete components. See the block diagram of the remote decoder in Fig. 6-4. The receiver preamp circuitry is contained within a small housing mounted on the keyboard input circuit board, and the decoder circuitry is on a separate board located on the left side of the tuner/timer. The decoder circuit board can be removed from its holder for easier servicing.

Because the remote system has an on-off function, it must be powered constantly from the 10 V that powers the tuner/timer control microprocessor. Most of the circuitry to decode the serial 16-bit

208

digital code is contained in IC401. This decoder IC is reset during initial power-up at pin 26 by transistors Q402 and Q403. For accurate timing, IC401 has a 400-kHz crystal oscillator for the master clock. The serial 16-bit data from the remote preamp is applied to Q401 and the output to pin 21 of IC401. You can see the 16-bit data on an oscilloscope at TP 403. When IC401 receives a 16-bit digital code, it stores the first 16-bit signal in the first count register and puts the second 16-bit signal into the second count register. These registers are then input into a coincidence detector. When the codes in both registers are identical, IC401 decodes the signal and outputs the proper logic codes to the rest of the circuitry.

When the proper 16-bit code is received for the on-off function, IC401 generates a positive pulse at pin 20 that can be scoped at TP 401. This pulse is then fed to the base of Q404, turning it on. The collector of Q404 pulls the remote power line low, which allows the power supply in the tuner/timer to toggle from off to on. If the system is already on, this pulse then causes the system to toggle from on to off.

When the correct 16-bit code is received from the channel-up function, IC401 outputs a positive pulse at pin 18 that is sent to the tuner/timer control microprocessor.

To troubleshoot the remote receiver and decoder, first confirm that the proper 16-bit code is received at TP 403 for the key being pressed. Then confirm the 400-kHz signal at pin 1. During reception of the 16-bit signal for power on-off, confirm the positive pulse at pin 20 of IC401. During reception of the 16-bit channel-up signal, confirm the positive pulse at pin 18 of IC401.

Function selection remote decoder

The other three decoding circuits—mode selection, slow speed, and slow tracking—develop the same resistance values as RCA model VFP170, which has a wired remote system. For example, when you select slow speed or slow tracking, a specific resistance is set up and the selected mode of operation is accomplished by the VCR.

During troubleshooting, you may, if one is available, sub the model VFP170 wired hand unit for the IR remote system to confirm correct operation of recorder functions. The wired hand unit can be plugged into the back panel of the VGP170. Thus you can determine whether the problem is in the IR decoder circuitry or in the recorder.

In Fig. 6-5 the IR remote mode selection is a 10-function type, identical to the F line. The mode function decoding circuitry decodes the incoming signal at IC401. The output of IC401 is a BCD code signal that is again decoded from 4 to 11 output lines by IC402. The 11 output lines are coupled to a hybrid IC (406), a resistor network IC with solid-state switches across each resistor. A high on an input of IC406 causes the appropriate internal switch to close and bypass a resistor. The resultant total resistance of IC406 is then output from pins 1 and 2 to a small connector of the remote plug.

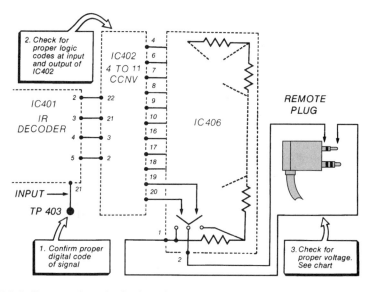

■ **6-5** *Remote decoder for function selection.* RCA Corp

The resistance output from the IR circuitry to the recorder during the 10 different modes is identical to the resistance used in the earlier F line machines. However, due to a different voltage source used in the VGP170 A/D converter (ADC) circuit, the voltage measured at this remote plug will be different.

When you service the mode selection area, always confirm the remote input 16-bit code first for its presence and proper signal levels. If the inputs are correct, then confirm the four decoder outputs of IC401 for each remote mode selection available. Confirm the output of IC406 and measure the voltage at the remote plug. If the voltages are incorrect, then, to help isolate the problem to either the tuner/timer unit or the recorder, substitute the VFP170 wired hand unit to check for proper voltages. If the voltages are still incorrect, the problem is probably within the machine.

Remote decoder slow-speed operation

During the slow-motion operation mode, eight different speeds are programmable by the IR remote system. The decoder chip (IC401) outputs digital codes at pins 6, 7, and 8 to control the slow speed. In Fig. 6-6, you can see these outputs coupled to the switching chip (IC405) and to bipolar transistors within IC407. These switches, which can be programmed to open or close, are connected across resistors within IC407, and they develop the correct value of resistance to be applied to the remote plug. The resistance range is the same range as the variable control of the wired hand unit, but it will only have eight possible resistances.

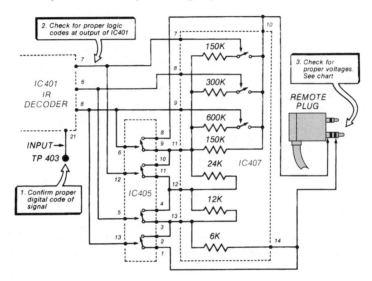

■ 6-6 *Remote decoder—slow speed.* RCA Corp

In slow speed, the IC401 outputs are all high. These outputs turn on all the switches, bypassing all of the resistors and creating a 0-Ω resistance. This action places the servo circuitry of the VCR machine in the fastest slow-motion speed.

To troubleshoot the slow-speed selection circuitry, always confirm the proper 16-bit serial input signal and the 400-kHz master clock oscillator with the scope first. If these pulses are correct, then confirm proper logic code outputs at pins 6, 7, and 8 while changing to slow speeds. Now measure the voltage at the output of IC407 to the remote plug for the proper level. Also, if available, sub in a wired remote hand unit to confirm the operation of the VGP170 machine.

Remote decoder slow tracking operation

The F model remote hand unit had a continuously variable control for slow tracking. The IR remote system uses a 32-position digital system for slow-motion tracking. Figure 6-7 shows that the slow-tracking circuitry is functionally similar to the slow-speed selection circuitry in that switches are activated to bypass resistors.

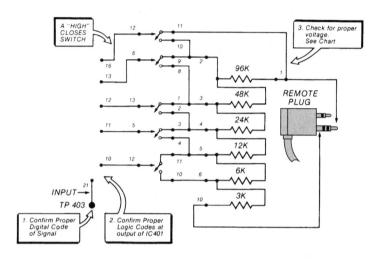

■ **6-7** Remote decoder for slow tracking. RCA Corp

When the 16-bit signal is received and decoded by IC401, it is output by a particular binary logic combination of the five outputs. These five outputs are passed to two solid-state switch chips (IC403 and IC404) to bypass various resistors within IC407. This determines the total resistance applied to the remote plug. This circuitry provides 32 possible resistance values for slow-motion tracking.

To service this equipment, do the following:

☐ Confirm the presence of 16-bit digital code at TP 403.
☐ Confirm proper logic codes at the output of IC401.
☐ Check for proper voltage at appropriate pins of IC407.

See Table 6-1 for the correct voltages at the pins of IC401.

■ Table 6-1 IC401 voltage output chart.

Button operation	16	13	Pin 12	11	10	IC407 outputs Voltage across pins 10 & 14
▼						1
15	0	0	0	0	0	6.59
14	0	0	0	0	1	6.55
13	0	0	0	1	0	6.50
12	0	0	0	1	1	6.45
11	0	0	1	0	0	6.39
10	0	0	1	0	1	6.33
9	0	0	1	1	0	6.26
8	0	0	1	1	1	6.20
7	0	1	0	0	0	6.13
6	0	1	0	0	1	6.05
5	0	1	0	1	0	5.98
4	0	1	0	1	1	5.84
3	0	1	1	0	0	5.80
2	0	1	1	0	1	5.70
1	0	1	1	1	0	5.60
Center	0	1	1	1	1	5.49
▲						
1	1	0	0	0	0	5.36
2	1	0	0	0	1	5.23
3	1	0	0	1	0	5.08
4	1	0	0	1	1	4.93
5	1	0	1	0	0	4.76
6	1	0	1	0	1	4.57
7	1	0	1	1	0	4.36
8	1	0	1	1	1	4.13
9	1	1	0	0	0	3.85
10	1	1	0	0	1	3.57
11	1	1	0	1	0	3.23
12	1	1	0	1	1	2.86
13	1	1	1	0	0	2.40
14	1	1	1	0	1	1.90
15	1	1	1	1	0	1.27
16	1	1	1	1	1	0.53

Remote control checks

The remote control circuit is responsible for decoding the 11 remote functions via the tuner/timer or camera inputs. Circuit operation is identical to the VFP170 remote control except for component value differences within IC807, which produce different voltages at IC807 input pin 13 and output pin 10. The wired remote hand unit used with the VFP170 gives the same results as the TGP1500 tuner/timer IR remote circuitry. The remote circuitry and points of service checks are shown in Fig. 6-8.

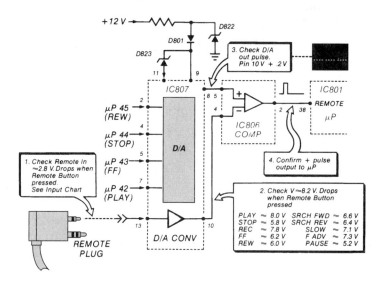

■ **6-8** *Remote operation control servicing diagram.* RCA Corp

If the circuit has no or incorrect remote operation, follow these steps:

1. Confirm the correct operation of the remote hand unit by checking the dc voltage to pin 13 of the IC807 DAC. The voltage at pin 13 should be as in the resistance-voltage chart.

2. Check the output of the amplifier in IC807 at pin 10. According to the chart in Fig. 6-8, when you press the play button on the remote hand unit the voltage at pin 10 should be about 8.0 V. When you press fast forward, the voltage should be about 6.2 V, pause should be very near 5.2 V.

3. Test for the presence of the D/A output at pin 8 of IC807. The voltage at pin 8 should be a pulse to the same voltage level as is occurring at pin 10 plus 50 mV. In some cases, it will go slightly below this value. The most important measurement is the dc value of the pulse amplitude. If the voltages at pin 8 or pin 10 are not as expected, suspect a defective IC807.

4. Confirm the presence of positive-going pulses at pin 2 of comparator IC806. Logic high pulses indicate that the D/A circuit has accepted the input command, and the microprocessor is instructed to accept the remote function determined by the BCD code at the input of the DAC. The

correct remote input resistance is shown in Table 6-2.

■ Table 6-2 Remote input resistance chart. RCA Corp

Mode	External resistance to ground	Pin 13 voltage (V)
Play	111.4 (kΩ)	2.6
Record	51.4	2.4
Frame adv	21.4	2.0
Slow	15.4	1.8
Search fwd	8.5	1.4
Search rev	6.4	1.2
F fwd	4.7	1.0
Rewind	3.4	0.8
Stop	3.2	0.6
Quick review	0.66	0.2
Pause	0	0

The preceding information was obtained from the RCA VCR-8 training manual. (Courtesy of RCA Consumer Electronics. Copyright 1982 by RCA.)

Zenith M line remote tuning systems

Zenith remote tuning systems are of two types: an up/down scan and a direct-access remote system. Both systems have 105-channel reception capability for full CATV-VHF-UHF versatility. They provide on-screen channel number display and time. A powerful microprocessor is used along with an MNOS nonvolatile memory.

The direct-access tuning system

The direct-access tuning system is shown in Fig. 6-9. The microprocessor chip has a 221-153 Zenith part number. The microchip continuously scans the keyboard every 5ms. When you press a key, the microprocessor identifies it and puts the proper divisor for the channel selected in the PLL. The PLL divides the sample frequency (the tuner local oscillator frequency divided by 256 in the prescaler) by the selected channel number. This frequency is then compared with the PLL to a divided-down 3.5-MHz crystal reference frequency so that the tuner oscillator assumes the accuracy and stability of the crystal reference.

The PLL generates an error signal whenever the system is not phase locked. The active filter processes the error signal, and the output voltage corrects the local oscillator tuning voltage so that

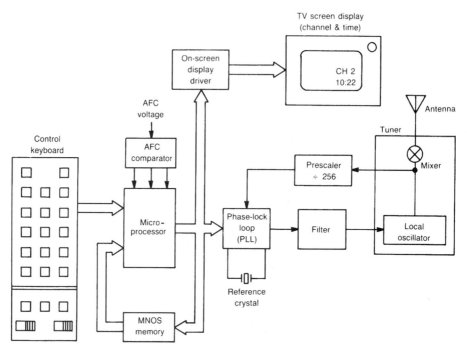

■ **6-9** *Direct-access tuning system block diagram.* Zenith Radio Corp

the error is reduced to zero and the system is locked to the correct frequency for the channel entered. The reference comparison frequency is approximately 1 kHz. The active filter takes the digital pulse output of the PLL and filters and simplifies the 1-kHz signal to convert it to the required dc analog voltage needed by the varactor tuning diodes. Power is continuously fed to the PLL and the microprocessor at all times (even when the receiver is turned off) as long as the ac line cord is plugged in.

Data is fed from the microprocessor to the on-screen display registers, which store the present channel and correct time information. The microprocessor uses data from the 60-Hz line to compute the correct time. The on-screen display driver has two outputs: one for the white letters and numbers, one for the black background. Input timing information is fed to the display driver from horizontal and vertical oscillator outputs from the 9-152 module. Appropriate timing signals are derived to display the desired information in the lower right corner of the screen. Properly timed blanking signals produce the black background portion of the on-screen display, and video signals produce the letters and numbers. See Fig. 6-10.

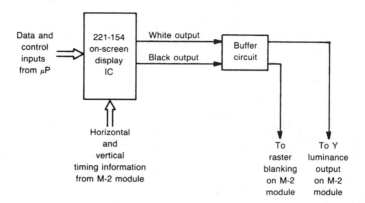

■ **6-10** *Screen display block diagram.* Zenith Radio Corp

An output of the microprocessor is also connected to the black driver circuit to provide interchannel raster blanking.

In the special AFC mode, the microprocessor searches for three parameters. In the AFC comparator circuit, the AFC voltage indicates whether the incoming signal is properly tuned and whether it is in a specified window between 1 and 5 V. The vertical pulse is also tested to determine the presence or absence of vertical sync pulses. A test is made to determine if the AFC voltage is above or below the 3-V threshold in the window. This sequence of events occurs only when the AFC mode switch is in the special AFC position.

Microprocessor control

A block diagram of the microprocessor is shown in Fig. 6-11. The microprocessor is a powerful, versatile device. It contains a (2K-×-8)-bit instruction ROM, containing a more than 2000-step operating program, and a 128-×-4 RAM for a scratch-pad memory. Eight input ports provide for input signals from the keyboard or the space command receiver. The full capacity of the system is used.

The oscillator input generates timing signals for control of the microprocessor and system operation. A 350-to-600-kHz clock frequency allows operation with each instruction cycle occurring during a three-clock-cycle period. A noncritical RC oscillator is used. A 200-Hz signal obtained from the PLL IC also provides timing information. The reset input initializes the microprocessor instruction set when power is applied to the system. A +5-V power supply is required. There are 12 independent latchable outputs and an 8-bit, latched programmed logic array (PLA). The outputs are used to perform bandswitching, video blanking, sound muting,

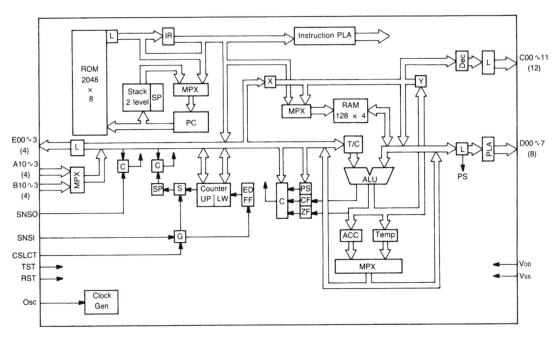

6-11 *221-153 microprocessor block diagram.* Zenith Radio Corp

keyboard scanning, and other functions. Data is fed out on the bus lines (PLL divider ratio, information for on-screen display, etc.).

An internal counter was added to the new microprocessor IC to add the channel-up and channel-down operations to the tuning system, independent of the remote receiver. These up/down frequencies are decoded by the microprocessor. The counter is checked periodically. If a proper frequency is detected directly by the microprocessor, the system is moved up or down to the next selected channel. The counter is used to count ultrasonic pulses that have been processed by the remote control preamplifier for correct logic level, without going through the remote receiver circuits. This allows direct reception of the up/down channel change commands by the microprocessor. Using this method, two extra functions are added to the tuning system by using the same remote receiver, which is capable of decoding only 16 different functions.

60-Hz buffer input circuit

The 60-Hz buffer input circuits are shown in Fig. 6-12. A 60-Hz signal from the remote control transformer is used in the 60-Hz buffer circuit for computing the correct time by the microprocessor. On the positive portion of the ac cycle, the transistor is turned on, rout-

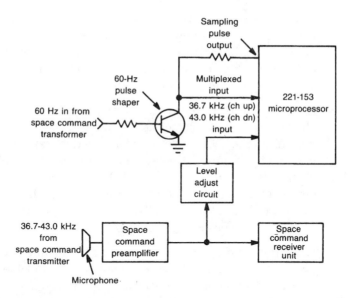

6-12 *Buffer and remote input circuits to microprocessor chip.* Zenith Radio Corp

ing the sampling pulse to ground. On the negative portion of the cycle, the transistor is cut off, and the sampling pulse is detected by an input going to the microprocessor. This technique effectively determines when a pulse edge occurs for use in time counting.

Screen readout display circuit

Figure 6-10 shows the screen readout display block diagram. Data output from the microprocessor is transmitted to the on-screen display IC221-154. Information on the channel tuned and time of day is recorded in a register in the display chip. The register is clocked by horizontal and vertical signals from the 9-152 module. This horizontal and vertical timing information positions the display in the lower right corner of the screen. Two outputs are generated by the on-screen display IC. A "white" output is created for the characters, and a "black" output for the background. They are fed to buffers to give the right amplitude and polarity. The buffer circuit allows interfacing to the 9-152 module in two places and overrides the video information to display the time and channel number on the screen.

Ultrasonic remote transmitter

The Zenith SC1600 remote system uses the 130-9 receiver. When the 221-134 chip is replaced by the 221-134-01, the receiver provides a momentary function at pin 11 of the IC. This function, through two diodes, will simultaneously pull down the channel-up (high) and channel-down (low) lines. When this occurs, the microprocessor board provides an on-screen display of both time and channel number. The on-screen display remains on for 4.5 s after you release the remote control button.

Another feature of the SC1600 is its ability to scan through the channels previously selected at the TV receiver. As the channel buttons on the TV receiver are depressed in sequence, the viewer makes a decision to either store or skip each channel. A skipped channel is indicated by both an LED at the set and a momentary display of the letters PO on the screen. The set LED is red for the skip condition. A saved (or stored) channel is indicated by a green LED on the receiver's front panel.

When the remote control unit buttons for channel high and channel low are pushed, only stored channels are available for viewing. No skipped channels are available. Thus, you see only selected channels when operating the remote.

The clock circuit has been updated to eliminate the sensitivity to line amplitude variations that may occur in some areas. The ac reference is still 60 Hz, but now the signal is ac coupled so that amplitude variations do not result in timing differences.

Figure 6-13 gives the circuit for the 124-20 remote control hand unit. The thick-film network determines the frequency being sent. A tap is used at the thick-film network to supply the 36.90-kHz time/channel recall frequency.

SC2500 remote hand unit

The SC2500 (see Fig. 6-14) has channel-up and channel-down functions, which are derived from two switch closures. These frequencies are derived by counting down (with the 221-148 chip) and by the 4.43-MHz crystal reference frequency. The 130-11A module is used as the remote receiver. These scan functions are obtained by having the microprocessor control board do the counting for the channel-up (36.72 kHz) and channel-down (42.95 kHz) frequencies. When you press these buttons, the stored channels are available for viewing. These channels are stored whenever a channel is selected on the front panel of the TV set and the enter key is depressed. Channels are not stored when a selection is made at the remote hand unit. This is done to avoid confusion and because the channel skip button is located only on the front of the TV receiver. It works very well because, generally, channels are not programmed often.

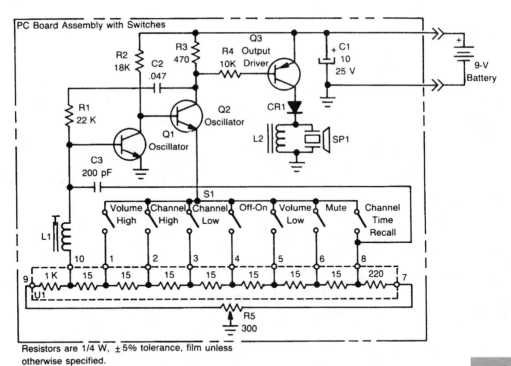

■ 6-13 *Diagram for SC1600 remote hand unit.* Zenith Radio Corp

Resistors are 1/4 W, ±5% tolerance, film unless otherwise specified.

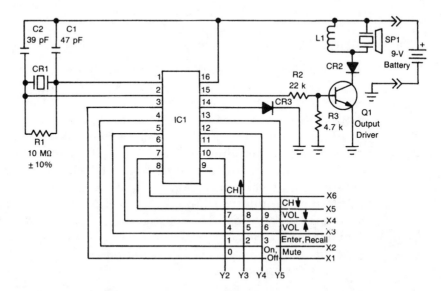

■ 6-14 *SC2500 remote hand unit circuit.* Zenith Radio Corp

Because of the addition of channel-up and channel-down and variations in IC sensitivity to ultrasonic signals, there are two pots in the system that affect performance. The only one you should ever adjust in the field is the range control on the back of the microphone/amplifier assembly. See Fig. 6-15 for this diagram. The other control is a factory adjustment only. Normal direct access of any channel from the hand unit is available.

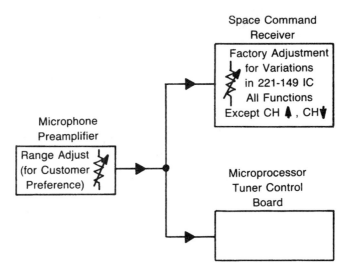

■ 6-15 *Sensitivity controls on SC2500 remote unit.*

Phenomenons solved

Volume control in the direct-access remote system has approximately 128 volume steps. However, to the set listener they are perceived as a smooth continuous volume increase or decrease. A problem that occurred with the G.I. 221-149 chip in early production receivers was that in the sliding of the remote/manual/off switch, a momentary drop of the 12-V supply would sometimes cause the volume control portion of the 221-149 chip to lock into a mute or a maximum volume level. In this case, the volume control buttons on the front panel of the TV receiver or at the remote hand unit had no effect. The solution was to unplug the ac line cord and then reconnect the TV receiver. The KX201 relay and zener diode CR208 (see Fig. 6-16) were added to prevent this lock-up occurrence.

A second phenomenon was sometimes evident when the set was first plugged into the ac power and the on-off switch pushed on: there would be a momentary sound burst. This only occurred

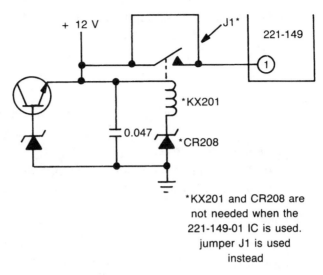

+ 12 V

J1*

221-149

①

*KX201

0.047

*CR208

*KX201 and CR208 are
not needed when the
221-149-01 IC is used.
jumper J1 is used
instead

■ **6-16** *Sound latch modification.*

within 2 s of IC power-up. The solution to both problems is in the design of the 221-149-01 chip. When this IC is used, the reed relay and zener are eliminated and a jumper bypasses the open contacts. This IC and circuit connections are shown in Fig. 6-16.

223

Zenith N line infrared remote control systems

This Zenith IR remote system offers a variety of features. All systems can now receive 112 TV channels. Some have keyboard access; another has a space phone and one for the projection TV set. A programmable memory allows any remote control set to be automatically turned off or on. The remote system is more compact with fewer parts and modules, and thus more reliable.

Features of IR remote system

1. IR transmitter and receiver for remote control operation
2. Complete IR unit on one plug-in module board
3. Use of PCM (pulse-coded modulation) IR system allows the new remote control functions to be added, which were not possible with ultrasonic systems.
4. Greater sensitivity and selectivity of the remote control system due to the use of the IR concept
5. Improved reliability of the remote control system

6. Preprogrammed channels allow channels to be scanned (up or down), bypassing unwanted channels
7. Digital channel number entry
8. Remote control of on-screen time and channel display, mute, and space phone functions
9. Programmable timer to turn set on or off at a preselected time
10. Instant response to remote power-on/power-off command
11. Sixty-four volume levels controlled either remotely or with front panel controls

System overview

The IR remote hand unit transmitter is built on a small PC board. A single I2L, 16-pin IC is used. Also included are three IR emitting diodes, a transistor, an oscillator adjustment potentiometer, a 4-×-8 matrix keyboard, and a 9-V battery.

The IR receiver consists of a detector and amplifier on a single PC board. The major parts include an IR optical filter, a photosensitive diode, an IC with high-gain amplifiers, two transistors, and an LC tuned circuit.

The tuning system control contains the microprocessor, which includes an internal PLL. An interface IC incorporates a quad comparator, an active filter for processing the tuning voltage, B+ and bandswitching circuits, and tuning-voltage supply and clamp circuits. The block diagrams in Figs. 6-17 and 6-18 illustrate the difference between the M and N models remote control systems.

Remote transmitter operation

After any key is pressed on the hand unit, the IC221-157 chip is turned on and draws between 4 and 6 mA total current. A PCM output waveform (see Fig. 6-19) is initiated. The code consists of a start bit, then five groups of a data bit, and its complement. The entire code thus consists of 11 bits of information. A single pulse represents the 0 state, a double pulse the 1 state.

The pulses are modulated by a 40-kHz clock signal to translate the signal to a higher frequency to avoid the usual frequencies, as shown in Fig. 6-20. The 11 bits are transmitted in about 56ms. This is repeated every 180ms as long as the transmitter key is depressed. Before transmission occurs, there is a 40ms delay after a

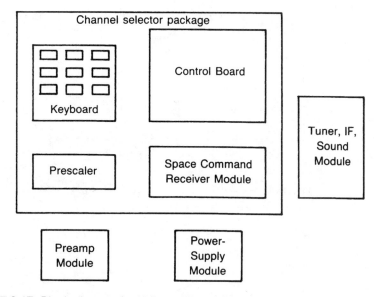

■ 6-17 *Block diagram for M line tuning system.*

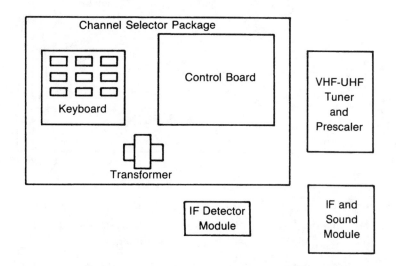

■ 6-18 *Block diagram for N line tuning system.* Zenith Radio Corp

key is depressed. The codes for all transmitter functions have the same period, but the 5-bit code is unique for each function.

The output pulse train from the IC is fed to an NPN amplifier transistor. See Fig. 6-21. The output is amplified to generate 1.2 A to drive the three IR, series-wired LEDs. A 1000-mF capacitor charged from the 9-V battery is the source of energy for the pulses. The transmitter has an internal 80-kHz RC oscillator. A crystal is not

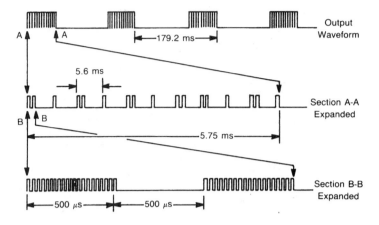

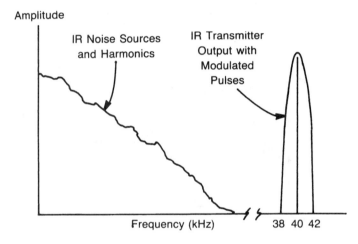

■ **6-19** *IR transmitter output waveform.*

■ **6-20** *Typical IR spectrum.*

needed because the system microprocessor operates asynchronously with respect to the transmitter.

All versions of the hand remote transmitter use the same code for
all common transmitter functions. Also, common to the direct-access hand unit versions is the PC board assembly. Remote-unit
battery life is about the same as for ultrasonic systems used in the
past.

Detector/preamplifier circuitry

The detector/preamplifier is located in the TV set, and IR light
from the hand unit can be received by the IR detector/preamplifier

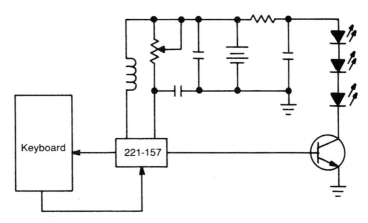

■ 6-21 *IR transmitter diagram.* <small>Zenith Radio Corp</small>

by direct or reflected radiation. The system is very insensitive to the surrounding area. The received IR light can normally only be affected by unusual room conditions, such as very dark walls. Ultrasonic systems were much more likely to be affected by the external surroundings.

Light from the transmitter passes through the IR optical filter to an IR photodiode. See Fig. 6-22. The peak sensitivity occurs at a wavelength of 960 nm. Refer to Fig. 6-23. The diode output is coupled to the IC, which amplifies the signal. The IC output to the

227

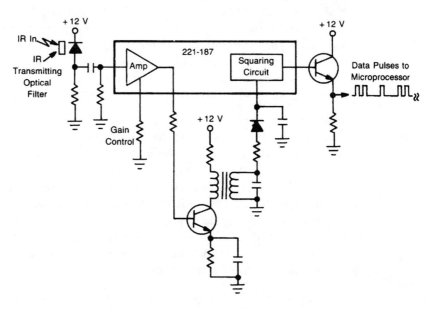

■ 6-22 *IR detector/preamplifier diagram.* <small>Zenith Radio Corp</small>

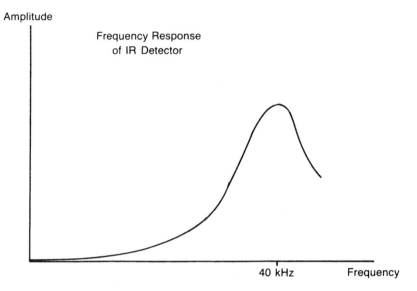

Amplitude

Frequency Response
of IR Detector

40 kHz   Frequency

■ **6-23** *Frequency response of IR detector.*

tuned circuit removes the 40-kHz modulation from the pulses. The tuned circuit output is fed to a squaring circuit in the same IC. This, in turn, is routed to an external NPN output driver transistor.

The preamplifier uses a 12-V supply derived from the standby transformer located on the tuning control board. The squared output signal consists of the pulses containing the serial data bits. It is transferred through a connector to the tuning control board. The pulses then pass through a noise-removing RC filter into the microprocessor for decoding. The decoding process is implemented in special hardware logic in the microprocessor and is controlled by the microprocessor software program contained in the ROM.

The program hunts for the start data bit and expects to receive the remaining 10 bits mentioned earlier. It samples past the tenth bit to ensure that the 10 bits received are valid and complete. If not, the sampling process is repeated. The decoding program will ignore invalid codes. If two keys on the hand unit are pressed at the same time, no IR signal is transmitted. When the data transmission has been decoded, the microprocessor activates the appropriate control outputs to achieve the desired control function. The IR detector/preamplifier is powered whenever the set is plugged into ac and the remote/manual switch is in the remote position.

Control module

The control module has an MNOS memory IC and uses a more complex version for the on-screen display IC for the space phone models to accommodate the dial-out features. A block diagram of the screen readout character generator is shown in Fig. 6-24. An extra 112-V power supply has been added in the N model control board to operate the on-off relay and the IR detector/amplifier. The relay and fuse for the space command transformer primary are located on the control board. See Fig. 6-25.

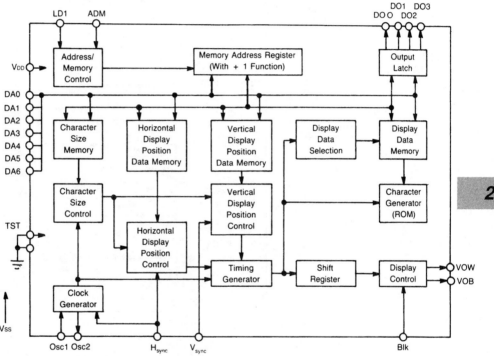

■ 6-24 *Character generator block diagram.* Zenith Radio Corp

The volume is adjusted by a DAC in the microprocessor. The pulse-width modulation (PWM) signal from the microprocessor is integrated by a small filter network, and 64 steps of dc voltage level are available for volume control. The last volume level is stored in the MNOS memory. If power to the TV set goes off and later comes back on, the system will operate at the last previously selected volume level.

The N models also feature an auto set on-off program. A separate control keyboard plugs into the main control board. The switches

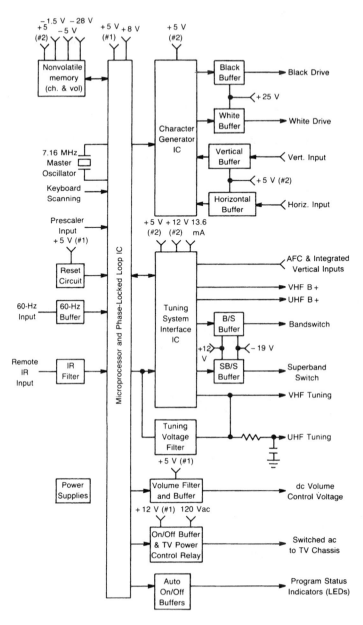

■ **6-25** *Space command remote control board block diagram used in the Zenith N line sets.* Zenith Radio Corp

and LED indicators are located on the main control board. Once the correct time has been set, the TV receiver may be programmed to turn on or off at any desired time. If the auto off time has not been programmed and the TV set has been placed in the auto on mode, the set will turn itself off after one hour of operation. Indicator lights show the status of the auto on and auto off functions when the TV set is in the automatic operation mode.

The basic tuning system can receive 112 VHF, UHF, and CATV channels, as can the manual tuning system. It can also be interfaced with space phone and projection TV features. The same interface IC is used in both manual and remote control versions of this tuning system.

The component counts of both active and passive devices have been reduced compared to previous systems. Many functions have been incorporated directly in the circuit ICs. New low-power semiconductor technology allows more complex integration of circuit functions and lower power dissipation for longer life. Two controls have been removed, eliminating the need for factory or field adjustments of the microprocessor oscillator and bandswitch clamp settings. The only remaining control is for horizontal adjustment of the on-screen display. The system has fewer modules and interconnecting plugs and cables.

Service considerations

Infrared radiation is invisible. The IR and ultrasonic remote control amplifier assemblies are similar in appearance and cannot be interchanged. Replace the amplifier assembly if it is defective and cannot be repaired.

As a first check of a faulty remote system, test the operation with a known good hand transmitter unit. Next, substitute for the detector/amplifier module. If the problem still exists, it is in the tuning system circuits. Troubleshooting the tuning system is simpler because there are fewer modules. Problems are therefore usually limited to the control module or the tuner unit.

The IR remote control system is more sensitive and selective. It is much more difficult to "accidentally" activate the tuning system. Power to the TV set may now be switched on and off instantaneously. A programmed automatic timer to turn the set on and off is also available. On some models, an upgraded space phone feature allows direct dialing of telephone calls from the remote control hand unit transmitter.

VCR microprocessor function control systems

7

This chapter reviews microprocessor control systems in VCRs. It explains how these microprocessor-controlled VCRs operate and gives troubleshooting tips on locating and correcting problems in these control systems.

VCR service considerations

When servicing a complex microprocessor-controlled VCR machine, you must develop a logic troubleshooting plan or approach. To determine this plan of action, look at the type of failures that could occur. Then develop a specific service procedure for each kind of fault. You can then develop each symptom into a flowchart system covering specific areas and thus not be concerned with areas that are not responsible for the problem.

After an initial analysis of the VCR, you can put the symptoms in various categories of a flowchart. One symptom, for example, might be that the machine does not respond to or responds incorrectly to input function commands. Another failure category might be that the input functions are accepted, but the mechanism does not respond by activating the proper mechanical functions, such as fast forward, rewind or loading, and so on.

Microprocessor chip considerations

Because of the small size and nearness to each other of the microprocessor chip pins, it is a good idea, when measuring the outputs of the pins, not to directly probe them. Instead, trace the pattern away from the microprocessor pins to where it connects to another component, such as a plug. This practice reduces the chance of shorting adjacent pins together and damaging the microprocessor. Observe normal MOS IC handling precautions when troubleshooting the microprocessor unit.

RCA TGP1500 VCR tuner/timer system control

VCR tuner/timer microprocessor

The functional block diagram in Fig. 7-1 shows the relationship between microprocessor IC102 and the power and oscillator input circuitry. The memory within the microprocessor is powered from the regulated 10 V at pin 21. During normal line voltage conditions, this 10 V is derived from regulator IC101. When a loss of ac power occurs, a small nicad battery, which is charged during normal tuner/timer operation, feeds power to IC103. This IC is a dc-to-dc voltage converter and develops a 10-V output during the time ac power is lost. The battery can supply power to the microprocessor and the 50-Hz clock circuitry for about one hour. This will maintain the microprocessor memory and timekeeping accuracy.

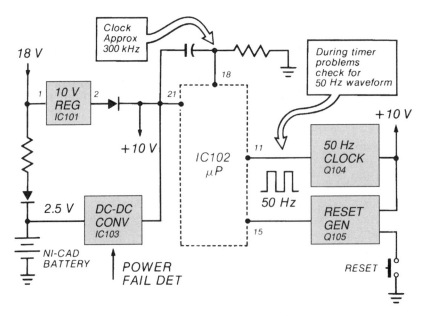

■ **7-1** *Block diagram of microprocessor, clock, and power source.* RCA Corp

Like all microprocessors, a master clock oscillator is required to sequence all of the operations within the microchip. An RC oscillator is used at pin 18 of IC102 to develop a signal of approximately 300 kHz.

Because the microprocessor timekeeping functions and memory must operate during a loss of ac power, you need a frequency source other than the normal 60-Hz power-line voltage. A combination of IC104 and Q104 develops this accurate frequency for the clock circuitry. A 50-Hz square wave is applied from IC104 to pin 11 of the tuner/timer control microprocessor, and this square wave is further divided within the microprocessor for the proper timing period.

If the tuner control or timer is operating improperly, be sure to confirm the +10 V at pin 21, the 300-kHz signal at pin 18, and the 50-Hz signal at the input of the microprocessor (pin 11). If they are incorrect, then troubleshoot the defective area before making any further checks.

Timer display & keyboard operation

The tuner/timer microprocessor generates eight scanning outputs that are passed to the display device as digit drivers and to the input keyboard matrix. See Fig. 7-2.

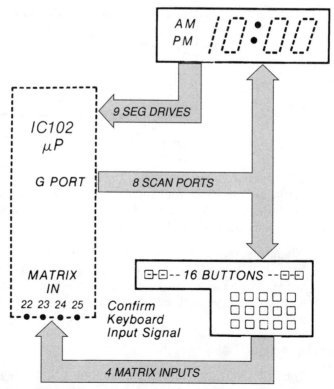

■ **7-2** *Timer display and keyboard block diagram.*

The timing chart in Fig. 7-3 shows that eight scanning pulses occur during a timer period of 6 ms. The nine segment drives are used in conjunction with the eight scanning outputs to generate the proper display readout.

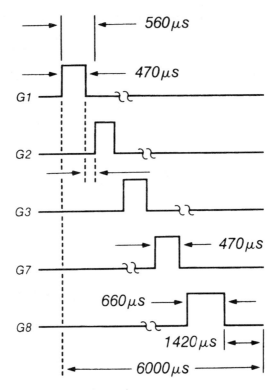

■ **7-3** *G-port output scanning pulses.*

The keyboard circuit switches the appropriate selected scanning output to one of the four input ports of the microprocessor, pins 22 through 25. This action informs the microprocessor of the instructions selected by the operator.

When making service checks, confirm with the scope that you have scanning pulses at the matrix input of IC102 for each keyboard button entry. If any pulse is missing for one keyboard entry, suspect the keyboard button contact or diode circuitry to be defective.

Channel selection

The TGP1500 tuner control system uses a 16-position digital channel selection circuit. Microprocessor IC102 has complete control of the digital channel selection circuitry. All operator requests for a new channel selection must be input to the microprocessor.

When a remote channel-up input command is received at pin 9 of microprocessor IC102, the microprocessor outputs one pulse at pin 7 that instructs the two shift registers (IC151 and IC701) to count up one position to the next channel.

Selecting a channel manually with the individual channel selection buttons is a bit more complicated in terms of the functions that occur in the tuner/timer circuitry. A manual input channel selection from the keyboard informs the microprocessor what channel has been selected. The microprocessor starts a series of operations to direct the two shift registers to that channel position. It does not, however, keep track of what channel position is presently displayed. When a request for a new channel is input manually from the keyboard, the microprocessor first outputs a series of pulses at pin 7 to increment the two shift registers upward until the microprocessor receives a low at pin 30. A low at pin 30 occurs when both shift registerICs are at position 16. The microprocessor then sends out the exact number of pulses to increment the shift registers to the position requested.

If, for some unknown reason, the two shift registers get out of synchronization, the microprocessor would not recognize that both ICs are at position 16 at the same time. To prevent this, IC701 is designated as the master shift register, and IC151 functions only as a slave. When IC701 reaches position 1, the position 1 output goes low and, through two diodes, pulls the channel-up and channel-down inputs of IC151 to a logic low. This low resets IC151 and places it in position 1, thereby synchronizing both ICs.

During channel selection troubleshooting, confirm the channel scan output at pin 7 of microprocessor IC102 during remote input, and check for a series of pulses when a new channel is selected at the keyboard. Then during manual resetting of the microprocessor or initial power-up conditions, confirm that the two shift registers are always reset to the channel 1 position.

RCA VFP170 VCR

The following information is a brief introduction to the VCR microprocessor system control.

System control

The system control microprocessor in the VFP170 VCR is responsible for controlling the operation of the entire machine. This is done by decoding various input data to generate microprocessor outputs that control the operation of the unit. Some input data is derived from the VCR function switches. Remote control input data via the DAC is also supplied to the microprocessor. The microprocessor has several inputs dedicated to sensing machine status and trouble conditions. Status inputs include tape end, cassette down, mode sense, and safety tab. Trouble inputs are dew, reel stop, cylinder lock, and low battery. The microprocessor also accepts an input from the memory counter that indicates when a preset time count on the tape counter has occurred, causing the machine to stop. For more details see Fig. 7-4.

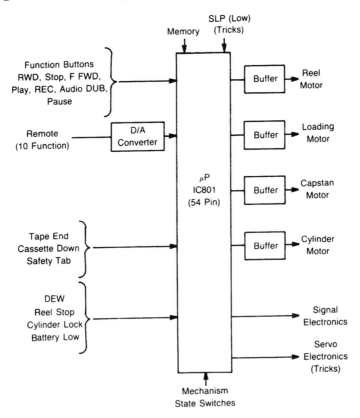

■ **7-4** *RCA VFP170 system control block diagram.*

After processing the various input functions, the microprocessor activates the appropriate output lines to provide the desired functions, including operation of the reel motor and loading motor by some buffer circuitry. The loading motor is activated to generate the various states of the VCR mechanism. The loading motor is responsible for removing the main brakes from the takeup and supply turntables during fast forward, reverse, and play. The loading motor is also activated to place the mechanism in the still/pause or in the record/pause mode of operation. This is done through feedback from the mode sense switch to the microprocessor.

The microprocessor also has several outputs controlling the capstan motor, cylinder motor, signal-processing electronics, and servo control electronics. Many of the inputs and outputs to the system control circuitry are made by connectors PG 801 and PG 802, as shown in Fig. 7-5.

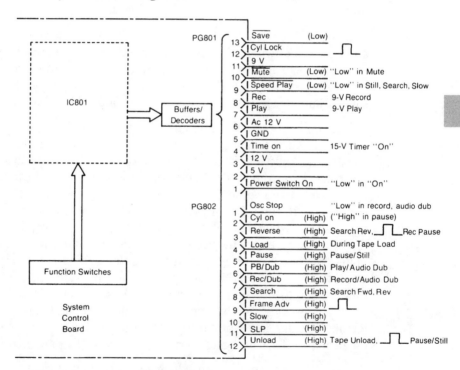

■ **7-5** *System control output lines.*

PG 801 pin 1 is the power switch on line. This line is logic low when the VCR is turned on. Pin 2 provides 5 V B+ from the switching regulator to the system control board, and pin 3 provides 12 V B+. Pin 4 provides the timer on command from the tuner/timer connector jack. This line goes to near 15 V when the tuner/timer activates to turn on the VCR. Pin 6 is a control line indicating that the unit is operating from ac derived 12 V instead of 12 V from the battery. Pin 7 is the play control output command line, and pin 8 is the record control line. Pin 9, not speed play, is a control line from the microprocessor that is activated (logic low) during nonstandard playback, such as when the VCR is operating in the still, search, or slow modes. At all other times the not speed play is a logic high.

Pin 10 is the not audio mute control line, which is pulled logic low in the audio mute modes, such as during the still/pause, search, and slow modes. Pin 11 is 9 V B+ to the system control circuit from the switching regulator. Pin 12 is the cylinder lock sense input, which goes logic high if the cylinder motor stops or slows considerably. The logic high on pin 12 during cylinder lock is a momentary pulse.

Pin 13 is the not save line from the system control microprocessor to the power-switching regulator circuit, which instructs the switching regulator to go into the power save mode, thus cutting off the 9-V supply and the servomotor B+ supplies while leaving the 5-V supply active to keep the system control circuit active.

PG 802 contains some additional control outputs. Pin 1 is the oscillator stop line applied to the audio circuit board assembly. This line will go logic low in record and audio dub, enabling the full erase oscillator to operate. In play operation, the line is logic high and turns off the audio erase oscillator. Pin 2 is the cylinder on control line to the cylinder motor. This line goes logic high in the play and record modes to turn on the cylinder. The capstan motor direction is reversed by the microprocessor pulling pin 3 logic high. This occurs during search reverse and for a short period when the unit is placed in the record/pause mode to back up the tape for about ½ second to provide the phase-match edit capability. Pin 4 provides a load condition to the servo and signal-processing circuits, indicating to them that the system is in the load operating mode. This signal does not control the loading motor.

Pin 5 is the pause control line, which goes logic high during record/pause and still/pause. Pin 6 is the playback and dub control line, which is logic high during playback or audio dub. Pin 7 is a record dub line, which is logic high during record and audio dub.

A logic high level on pins 6 and 7 indicates that the unit is to operate in the audio dub mode. The search line (pin 8) goes logic high during the search modes of operation, both forward and reverse. Frame advance operation is activated by a logic high pulse from pin 9 fed to the servo, causing the capstan servo to advance the tape by one frame with each logic high pulse. Pin 10 is the slow control line. This line goes logic high only during the slow mode of operation. The SLP high line, pin 11, is fed to the system control microprocessor to instruct the microprocessor that the tape is being played back in the SPL mode and that the features of slow, search, and frame advance can be performed. The unload line (pin 12) instructs the signal-processing electronics to be in mute because the mechanism is in unload operation.

Some of the preceding information was taken from the RCA VCR-6 workshop training manuals #8119 and #8204 (copyright 1981), courtesy of RCA Consumer Electronics.

RCA VFT190 VCR microprocessor system control

System control overview

The VFT190 VCR has a single-chip, 4-bit microprocessor (IC6002) along with associated electronics located on two circuit boards to virtually control the entire VCR machine. The system control 1 timer board accepts input commands, processes data (IC6002), and provides the necessary timing functions for the mechanism. It is also responsible for controlling the VCR in the timer control mode. The system control 2 board provides loading-motor driver circuitry and necessary regulated B+ voltages to the electronics.

The block diagram (see Fig. 7-6) of the system control circuitry shows the important role the microprocessor plays in the control and operation of the machine functions. Microprocessor IC6002 scans the mode select board to determine if a new mode has been requested by the operator.

When a new instruction is given, the microprocessor first checks the safety sensors for any trouble before it executes the instructions. If no trouble is found, the VCR goes into the new mode.

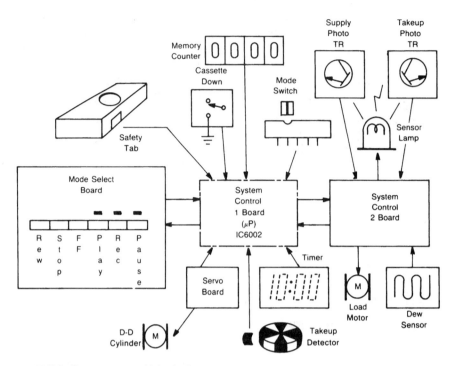

■ **7-6** *System control block diagram.* RCA Corp

The VFT190 has the following safety features to detect troubles that could damage the machine or tape:

☐ Dew sensor: detects moisture or condensation within the machine.
☐ Sensor lamp burnout detector: places VCR in the stop mode if the sensor lamp becomes defective.
☐ Cassette compartment down detect: senses whether the cassette compartment is completely down.
☐ Takeup detector: monitors for the takeup reel rotation during play, rewind, and fast forward.
☐ Supply sensor: checks for end of tape leader in play, record, or fast forward mode.
☐ Takeup sensor: checks for beginning of tape leader in rewind mode.
☐ Timer set: puts power-on and power-off function in control of timer.
☐ Power interrupt: shuts machine off instantly when loss of ac power occurs.

Mode select circuit operation & servicing

The microprocessor scans the mode select circuitry with two of its four scanning outputs. The four scanning outputs are timed, but the waveforms are not constant frequencies as the 60-Hz, real-time, interrupt oscillator signal is fed to input pin 30 and causes a slight shift in timing. This can be measured at TP 6005. The microprocessor also has a built-in RC master oscillator at pin 40 that is internally divided down to develop the scanning pulses. See Fig. 7-7. The frequency of the oscillator is adjusted by R6001 to make the largest negative portion of the C0 pulse 1.2 milliseconds. The two scanning outputs used in the mode select circuitry are inverted and switched to one of the four B port inputs of the microprocessor to determine what mode of operation has been requested. The microprocessor then monitors the B port inputs, and when it sees an inverted C0 or C1 pulse, the microprocessor will initiate the appropriate instructions to place the VCR in that mode of operation.

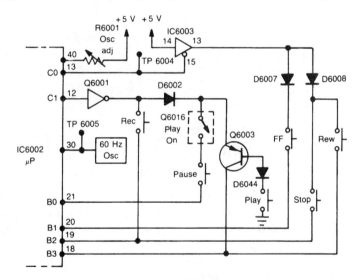

243

■ **7-7** *Microprocessor mode select circuits.*

Servicing the mode select circuitry first requires you to scope the 60-Hz square wave at TP6005 and to check the scanning C port outputs of microprocessor IC6002. Check for inverted C port signals at the output of IC6003 pin 13 and the collector of Q6001. While monitoring the appropriate B port of the microprocessor, press the corresponding mode switch and look for the inverted C port signal.

Example

A faulty machine has symptoms of no operation when put in the play mode, and the play LED does not light up. To check the play mode switching circuitry, scope the C1 port of microprocessor IC6002 and the collector of Q6001 for scanning pulses. While pressing the play button, scope the microprocessor B3 port for the C1 pulse. If it appears at B3, then the play mode switching circuitry is operating correctly. The problem is then in the microprocessor or the system control circuitry.

Cassette down detect checks

The cassette down detect circuit on most VCRs detects the position of the cassette holder by a cassette down lock lever. If you don't push it down and lock it, the videotape could get damaged, so stop all mechanism operation until the cassette down switch, located on the bottom of the mechanism, detects complete cassette holder closure.

When the cassette compartment is pushed down, pin 12 of IC6003 is grounded, which makes the output at pin 11 go low during the time that the C0 pulse at pin 15 goes low. If the cassette down switch is not closed, the output of the IC will not go low during the low periods of the C0 pulse.

The following faults can occur:

□ VCR stays in the stop mode.
□ Mechanism function keys, except eject, inoperative.

Servicing the cassette down detect circuitry requires you to scope the A0 input and the C0 output of the microprocessor simultaneously for the proper waveform. If not, suspect the cassette down switch or IC6003.

Dew sensor operation & servicing

The dew sensor is a special variable resistor that changes its resistance with ambient humidity. See Fig. 7-8. Without the presence of dew, the voltage across the sensor is normally low because of its low resistance. Transistors Q6516, Q6517, and Q6518 are connected as a Schmitt trigger configuration. When the voltage across the sensor gets high enough to exceed the trigger level of the Schmitt trigger, a logic high level output appears at its output. The logic high output turns on the dew indicator LED and triggers the auto stop line, which then places the VCR in the stop mode.

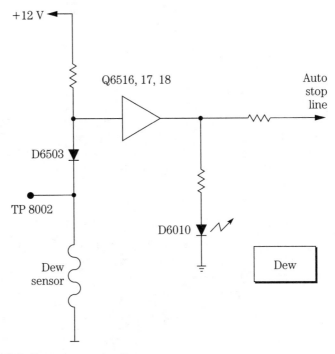

■ **7-8** *Dew sensor circuit.* RCA Corp

The following symptoms are possible:

☐ Dew LED on
☐ VCR will not load or goes to stop mode and then unloads the tape

When servicing the dew sensing circuitry during symptoms of VCR in stop mode and dew LED on, you can make a quick check by grounding TP 8002. If the problem clears, then the dew sensor is defective. If the problem does not clear, suspect D6503, Q6516, Q6517, or Q6518.

Tape sensor lamp checks

The incandescent sensor lamp provides light to the tape end sensors when the start or end of tape is reached by activating the appropriate phototransistor. Voltage is fed to the sensor lamp at turn-on, whether the cassette holder is in the down or up position. During normal operation, the voltage across the lamp should be about 4.2 V. This can be checked from TP 8001 to ground. This voltage is not enough to turn on zener diode D6504; thus the voltage on the auto stop line should be 0 V. If the lamp opens, the voltage at TP 8001 would rise, causing D6504 to conduct and producing a 0.6-V level on the auto stop line. This level makes the VCR stay in the stop mode.

The following symptoms are possible:

☐ No VCR operation
☐ VCR stays in the stop mode

When servicing this circuit during a malfunction, you need to look at the sensor lamp. If it is off, measure the voltage at TP 8001. A voltage lower than 4 V indicates the resistor feeding the lamp could be open; if the voltage is higher than 5.6 V, suspect an open lamp.

Cylinder detect operation & servicing

Under normal conditions the cylinder rotates at 1800 rpm, keeping the voltage of the motor drive circuit (IC201, pin 8) high. The logic high signal keeps cylinder lock transistor Q232 turned on, thus keeping the auto stop low. See Fig. 7-9.

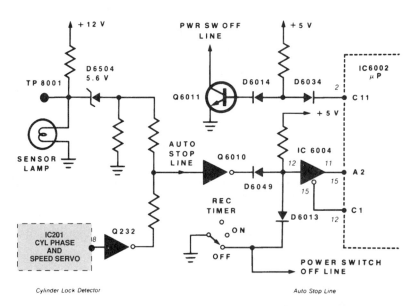

■ **7-9** *Cylinder lock detector and auto stop line.*

If the cylinder motor slows appreciably or stops, the voltage output of the motor drive circuit goes logic low, which turns off Q232. This allows the auto stop line to go to 0.6 V and places the VCR in the stop mode.

If the VCR shuts down (goes to stop mode), measure for a logic high at IC201 pin 8. If there is none, suspect IC201, IC202, or associated circuitry in the cylinder drive area.

Note: If the level is low on pin 8 of IC201, you can ground the auto stop line to keep the VCR from going to the stop mode, which allows the testing of the cylinder servo system.

Auto stop circuit operation & servicing

The auto stop line drives the input of inverter Q6010. A normal low on the input of Q6010 generates a logic high on its output, which allows the input of IC6004 pin 12 also to be high. The high input to this gated buffer causes the output to be high when the C1 pulse from the microprocessor is low. Again see Fig. 7-9.

If one of the previously described safety features causes a high on the auto stop line, it generates a low at the input of IC6004 pin 12, which also makes the output low while the C1 pulse is low. The microprocessor is continually scanning the output of IC6004 pin 12, and when a low occurs when the C1 pulse is low the microprocessor places the machine in the stop mode. It does this by allowing pin 2 of the C11 port to go high. This lets Q6011 turn on and places a low on the power-switch off line, thus shutting down the 12-V regulator. When the microprocessor permits the power-switch line to go high, the +12 V returns and the microprocessor is reset, placing the machine in the stop mode.

The following symptoms can occur:

☐ VCR shuts down (goes to the stop mode)
☐ Stays in the stop mode (will not load)

Servicing the auto stop line and associated circuitry requires scoping the C1 output and A2 input of the microprocessor simultaneously for the proper waveforms. If the main power switch is in the off position, then, when the C1 pulse is low, the A2 port will be low. If the power switch is not in the off position, then, when the C1 pulse is low, the A2 input to the microprocessor should be high. If not, check for a high on the auto stop line or suspect Q6010, D6049, or IC6004.

Takeup turntable detector: Operation & servicing

The takeup detector is linked mechanically to the digital tape counter. A ring magnet is located on a shaft at the bottom of the digital tape counter where a Hall-effect sensor (IC6551) is located nearby. See Fig. 7-10. When the takeup turntable rotates, the digital tape counter rotates and the Hall-effect IC changes its con-

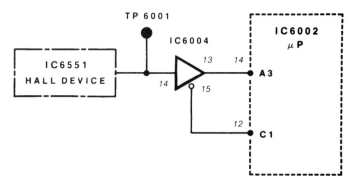

■ **7-10** *Takeup detector.*

duction characteristics with each passing of either a north or a south pole of the ring magnet. This change causes a changing squarewave voltage to appear at the output of the Hall-effect chip, which is passed onto TP 6001 and the input of IC6004 pin 14. The square wave appearing at the input of IC6004 causes an interrupted C1 pulse to be coupled to the A3 input of the microprocessor. This action signals the microprocessor that the takeup turntable is rotating normally.

The following symptoms can occur:

☐ VCR loads and then shuts down
☐ VCR goes to stop during fast forward and rewind modes

Troubleshooting requires you to scope TP 6001 and look for a square wave. If a square wave is not present, suspect the Hall-effect device IC6551 of mechanical linkages and drive belts plus the digital tape counter.

Tape end sensors operation

The supply sensor detects the end of the tape leader on the supply turntable. When the light appears on the face of phototransistor Q6551, it conducts, placing a low at the input of Q6512. The output of Q6512 then goes high, making the output of Q6514 go low, which low is passed to the A3 input to pin 14 of IC6002. The microprocessor, upon seeing this low, places the VCR in the stop mode.

The following symptoms are possible:

☐ VCR will not enter forward mode (goes to stop)
☐ VCR shuts down

To service the supply sensor, use a voltmeter to measure for the correct voltages at the inputs of Q6512 and Q6514.

Time recording operation & servicing

Unattended VCR recording is made possible by the timer function of the timer/clock circuit including timer IC6005. When the on-off timer switch is put into the timer mode, three things occur to instruct the VCR that it has been placed into the timer record mode:

1. Through the timer switch, the base of transistor Q6014 is grounded, causing the transistor to conduct and simulate the stop button being pressed. This signals the microprocessor to place the VCR in the stop mode by passing the inverted C0 port output to the B2 port input of the microprocessor. See Fig. 7-11.

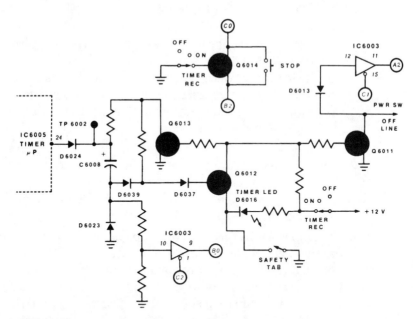

■ **7-11** *Timer-set circuit.* RCA Corp

2. Through the timer switch, +12 V is used to turn on Q6011, pulling the power-switch off line low, thus shutting down the switch +12-V regulator and the VCR.

3. The 12 V also powers a latch circuit consisting of Q6012, Q6013, D6037, D6039, and C6008. With the output of timer IC6005 at pin 24 low, the latch circuit is turned off.

When the programmed on time occurs, pin 24 of the timer IC causes TP 6002 to go high. This high causes C6008 to start charging. The charging current turns on the latch, thus turning off Q6011. With this occurring, the switched 12-V regulator is turned on. The charging current also causes the output of tri-state buffer IC6003 to be momentarily high while the C2 pulse is low at pin 1. The output of this buffer is passed to input port B0 of the microprocessor. This action instructs the microprocessor that a timed recording is requested, and the microprocessor places the VCR into the record mode.

If the safety switch (record lock-out) is open because the tab in the cassette is removed, this keeps the latch from being turned on and doesn't let Q6011 turn on and switch the 12-V regulator off.

A symptom of malfunctioning is no timer record operation. If this occurs, check the following items:

1. Check for an inverted C0 pulse at the B2 input of the main microprocessor and verify that transistor Q6011 is turned on. Q6011 pulls the power-switch off line low. Also verify that the latch circuit is powered and present to accept instructions from the timer microprocessor. If any one of these are not operating correctly, repair the associated circuitry before going on to the next check.

2. Monitor TP 6002 for the presence of a logic high when the programmed start time occurs. If this does not appear, suspect the timer microprocessor IC6005. If TP 6002 indicates a high, check for the momentary C2 pulse at the B0 input port of the main microprocessor and the operation of the latch circuit.

3. To help isolate a timer circuit problem, place the power switch in the timer mode and attach a clip lead from TP 6002 to TP 6003. If the VCR now turns on in record mode, suspect a defective timer microprocessor chip. If the VCR turns on momentarily and then shuts off, suspect a faulty time constant circuit or IC6003. You can detect this situation by watching the power-on indicator LED. If the VCR remains in the off mode during this clip lead test, suspect a faulty latch circuit.

Mode sense switch circuit operation & checks

The mode sense switch (part of the tape transport) informs the microprocessor what mode the tape transport mechanism is in. When the microprocessor places the VCR in the play mode, it switches power to the loading-motor circuit to load the tape. While the loading motor is powered up, the microprocessor scans the A input ports for a logic low during the time that the C3 output port is low to determine the position of the mode sense switch. When the switch reaches the play position, it indicates that loading is completed. Then the microprocessor removes power from the loading motor and switches power to the playback circuitry.

The following are possible faults:

☐ No VCR play operation
☐ VCR tries to load, then unloads

For troubleshooting, connect one channel of a dual-trace scope to the C3 output and the other channel to the appropriate A input port. Prime suspects would be IC6004 and microprocessor IC6002.

Stop to play operation & servicing

The functions and microprocessor operating modes have already been covered. But what happens during an operator command to place the VCR mechanism into the play mode? When the VCR is in the stop mode and the operator presses the play button, eight separate circuit functions occur:

☐ The base of Q6003 is pulled low, turning on the transistor and applying an inverted C1 pulse to input B3 of microprocessor IC6002. See Fig. 7-12.
☐ The play output, pin 35 of the microprocessor, goes low, generating a high output at the output of Q6004. This action turns on the play LED and instructs the play circuitry to assume this mode.
☐ The output at pin 8 of the microprocessor goes high, directing the loading-motor, voltage-control circuit (consisting of Q6507, Q6508, Q6510) to generate an output to TP 6504 and the loading-motor drive circuit of about 8 V.
☐ The load command output at pin 25 goes high to initiate power to the loading motor and start loading tape into the mechanism.
☐ During loading, the loading motor engages the proper levers and gears to load tape into the mechanism. A linkage is connected to the mode sense switch, which moves in the load direction and

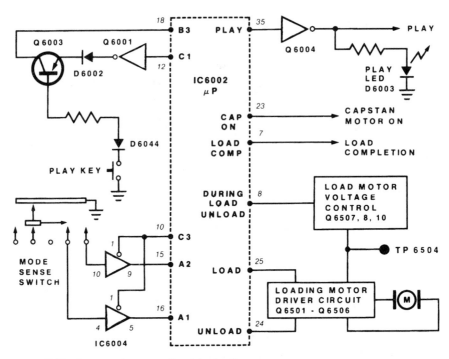

■ 7-12 *Stop to play operation block diagram.*

first grounds the input to pin 4 of IC6004, causing a low output to the microprocessor during low periods of C3.

☐ When this occurs, the microprocessor causes pin 23 to go high, which activates the capstan motor to move the tape.

☐ After a short time, the loading motor completes loading of the tape. It does this by grounding pin 10 of IC6004 through the mode sense switch, causing a low output to be sent to the microprocessor during low periods of scan pulse C3.

☐ The final step is to instruct the circuitry to go from E-E to play mode, by the microprocessor instructing pin 7 to go high.

A possible fault is no VCR play or improper play operations.

The eight functions must occur in sequence, or the microprocessor will place the VCR into stop. Several safety and trouble sensors can interrupt this sequence and cause the microprocessor to place the VCR in the stop mode. The best service procedure is to follow the eight steps to determine at which point the sequence is interrupted. This will help you to determine which circuitry or safety sensors are faulty. Now check out all circuitry in the section where the interrupt occurred.

The preceding information and diagrams are supplied courtesy of RCA Consumer Electronics Company in training manual VCR-7 #8134 (copyright 1981).

JVC HR-7300 U VCR microprocessor control system

JVC HR-7300 features "feather touch" control operation. Just a light touch of the buttons or remote control unit keys supplies mode command signals to circuits, motors, switches, and solenoids to set up the selected mode.

Internal sensors protect the machine and the tape. Through continuous monitoring of these sensors, the control system decides whether to continue or to stop the mode in progress or to shift to another mode.

A built-in microcomputer helps to detect and control the operating modes. The microprocessor is preprogrammed—the user cannot alter it. Although a basic understanding of the principles of a microcomputer is helpful, for practical troubleshooting an understanding of which input signals produce specific output signals is more important.

In the following circuit description, "mechanism control" is shortened to "mechacon." The block diagram contains input and output data for reference during service.

Block diagram description

See Fig. 7-13. The mechacon circuit receives mode command signals from the operation keys and mode detect signals from the sensors, and produces signals for driving the motors and solenoids to set up the required modes. Mode control signals are also sent to the proper circuit boards.

These control functions are performed by the CPU of IC2, which is a one-chip, 4-bit microcomputer. In the block diagram, the input signal generators from the function keys and sensors are shown at the left of the CPU; the motors and solenoids controlled by the CPU output signals are located at the right along with the circuit board connectors supplied by the CPU signals.

The CPU has only two sets of input ports (A and B), totalling 8 bits, whereas 14 inputs are obtained from the operation keys and sensors. For this reason, IC1 multiplexer is provided as an input expander. Using the 3-bit bus select signal from CPU port H (strobe data irrelevant), it selects one output from among four inputs and

253

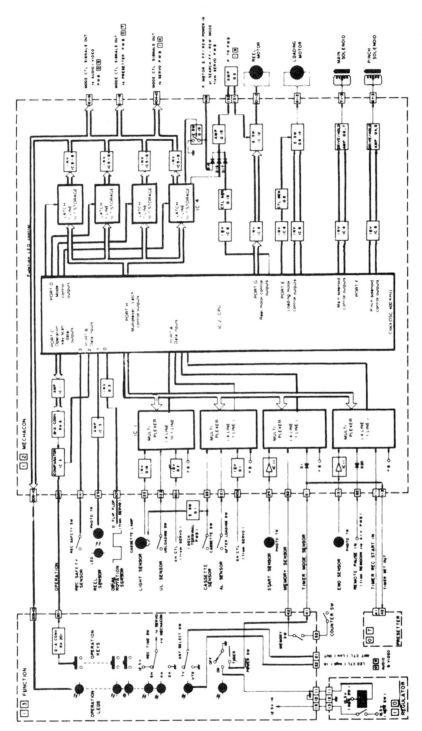

■ 7-13 *Mechacon block diagram.* JVC Corp.

VCR microprocessor function control systems

data irrelevant), it selects one output from among four inputs and sends it to the CPU input ports.

Thus, the four 4:1 multiplexer circuits of IC1 supply 4-bit outputs to the CPU input A ports from 16 inputs (in practice, four input terminals are fixed), and the remaining operation and sensor signals go directly to the input B ports. At the same time, four 7-bit latches of IC4 function as output expanders. The 4-bit outputs of the CPU D ports are expanded to 28 latched outputs. Latch positions are determined by the 3-bit bus select from the CPU H ports and the strobe data.

IC4 outputs are fed through open-collector inverters as either low or open (high when connected to other boards) outputs to other circuit boards. Drive signals for motors and solenoids are obtained directly through inverters from CPU output ports E, F, and G.

Overall signal flow

During a selected mode, a high from the IC3 comparator goes to the CPU input port B to signify that the mode is being held. At this time, the 4-bit operation key scan data are obtained from CPU C ports in a cycle of about 7.5ms (133 Hz) for the binary range 0000 to 1111. The digital sequence goes through the IC11 buffer and the RA6 DAC to become a sequential voltage in 16 steps from 0 V to about 9.5 V, which is fed to the comparator at 133 Hz.

The comparator output remains high as long as an operation key is not pressed. The 4-bit multiplexer/latch control data of the H port control multiplexers to allow acceptance of the mode detector signals; the latch circuits are controlled to latch the mode outputs. Outputs are also obtained from other output ports according to the mode.

When an operation key is pressed, a fixed dc voltage, determined by the resistance combination of function board RA1 DAC goes to the noninvert input of the comparator. At the same time, the 16-step scan data are applied to the invert terminal. The comparator produces either a high or a low output.

If the scan data are higher than the fixed input from the operation key, low output from the comparator goes to CPU port B. The CPU interprets this as pressing an operation key, resets port C, and sends a new 4-bit output sequence of 0000, 0001, etc. As a result, the comparator output again becomes high. When one of the 16 steps from the operation key to the comparator becomes low, a low comparator output goes to CPU port B. By detecting this low together with the output status of port C, the CPU can detect which specific operation key has been pressed.

The CPU also detects other input port data, including timer, cassette switch, cassette lamp, and sensors. Data pertaining to the depressed key are checked—for example, is it the same as the mode in progress? Is a shift to the new mode select possible from the present mode? Outputs corresponding to the operation key are then sent to the motors, solenoids, and circuit boards.

From port D, the 4-bit output goes to the IC4 latch, resulting in 28 latched outputs (in practice, five are not used) that are sent through open-collector inverters to the circuit boards. Control signals also go to the function board for lighting the LEDs corresponding to the depressed operation key.

Three bits of the 4-bit port E output are for loading-motor control. They are fed through inverters to the control generator for determining motor torque and to electronic switches Q9 to Q14, which select motor direction.

For example, in the play mode, rotation is in the loading direction. When the loading mechanism begins operation and the unloading (UL) switch is off, the CPU detects the start of loading. At the end of loading, the after-loading (AL) switch comes on, at which time the CPU detects the end of loading and stops the loading motor. The unloading process is the opposite of this.

The 4-bit port F output is divided into 2 bits each. These bits go by inverters to the solenoid drive and hold amplifiers for switching the main and pinch solenoids on and off according to mode. The pinch solenoid is driven after completion of loading (AL switch on) during play and recording.

Four bits from port G are fed through an inverter to electronic switch IC12 for controlling forward and reverse rotation of the reel motor. Rotational torque is controlled by drive voltage from the servo board to D16 during search fast forward and rewind (S-FF and S-rew). During ordinary fast forward and rewind, supply is from port D with control through an inverter and control generator (Q15) at D17. Latch IC3 provides control through D15 during unloading, at short rewind, at the start of FF/rew and in the idler mode (during which the reel idler shifts towards the supply of takeup reel disk).

During play/rec, takeup is driven mechanically by the capstan motor. The select bus from port C selects the sensor state data required for the particular mode and feeds them to the CPU as auto stop data.

Operation key-in circuit

Note: The mechacon circuit is completely controlled by the CPU, thus eliminating the need for complex drive and other related circuitry.

As shown in Fig. 7-14, when the sub power switch is set from off to on, an approximately 60ms high pulse from IC3 pin 2 goes to the reset terminals of the CPU, resetting the CPU and producing the stop mode. All port outputs are at the stop mode at this time.

The 4-bit operation key scan data output from port C covers the binary digits from 0000 to 1111 in 0.16ms increments, and then produces 1111 for approximately 5ms. Each cycle is about 7.5ms (133 Hz) long.

Through the IC11 buffer converter, the 4-bit output goes to RA6. The RA6 DAC converts the data to a 16-step output from 0.15625 V to 9.63125 V, which goes to the invert pin 6 of the IC3 comparator. At the noninvert input, as long as an operation key is not pressed, 10 V is supplied through R45 and R46. The normally high comparator output goes to CPU port B, instructing the CPU that an operation key is not pressed.

Pressing an operation key sends a fixed voltage corresponding to the particular key to the noninvert input for the comparator, where it is compared with the key scan data. The voltage obtained by pressing each operation key is limited to one of the 16 steps according to the 4-bit key scan data.

Example

Assume the play key is pressed; see Fig. 7-15. This applies 2.99 V to the comparator noninvert input. At this time, when the voltage at the invert input from the key scan data goes higher than 2.99 V (as when the 4-bit data exceeds 5), the comparator low output goes to CPU port B, indicating to the CPU that an operation key has been pressed. The key scan counter is reset, and the 4-bit scan data from port C increment sequentially from 0000, 0001, etc. Because the play key is pressed, the comparator output becomes high at the 0000 data poll, supplying the equivalent of a no response to port B2. After incrementing in sequence, the comparator output becomes low when the poll reaches 0101. This provides a yes response to port B2. The CPU thus recognizes that the play key has been pressed, and it enters the play mode. At the same

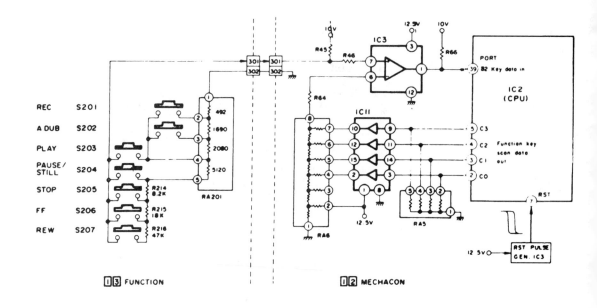

REC   S201
A DUB   S202
PLAY   S203
PAUSE/
STILL   S204
STOP   S205
FF   S206
REW   S207

RA201
R214 8.2K
R215 18K
R216 47K

492
1690
2080
5120

IC3
IC2 (CPU)
IC11
R45
R46
R66
R64
RA5
RA6

PORT
39 B2 Key data in
5 C3
4 C2 Function key scan data out
3 C1
2 C0
7 RST

RST PULSE GEN. IC3

☐③ FUNCTION   ☐② MECHACON

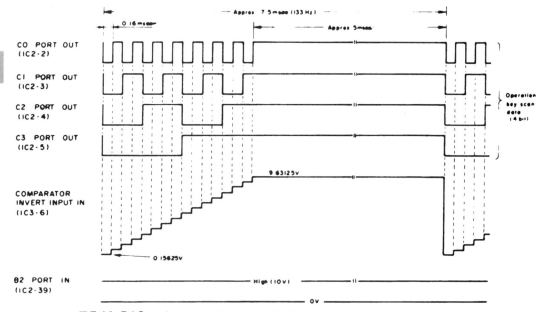

CO PORT OUT (IC2-2)
C1 PORT OUT (IC2-3)
C2 PORT OUT (IC2-4)
C3 PORT OUT (IC2-5)

COMPARATOR INVERT INPUT IN (IC3-6)

B2 PORT IN (IC2-39)

Approx 7.5 msec (133 Hz)
0.16 msec
Approx 5 msec

Operation key scan data (4 bit)

9.63125V
0.15625V

High (10V)
0V

■ **7-14** *DAC and comparator outputs in stop mode.*

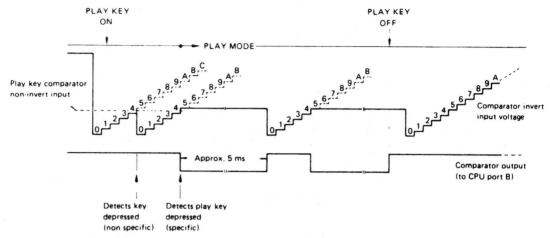

PLAY KEY
ON

PLAY KEY
OFF

PLAY MODE

Play key comparator
non-invert input

Comparator invert
input voltage

Approx. 5 ms

Comparator output
(to CPU port B)

Detects key
depressed
(non specific)

Detects play key
depressed
(specific)

■ 7-15 *Output waveforms with play key depressed.*

time, the key scan data stop incrementing, and the 0101 output is produced for about 5ms.

The CPU clock operates at 400 kHz, and one instruction cycle is 10µs, so about 500 instructions can be performed in the 5ms period. However, to avoid errors, the process is repeated and then implemented. When the play key is off, as indicated in Fig. 7-14, the key scan data remains at standby for one cycle of 7.5ms.

When the channel key of the remote control unit is pressed, the comparator output goes low. With port B low for two polling cycles, the channel-up command is recognized.

Therefore, the CPU is able to determine which key has been pressed and execute the instructions according to the mode.

CPU input signals & functions

Table 7-1 indicates the CPU input port signals, their objectives, high (H) or low (L) levels according to mode, and required conditions. Although the table lists the input port signals with respect to mode, each input signal is checked individually at the CPU as the mode continues.

Expect during loading or unloading, a change in input signal other than the operation signal initiates the auto stop mode. Also, to protect the set and the tape, the CPU timer functions during loading, unloading, pause, and still. If the particular mode continues for longer than a predetermined period, the auto stop or emergency mode is entered.

259

Table 7-1. Input Port Signals versus Modes.

CPU input port (IC2)	Input expander (IC1)		Detect signal (Sensor name)	Detected condition	Detection method
B	0		Drum flip-flop (Drum rotation sensor)	Head drum rotating?	Head drum magnets detected by pick-up head.
	1		Take-up reel FG (Reel sensor)	Tape stack or jammed inside set?	Reel sensor detects take-up reel disk rotation.
	2		Operation	Operation key depressed?	Detected by computer circuit from DAC.
	3		REC safety SW (REC safety sensor)	Does cassette contain important or costly pre-recorded program?	REC safety switch detects presence or absence of REC safety tab on cassette case.
A	0	4C	Tape beginning photo TR (Start sensor)	Tape at beginning position?	Clear leader tape segment passes cassette lamp light to trigger start sensor.
		5C	Memory and counter SW (Memory sensor)	Tape at memory command position?	With memory switch on, when counter decrements from 0000 to 9999 counter switch becomes on.
		6C	Power SW (Timer sensor)	Timer mode?	Sub power switch set to timer mode.
		7C	————	————	(+10 V applied)
	1	4D	Tape end photo TR (End sensor)	Tape at end position?	Clear leader tape segment passes cassette lamp light to trigger end sensor.
		5D	Remote Pause	REC Pause mode?	Pause mode set from remote control unit.
		6D	Timer REC start	Timer REC start command available?	From timer circuit.
		7D	————	————	(+10 V applied)
	2	4A	Cassette lamp (Light sensor)	Cassette lamp lighted?	Cassette lamp current flow detected.
		5A	Unloading SW (UL sensor)	Tape present in cassette case?	UL switch triggered by loading ring at loading start and unloading end.
		6A	PB CTL signal	LP mode?	From SERVO circuit
		7A	————	————	(+10 V applied)
	3	4B	Cassette SW (Cassette sensor)	Cassette tape set in proper position?	Cassette tape triggers cassette switch.
		5B	After loading SW (AL sensor)	Loading complete?	Loading ring triggers AL switch at completion of loading and at start of unloading.
		6B	Rec time SW or CTL signal	EP mode?	From SERVO circuit
		7B	————	————	(+10 V applied)

Symbols ———— : irrelevant, H : high input, L : low input, ⊓⊔ : pulse input
* Normal High input except Low in Ep or Lp mode

| Input port states | | | | | | | | | | | | | | | | |
| Stop | | Play | | | | | REC | | | A.Dub | | | FF | REW | Timer | |
Un-loading	Stop	Load-ing	Play	Still	Search FF	Search REW	Load-ing	REC	Pause	Load-ing	A.Dub	Still			Stand by	REC
⊓⊔	–	⊓⊔	⊓⊔	⊓⊔	⊓⊔	⊓⊔	⊓⊔	⊓⊔	⊓⊔	⊓⊔	⊓⊔	⊓⊔	–	–	⊓⊔	⊓⊔
⊓⊔	–	⊓⊔	⊓⊔	–	⊓⊔	⊓⊔	⊓⊔	⊓⊔	–	⊓⊔	⊓⊔	–	⊓⊔	⊓⊔	–	⊓⊔
–	–	–	–	–	–	–	–	–	–	–	–	–	–	–	–	–
–	–	–	–	–	–	–	L	L	L	L	L	L	–	–	L	L
–	–	H	–	–	–	H	H	–	–	H	–	–	–	H	–	–
–	–	–	–	–	–	–	–	–	–	–	–	–	–	H	–	–
–	–	–	H	H	H	H	–	H/L	H/L	–	H	–	H	H	L	L
H	H	H	H	H	H	H	H	H	H	H	H	H	H	H	H	H
–	–	H	H	H	H	–	H	H	H	H	H	H	H	–	H	H
–	–	–	–	–	–	–	L	–	–	L	–	–	–	–	–	–
–	–	–	–	–	–	–	–	L/H	L/H	–	–	L	–	–	H	L
H	H	H	H	H	H	H	H	H	H	H	H	H	H	H	H	H
L	L	L	L	L	L	L	L	L	L	L	L	L	L	L	L	L
H	L	–	H	H	H	H	–	H	H	–	H	H	L	L	H	H
*	*	*	*	*	*	*	*	*	*	*	*	*	*	*	*	*
H	H	H	H	H	H	H	H	H	H	H	H	H	H	H	H	H
L	–	L	L	L	L	L	L	L	L	L	L	L	L	L	L	L
H	H	H	L	L	L	L	H	L	L	H	L	L	H	H	L	L
*	*	*	*	*	*	*	*	*	*	*	*	*	*	*	*	*
H	H	H	H	H	H	H	H	H	H	H	H	H	H	H	H	H

261

CPU functions

The CPU functions according to mode are indicated in Table 7-2 for reference during service.

Mechacon operations (other than normal)

In addition to setting up the selected operating modes, the mechacon circuit performs these following functions in order to protect the tape and machine.

Sub power switch on requirements

1. Cassette sensor: Completely inoperative unless cassette switch is on. If the cassette switch changes from on to off while a mode is in progress (after UL), the stop mode is entered.

2. Light sensor: Inoperative if cassette lamp fails. If failure occurs during an operating mode (after UL), the stop mode is entered.

3. Record safety sensor: If the record safety switch is not on, recording (including record pause) and audio dub (including audio dub pause) are inoperative. If the switch state changes from on to off during these modes, UL is performed and the stop mode entered.

4. Sub power switch: If the UL switch is off when the sub power switch is set to on, UL is performed.

5. Channel key: The channel key of the remote control unit is operative only during the stop, UL record pause, FF, and rew modes.

6. Start sensor: If on during the rew mode, the rew mode becomes inhibited. When the start sensor switches on during rewind or search rewind (after UL), the stop mode is entered.

7. End sensor: When the end sensor is on, play, recording, and FF are inoperative. If these modes are in progress and the end sensor switches on (after UL), the stop mode is entered.

8. Reel sensor: When the AL switch is on during play, recording, audio dub, search FF, or search rew, and if the takeup reel disk rotation stops, then after about 3 s UL is performed and the stop mode is entered. This limitation does not apply to pause/still mode. If the UL switch is on during FF/rew, and if takeup reel disk rotation stops, then after about 4.2 s the stop mode is entered.

9. The drum motor rotates when the UL switch is off.

Table 7-2. Output Port Signals versus Modes.

Symbols: H : high output, L : low output, ⊓ : high pulse output, ⊔ : low pulse output, (↗) : rising component employed, * : Ep mode or Lp mode high output

CPU (IC2) input port		IC3	Output signal	(level)	Unloading	Stop	Loading	Play	Still	Search FF	Search REW	Loading	REC	Pause	Loading	A.Dub	Still	FF	REW	Standby	REC
E	0		Loading motor power ctl	(low)	L	H	L	H	H	H	H	L	H	H	L	H	H	H	H	H	H
	1		Loading motor reverse ctl	(high)	H	H	L	H	H	H	H	L	H	H	L	H	H	H	H	H	H
	2		Loading motor forward ctl	(high)	L	H	H	H	H	H	H	H	H	H	H	H	H	H	H	H	H
	3		Reel motor FF/Rew power ctl	(low)	H	H	H	H	H	H	H	H	H	H	H	H	H	L	L	H	H
F	0		P. solenoid hold ctl	(high)	L	L	L	H	H	L	L	L	H	H	L	H	H	L	L	H	H
	1		P. solenoid drive ctl	(high)	L	L	L	⊓	L	L	L	L	⊓	L	L	⊓	L	L	L	⊓	L
	2		M. solenoid hold ctl	(high)	H	L	H	H	L	H	H	H	H	L	H	H	L	H	H	L	H
	3		M. solenoid drive ctl	(high)	L	L	⊔	L	L	L	L	⊔	L	L	⊔	L	L	⊔	⊔	L	L
G	0		Reel motor forward − ctl	(high)	L	H	H	H	H	H	L	H	H	H	H	H	H	H	L	H	H
	1		Reel motor reverse + ctl	(high)	H	L	L	L	L	L	L	L	L	L	L	L	L	L	H	L	L
	2		Reel motor forward + ctl	(high)	L	L	L	⊓	L	H	L	L	⊓	L	L	⊓	L	H	L	L	L
	3		Reel motor reverse − ctl	(high)	H	H	H	⊔	H	L	L	L	⊔	H	H	⊔	H	L	H	H	H
D	0	1B	——		–	–	–	–	–	–	–	–	–	–	–	–	–	–	–	–	–
		2B	D/cap. motor stop ctl	(low)	H	L	H	H	H	H	H	H	H	H	H	H	H	L	L	H	H
		3B	Pause/still LED ctl	(high)	L	L	L	L	H	L	L	L	L	H	L	L	H	L	L	H	L
		4B	Video REC start ctl	(high)	L	L	L	L	L	L	L	L	H	H	L	L	L	L	L	H	H
		5B	Audio dub ctl	(high)	L	L	L	L	L	L	L	L	L	L	L	H	H	L	L	L	L
		6B	CH lock ctl	(high)	L	L	L	H	H	H	H	H	H	L	L	H	L	L	L	H	H
		7B	EP LED ctl	(high)	*	*	*	*	*	*	*	*	*	*	*	*	*	*	*	*	*
	1	1A	——		–	–	–	–	–	–	–	–	–	–	–	–	–	–	–	–	–
		2A	Search FF ctl	(low)	H	H	H	H	H	L	H	H	H	H	H	H	H	H	H	H	H
		3A	Play LED ctl	(high)	L	L	H	H	H	H	H	H	H	H	H	H	L	L	H	H	H
		4A	Video E-E ctl	(low)	H	H	H	L	L	L	L	H	H	H	H	L	L	H	H	H	H
		5A	Audio PB mute ctl	(high)	L	L	L	⊓	H	H	H	L	L	L	L	L	L	L	L	L	L
		6A	CH UP ctl		(↗)	(↗)	(↗)	L	L	L	L	L	L	(↗)	L	L	L	(↗)	(↗)	L	L
		7A	LP LED ctl	(high)	*	*	*	*	*	*	*	*	*	*	*	*	*	*	*	*	*
	2	1C	——		–	–	–	–	–	–	–	–	–	–	–	–	–	–	–	–	–
		2C	Search rew ctl	(low)	H	H	H	H	H	H	L	H	H	H	H	H	H	H	H	H	H
		3C	Audio dub LED ctl	(high)	L	L	L	L	L	L	L	L	L	L	H	H	H	L	L	L	L
		4C	Audio E-E ctl	(low)	L	L	L	H	H	H	L	L	L	H	H	H	L	L	L	L	L
		5C	Servo rec ctl	(high)	H	L	H	H	H	H	L	L	L	H	H	H	H	H	H	L	L
		6C	——		–	–	–	–	–	–	–	–	–	–	–	–	–	–	–	–	–
		7C	Raw LED ctl	(high)	L	L	L	L	L	L	H	L	L	L	L	L	L	L	H	L	L
	3	1D	R.M. UI/idler power ctl	(high)	H	L	L	⊓	L	L	L	L	L	L	L	L	⊓	⊓	L	L	L
		2D	Pause/still ctl	(high)	L	L	L	L	H	L	L	L	L	H	L	L	H	H	H	H	L
		3D	Rec LED ctl	(high)	L	L	L	L	L	L	L	H	H	H	L	L	L	L	L	H	H
		4D	Audio rec start ctl	(high)	L	L	L	L	L	L	L	L	H	H	L	H	H	L	L	H	H
		5D	Search FF/rew ctl	(low)	H	H	H	H	H	L	L	H	H	H	H	H	H	H	H	H	H
		6D	——		–	–	–	–	–	–	–	–	–	–	–	–	–	–	–	–	–
		7D	FF LED ctl	(high)	L	L	L	L	L	H	L	L	L	L	L	L	L	H	L	L	L
C	0 1 2 3		Operation key scan data																		
H	0 1 2 3		Strobe data S0 / S1 / S2 Bus select for IC1 S0 / S1 / S2 Bus select for IC3																		

10. Drum rotation sensor: If the drum motor (video heads) rotation stops with the UL switch off, then after about 3 s UL is performed and the stop mode is entered.

11. Memory sensor: During rewind with the memory switch of the function board on, when the tape counter indication decrements from 0000 to 9999, the stop mode is entered.

12. The UL motor rotates in the forward direction when the play LED is lighted and the AL switch off. When the stop LED is lighted and the UL switch is off, the motor rotates in the reverse direction.

13. AL sensor: During UL, if the period between UL switch off and AL switch on exceeds 10 s, UL is performed and the stop mode is entered.

14. UL sensor: During UL, if the period between AL switch off and UL switch on exceeds 10 s, the mechanism stops and the emergency mode is entered.

15. Pause/still overtime sensor: If the pause or still mode continues for more than 5 to 6 min, UL is performed and the stop mode is entered.

16. Auto rewind: During play/record, audio dub, FF, and search FF, when the end sensor functions and auto stop is produced (after UL), the rewind mode is entered; however, if the stop key is pressed during UL, the auto rewind mode is not entered.

17. Short rewind: When the stop mode is produced from FF or rewind, short rewind is performed for 240ms; then the stop mode is entered.

18. The capstan motor rotates when the UL switch is off. However, this limitation does not apply to pause/still.

19. When the remote control unit is connected, control can be performed by either the local or remote operation keys. If both are used, the most recently pressed key instructs the mode. When stop is pressed, however, the stop mode has priority regardless of the pressing sequence.

20. During recording, the remote pause mode has priority over the local and remote operation keys, but this does not apply to the stop mode.

Sub power switch to timer

1. If the record safety switch is off, record start is inhibited, and at prestart the stop mode is entered.

2. While a mode is in progress with the sub power switch on, if the switch is set to timer the mechanism stops; however, at the timer start time, record or record pause becomes the record mode.

3. During time recording, the prestart (high) signal initiates loading 10 before the timer start time. Then at record start, the pinch roller engages to yield the recording mode.

The preceding information is supplied courtesy of the JVC Corp. (subsidiary of Victor Company of Japan, Ltd.) through VCR service manual #8203.

Troubleshooting computer monitors

8

This chapter will feature the Sencore CM2000/2125 computer monitor analyzer.

A computer monitor operates somewhat like a television without a tuner or an IF section. Instead of receiving an RF signal, converting it to an IF signal, and detecting the signal to produce video, a monitor receives the video information straight from the computer through red, green, and blue (RGB) video lines. Horizontal and vertical synchronizing pulses supplied from the computer lock the picture in. There are several types of computer monitors. Each monitor receives an input signal from the computer and converts the signal into a graphic image. A photo of the Sencore CM2125 monitor analyzer is shown in Fig. 8-1.

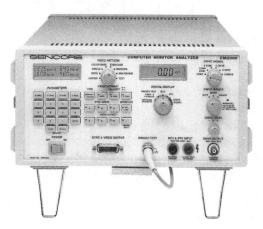

■ **8-1** *Photo of CM2000/CM2125 SENCORE monitor analyzer.*

Monitor types

There are two common types of monitors: digital and analog. A digital computer monitor receives TTL signal levels and produces colors through combinations of "1's" and "0's" as shown in Fig. 8-2. Monochrome digital monitors have one or two video inputs and display one or two shades of amber, green, or black and white.

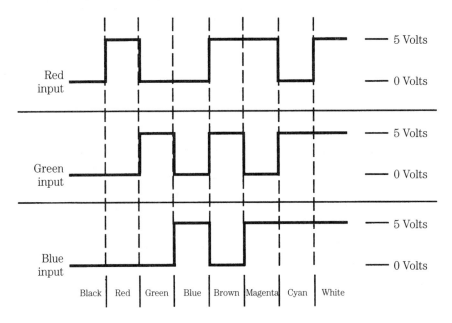

■ 8-2 *Alternating TTL levels from 1's and 0's produce shades of gray or colors in digital computer monitors.*

Three, four, or six video input lines may be used for color digital computer monitors: red, green, blue, red intensity, green intensity, or blue intensity. The intensity lines are used in digital monitors to vary color saturation. Color digital monitors can 8, 16, or 64 colors depending on the number of video inputs. Using TTL signal levels limits the number of colors displayed by the color digital monitor.

Three video input lines are used for color analog computer monitors: red, green, and blue. A single input line is used for analog monochrome computer monitors to produce shades of gray. Colors or shades of gray are created by varying a voltage between 0.0 and 0.7 volts peak-to-peak. An infinite number of colors or shades of gray are possible, as shown in Fig. 8-3.

Because of the low resolution of early computer monitors, picture quality and clarity was extremely poor. To improve resolution of

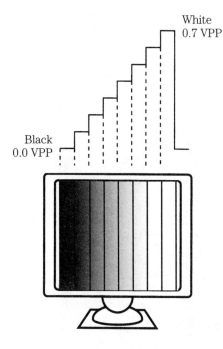

■ **8-3** *Varying voltage levels from 0.0 to 0.7 volts peak-to-peak produce infinite shades of gray colors in an analog monitor.*

White
0.7 VPP

Black
0.0 VPP

these monitors, high resolution monitors were developed. These monitors have faster scanning frequencies and more displayed pixels. More pixels are displayed in less time, thus increasing the monitors bandwidth and vastly improving picture quality. For example, the NTSC television system uses a scanning frequency of 15.7 kHz and produces a bandwidth of 4.2 MHz. The VGA computer format uses a scanning frequency of 31.5 kHz and produces a bandwidth of 25.2 MHz.

Sync input methods

To display an image, a monitor requires two synchronizing signals for the scan circuits: horizontal sync and vertical sync. Computers operate at different scan frequencies for each format, as shown in Fig. 8-4.

A multiscan monitor can receive and lock to a range of scanning frequencies within in its specifications. The monitor automatically locks to the frequency applied to the output. For example, one multiscan monitor model will sync to horizontal frequencies between 15 kHz and 35 kHz. If this monitor receives an MDA format (see Fig. 8-4) the horizontal circuits will automatically sync to 18.5 kHz and the vertical circuits will sync to 50 Hz.

Mode	Horizontal frequency (kHz)	Vertical frequency (Hz)	Horizontal resolution (pixels)	Vertical resolution (lines)
CGA (Color Graphics Adapter)	15.7	60	640	200
MDA (Monochrome Display Adapter)	18.4	50	720	350
HGC (Hercules Graphics Card)	18.4	50	720	350
EGA (Enhanced Graphics Adapter)	21.8	60	640	350
PGC (Professional Graphics Controller)	30.5	60	640	480
VGA (Video Graphics Array) 1	31.5	70	640	350
2	31.5	60	640	480
3	31.5	70	720	400
Apple MAC II	35.2	67	640	480
Super VGA	35.2	56	800	600
8514 A	35.2	87	1024	768
XGA (Extended Graphics Array)	35.2	87	1024	768

■ **8-4** *Computer monitor's use higher scan rates and more displayed pixels for improved performance capability.*

Computer monitors use three different sync input schemes. The first method uses separate vertical and horizontal sync inputs. The second method uses a vertical and horizontal composite sync input. The third method uses vertical and horizontal composite sync on a video line (usually green). For example, Apple Macintosh® monitors use a composite sync signal on the green video input line.

Resolution

Resolution refers to the maximum number of light-to-dark transitions a monitor is able to produce. Resolution is measured in pixels or lines. (*Horizontal resolution* is almost always defined by pixels, whereas *vertical resolution* may be specified in vertical lines or pixels.)

A *pixel* (picture element) is the smallest area of light or dark the monitor can produce. The number of pixels displayed from top to bottom of the screen is vertical resolution or vertical lines. The number of pixels displayed across the screen is horizontal resolution. Refer to the drawing in Fig. 8-5.

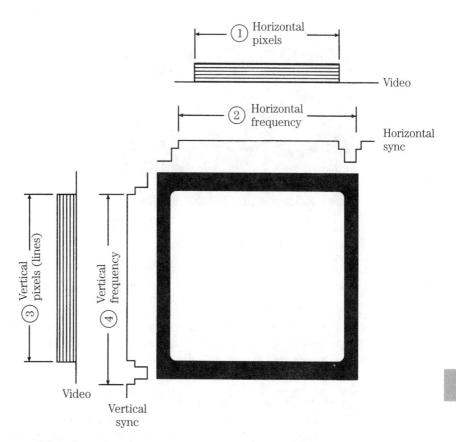

■ **8-5** *A monitor's resolution is described in pixels or lines.*

Good resolution is needed in order to produce a crisp picture. Four factors contribute to a crisp picture:

☐ Bandwidth
☐ Dot Pitch
☐ Refresh Rate
☐ Scanning Method (Progressive or Interlace)

The bandwidth of a monitor is the maximum frequency that the video circuits can pass. Bandwidth determines the fine detail of the picture. If the frequency response of the video circuit decreases, the small images and fast transitions will appear to be out of focus or blurry.

Dot pitch is the distance between like colors in the shadow mask—for example, the distance between the center on one "red" hole and the next "red" hole as shown in Fig. 8-6. Dot pitch determines the smallest size pixel a color CRT can produce. The smaller the

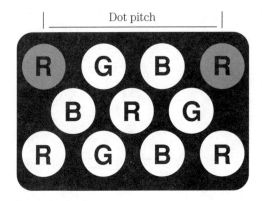

■ **8-6** *Dot pitch is the distance between like colors.*

dot pitch, the sharper the image. Typical values of dot pitch are between 0.26mm and 0.31mm.

Refresh rate is the time it takes to display a full frame of video information. If the refresh rate of a monitor is 60 Hz, it takes 1/60 of a second to display a full picture.

Two methods may be used to create vertical scan: progressive scan or interlace. Progressive Scan sweeps the picture tube once to produce a full frame of video. Interlace Scan uses two fields (even and odd) of sweep to produce a full frame of video.

A disadvantage of interlace scan is "half-line" jitter, which causes the picture to flicker. Interlaced monitors enable high resolutions while keeping the bandwidth lower than what would be required by a noninterlaced monitor with the same resolution and vertical scan frequency.

Input connectors

The input connectors on computer monitors take on a wide variety of wiring configurations and physical shapes and sizes. Some computer monitors take a 9 pin subminiature D (D-Sub) connector, others a 15 pin D-Sub, others a 15 pin high density D-Sub, and still others use BNC connectors (see Fig. 8-7). The CGA, EGA, MDA, and PGC computer monitor formats all use the 9 pin D-Sub, but their wiring configurations are different. Some of the more common connectors are illustrated in Fig. 8-7.

Aspects of the Sencore CM2000/CM2125

The following text will help you use the CM2125 to its fullest capabilities. This section covers both understanding monitors and troubleshooting monitors, and it uses the CM2125 as an example.

272

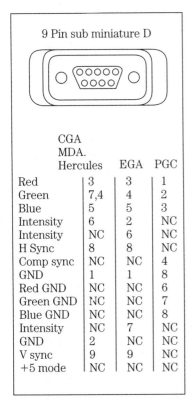

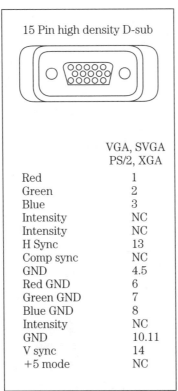

	9 Pin sub miniature D			15 Pin high density D-sub	15 Pin D-sub
	CGA MDA. Hercules	EGA	PGC	VGA, SVGA PS/2, XGA	Apple, Mac
Red	3	3	1	1	2
Green	7,4	4	2	2	5
Blue	5	5	3	3	9
Intensity	6	2	NC	NC	NC
Intensity	NC	6	NC	NC	NC
H Sync	8	8	NC	13	NC
Comp sync	NC	NC	4	NC	3
GND	1	1	8	4.5	11
Red GND	NC	NC	6	6	1
Green GND	NC	NC	7	7	6
Blue GND	NC	NC	8	8	13
Intensity	NC	7	NC	NC	NC
GND	2	NC	NC	10.11	14
V sync	9	9	NC	14	NC
+5 mode	NC	NC	NC	NC	NC

■ 8-7 *Computer monitors use a variety of connectors and wiring configurations to hook to the video circuit output.*

You can use this chapter two ways: either as a reference for how to do a specific test, or as a step-by-step troubleshooting guide.

The Trouble Tree

The "Trouble Tree" will help you decide which tests and signal injections to do for a given symptom. It outlines a logical troubleshooting sequence that will lead you to the defective stage in the least amount of time. The "Trouble Tree" is shown in Fig. 8-8.

The following applications will provide you with specific details and procedures for troubleshooting defective monitors. After you have become familiar with the test procedures, you will be able to troubleshoot following just the steps outlined by the "Trouble Tree." Begin your troubleshooting by selecting the "Trouble Tree" path that best fits the symptoms you have observed.

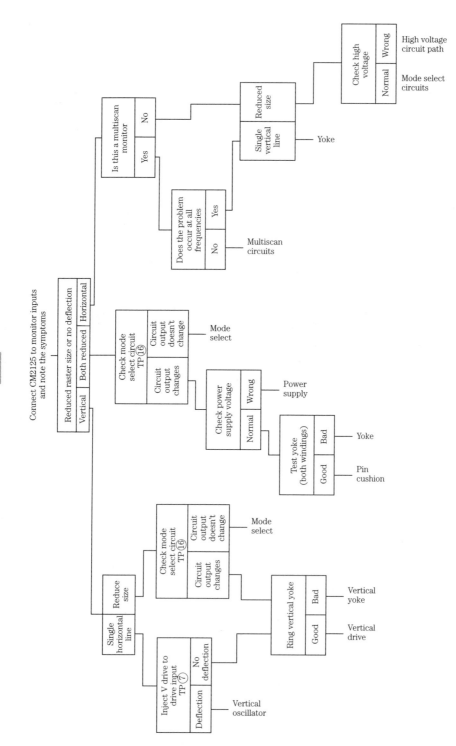

■ 8-8 Select the "Trouble Tree" path that most closely matches the symptom of the computer monitor you are servicing.

Monitors

The CM2125 provides the signals necessary to service all types of monitors. These include RGB computer monitors, data display terminals, monochrome computer monitors, RGB video monitors and specialized display monitors requiring noncomposite video inputs. These monitors fall into two basic types: digital and analog. They can be either black and white or color.

Video adapter cards

Monitors that are connected to computers receive their signal from a video graphics adapter card or circuitry located inside the computer. The adapter card generates the video and sync signals needed by the monitor. There are several different video graphics standards, such as color graphics adapter (CGA), enhanced graphics adapter (EGA), and video graphics adapter (VGA). Each standard produces different sync frequencies and pixel counts, and each video adapter card requires a compatible type monitor. Multiscan monitors work with any type of video graphics adapter card because they can sync to a wide range of frequencies.

The video circuits amplify the input signals to a level that is sufficient to drive the CRT. They also set the correct bias for the CRT and provide brightness and contrast control. Color monitors have 3 sets of identical amplifiers—one for each channel of the RGB signal. Each channel must function identically in order for the monitor to produce proper color. Note block diagram in Fig. 8-9.

Because of the fast scanning frequencies and high resolutions in monitors, the bandwidth of the video amplifiers is usually quite high. Bandwidths of 50 MHz or more are not uncommon. Contrast this with the 4.2 MHz, or less, response of most television receivers.

Most monitors receive separate horizontal and vertical sync inputs that feed directly into the horizontal and vertical oscillators via a buffer. Some monitors use a composite sync input in which both the vertical and horizontal sync is fed in on the same pin. These monitors require a V&H sync separator stage to separate the sync signals before they are fed to the oscillators. Refer to Fig. 8-10.

On some monitors the composite sync signal is fed in on the green video input line. In these monitors, the sync must first be separated from the green video before the horizontal and vertical sync can be separated from one another.

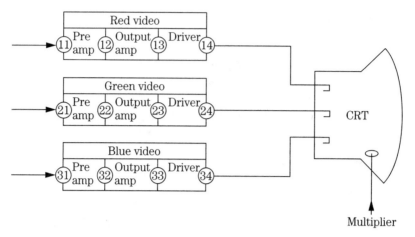

■ **8-9** *Video circuits block diagram.*

276

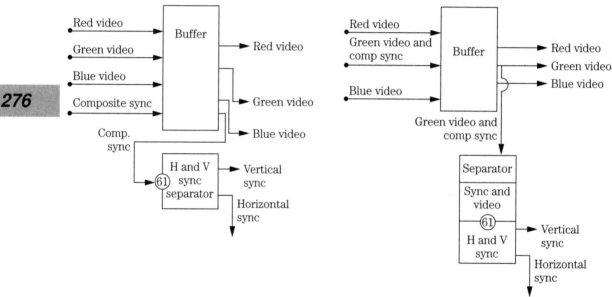

■ **8-10** *Some monitors have a composite sync input while others receive sync on one of the video lines.*

Several monitor standards (PGC, MCGA, and VGA) have multiple graphics modes. The VGA standard, for example, has three modes, as Fig. 8-11 shows. VGA 1 and VGA 3 differ only in the number of pixels that are displayed. With everything else equal, the raster in VGA 1 (350 vertical pixels) would have less height than the raster in VGA 3 (480 vertical pixels), and the display would appear compressed.

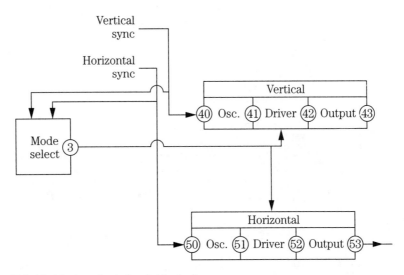

■ 8-11 *Mode select circuit block diagram.*

A mode select circuit, used in some monitors, compensates for the compressed display that results from these different graphic modes. The mode select senses the input and tells the vertical driver to adjust the driver current to produce a full raster. The polarity of the horizontal and vertical sync pulses forms a code that tells the mode select circuit what graphics mode is applied. Figure 8-12 shows the polarity code. Test the mode circuits by changing the sync polarities and checking for proper raster height.

Mode	Horizontal resolution	Vertical resolution pixels	Horiz. sync polarity	Vert. sync polarity
1. VGA	640	350	(+)	(−)
2. VGA	720	400	(−)	(+)
3. VGA	640	480	(−)	(−)

■ 8-12 *Standards for the three VGA modes.*

Vertical & horizontal circuits

The vertical and horizontal circuits each consist of an oscillator, driver, output, and yoke. The *oscillator* is synchronized to the incoming video. It develops a signal that is amplified and converted to a current waveform by the *driver*. The *output* stage provides sufficient current to drive the deflection yoke. The *yoke* produces the magnetic field necessary to move the electron beam up and

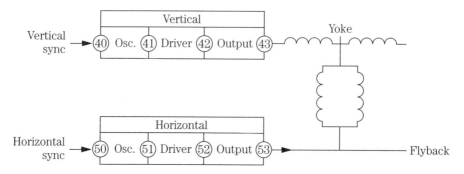

8-13 *Vertical and horizontal circuits block diagram.*

down and back and forth across the face of the CRT. Note the block diagram in Fig. 8-13.

Problems in the oscillator result in no deflection or loss of sync. A problem in the driver, output or yoke results in no deflection, partial deflection, or poor linearity.

High voltage & power supply circuits

The horizontal circuits have a second function besides providing deflection: They provide the drive signal to the flyback transformer that creates the focus and high voltages, and other scan-derived power supply voltages. Note circuit in Fig. 8-14

During normal operation, a large pulse is produced at the collector of the horizontal output transistor. The output connects to the primary of the flyback transformer so the pulses are induced into the flybacks secondary windings. The pulses are stepped up and rectified to produce the focus and high voltage, and then rectified to produce the dc voltages used to operate the monitor. Because these voltages depend on the pulse at the output transistor that occurs from horizontal scanning, they are called *scan-derived*.

Using the computer monitor analyzer

The CM2000/CM2125 improves troubleshooting effectiveness through a technique called "Functional Analyzing." This method is made up of two parts: signal injection and signal tracing. Signal substitution lets you inject "known good" signal into the circuits under test.

Once you narrow the problem to a single stage, use signal tracing to find the faulty component. As you signal trace, compare the

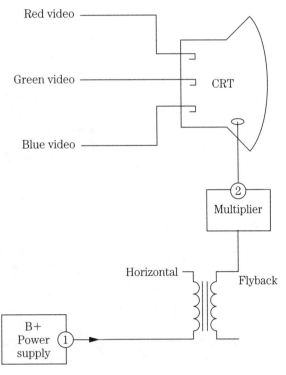

■ **8-14** *High voltage and power supply circuit block diagram.*

voltage levels, frequencies, and waveshapes to those on the service manuals.

The computer monitor analyzer provides the ability to analyze computer monitors and isolate defective stages when troubleshooting. This info will quickly familiarize you with the features and operation of the analyzer to get you started making the best of this test instrument. The front panel controls of the CM2000/2125 analyzer is shown in Fig. 8-15.

Connecting to a monitor

The CM2125 sync & video output jack provides all the signals needed to connect to the input terminal of a computer monitor. Most computer monitors use one of several standard types of input connectors. The interface connectors adapt the signals from the sync & video output jacks to the standard connector on the monitor you are servicing. See Fig. 8-16 to select the interface connector that matches the monitor you are servicing.

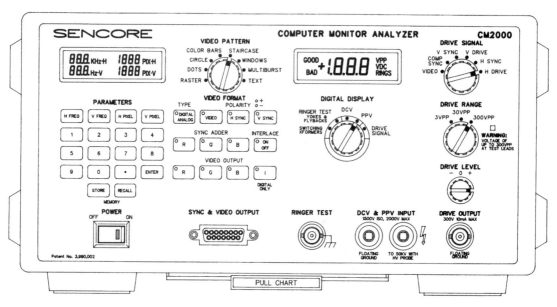

■ **8-15** *Front panel controls.*

Format	Storage location	Connector
CGA	0	1
Hercules, MDA	1	1
EGA	2	2
PGC 1	3	3
PGC 2	4	3
MCGA 1,VGA 1	5	4
VGA 2	6	4
MCGA 2,VGA 3	7	4
Super VGA	8	4
815A, XGA	9	4
1024 × 768	10	5
1280 × 1024	11	4
MAC II	12	4
Micro VAX	13	6 (BNC)
Sun color 1152 × 900	14	6 (BNC)
IBM RS6000 color 6091, 5081	15	6 (BNC)
HP 98789A, 98754A	15	6 (BNC)
Apollo DN2500, 3000, 3500, 4500	16	6 (BNC)
IBM RS6000 monochrome 8508	17	6 (BNC)
Apollo 19" color	18	6 (BNC)
Radius 1152 × 882	19	6 (BNC)

■ **8-16** *CM2000 format storage locations and interface connectors for common monitor formats.*

To connect the CM2125 to a monitor

1. Turn off the power switch to both the CM2125 and the monitor.
2. Plug the matching interface connector into the sync & video output jack.
3. Plug the monitor signal input cable into the interface connector. If the monitor does not have a cable, or if the cable is too short, use the (optional) output extension cable between the sync & video output jack and the interface connector.
4. Turn on the CM2125 (wait to turn on the monitor until you have chosen the signal format).

Choosing the signal format

Each type of computer monitor receives a particular set of signals from the computer it is connected to. This signal format can be classified by the type of computer or video adapter circuit which the monitor was designed to work with.

The signal format includes the following: horizontal and vertical scan/sync rate, the number of horizontal and vertical pixels (smallest possible area of either light or dark), the polarity of the video signal and sync pulses, whether the signals are digital (TTL) or analog, whether sync is added to any of the video signals, and whether the signal is interlaced or not.

There are two ways to choose the correct signal format. The most common computer monitor formats are listed in Fig. 8-16. These setups are stored in the CM2125's memory locations as listed. For these monitors, simply recall the stored format.

To recall a stored format

1. Press RECALL
2. Enter the desired format number
3. Press ENTER

If the monitor you are servicing is not listed in Fig. 8-16, determine the monitor's signal format from the owner's manual or service manual specifications. Enter the signal parameters using the CM2125 parameters and video format keys. Refer to the CM2125's "Pull Chart" or "Operations and Application Manual."

Once you have entered a new format, you can store it in memory for future recall. Memory locations 20–39 are available for storing new formats from the front panel.

Now that you have selected the correct signal format for the monitor you are servicing, turn on the monitor and proceed with testing.

Note: Some monitors are *multimode*, meaning they are capable of operating at two or more formats. For example, there are 3 VGA listings in Fig. 8-16. Test multimode monitors with each of the appropriate formats to ensure that they are properly in each mode.

Other monitors are *multiscan*, capable of operating over a wide range of signal formats. For example, some multiscan monitors are capable of operating CGA, EGA, VGA, and Macintosh formats. Test multiscan monitors with several different formats within the monitor's operating range.

Selecting video patterns

You will use each of the CM2125 video patterns to perform one or more tests of the monitor's operation. The following is a description of each pattern and its uses in troubleshooting and adjusting monitors.

To view the complete pattern, be sure that the "R", "G", and "B" video output buttons are all selected as indicated by the lighted LED on each button.

Raster This pattern produces a full-screen box, surrounded by a 1-pixel-wide white border.

Use this pattern to test color purity and high voltage power supply regulation. In "+" *video polarity*, with all the video output buttons on, the box should be pure white with no coloration. In "–" *video polarity*, the box switches to black. The outside white border should remain straight and ripple free in either polarity. Any change in the height or width of the border as you switch video polarity indicates less than perfect high voltage power supply regulation.

Dots This pattern produces either 9 rows by 13 columns (at higher resolutions), or 11 rows by 15 columns of 1 pixel dots.

Use this pattern to test static and dynamic convergence. Check for white dots with no color fringing. Color fringing on dots near the center indicates static misconvergence. Color fringing on dots near the corners indicates dynamic misconvergence.

Circle This pattern produces two centered circles and four corner circles on a 1-pixel-wide cross hatch display.

Use this pattern to test the monitor's linearity and convergence. Check that each line is straight and that each box is square and the same size throughout the raster. Also check that each circle is round rather than egg-shaped. Unequal spacing between vertical lines indicates horizontal nonlinearity. Unequal spacing between horizontal lines indicates vertical nonlinearity. If the CRT is converged properly, each line will be a single, white line without any colored fringing.

Color bars This pattern produces two rows of eight bars consisting of the three primary colors (red, green, blue), three secondary colors (yellow, cyan, magenta), plus black and white, as shown in Fig. 8-17.

Black	Blue	Green	Cyan	Red	Magenta	Yellow	White
White	Yellow	Magenta	Red	Cyan	Green	Blue	Black

■ **8-17** *Bar sequence produced by the CM2000 color bars pattern.*

Use this pattern to test the monitor's ability to produce proper colors. Check that each color bar is present. A missing bat or wrong color sequence may indicate that a video channel is connected incorrectly or is defective. Also check that the colors are uniform in intensity from top to bottom and left to right. Non-uniform bars may indicate problems in the video amplifiers.

The color bars sequence shown in Fig. 8-17 is for "analog" type format ("+ video polarity). When "digital" type is selected, the pattern changes slightly, depending on the setting of the "1" output. With the "1" output on, the bar sequence is similar to the "analog" type with the bottom row of bars being brighter than the top row. When the "1" output is off, the top and bottom row of bars are the same brightness.

Staircase On analog monitors, this pattern produces 16 evenly spaced bars ranging from black to 100% white (or amber or green), depending on monitor phosphor.

Use this pattern to test the brightness and contrast linearity of analog and monochrome digital monitors. A properly operating analog monitor or monochrome digital monitor will display 16 distinct bars ranging from black to white. On a color monitor, each step should be a pure shade of gray with no hint of color.

Color digital monitors, which are only capable of 2 signal levels, do not reproduce this 16-step pattern. Instead they produce color bars having the same sequence as the Color Bars pattern, with the exception that the top row of bars is on the left of the screen and the bottom row is on the right half of the screen.

Windows This pattern produces five white windows (four corners and center) on a black background. See Fig. 8-14.

Use this pattern to test the monitor's power supply regulation. Check for clear, distinct transitions between the black and white portions. All the white boxes should be the same brightness level and the entire screen should be free of ripple. The pattern should lock in with no "bounce" as you switch between "+" and "−" video polarity.

Multiburst This pattern produces five sets of vertical and horizontal multiburst lines. The lines in each set are grouped according to line width. The lines in the first group are 1 pixel wide, the second group 2 pixels wide, the third group 3 pixels wide, etc.

Use this pattern to test monitor resolution. Test horizontal pixel resolution by examining the vertical lines and test vertical pixel resolution by examining the horizontal lines. Both the vertical and horizontal 1-pixel-wide lines should be individually distinct on a properly operating monitor.

Text This pattern produces a screen filled with upper- and lowercase text characters to duplicate user conditions.

Use this pattern to test the final performance of a monitor. All the characters on the screen should be focused and easy to read.

Drive signals

The drive signals provide known-good substitute signals for troubleshooting monitors. To use the troubleshooting drive signals, first connect the monitor to the CM2125 sync & video output jack and choose the correct signal format for the monitor you are servicing. Then, use the substitute drive signals to inject into the area of the suspected defect to locate the defective stage. When you substitute a good signal beyond the defective stage, normal monitor operation will be restored.

The following is a description of each drive signal and how to use it in troubleshooting monitors. See Fig. 8-18 for a typical monitor including the numbered test points that will be referenced in the following discussion.

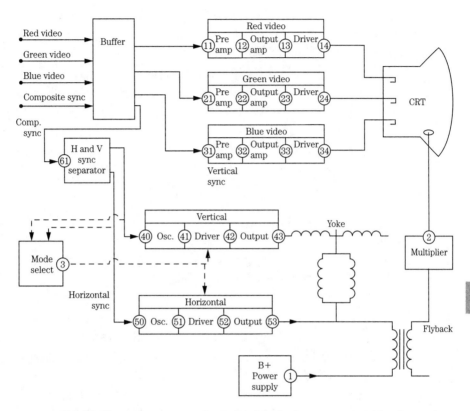

■ **8-18** *Compare your monitor to this block diagram as a guide when substituting drive signals.*

Video This signal provides a standard video signal corresponding to the green portion of whichever video is selected. Use it to substitute into video stages including the red, green, and blue channels. (Test Points 11, 12, 13, 14, 21, 22, 23, 24, 31, 32, 33, and 34)

The video drive signal produces the color of the channel into which it is injected. Use the Raster video pattern with the video drive signal for most troubleshooting.

Comp sync This signal provides combined vertical and horizontal sync. Use it to substitute at any point before the sync separator in monitors that use composite sync input. (Test Point 61)

V sync This signal provides vertical sync, timed with the video output signal. Use it to substitute into the vertical stages before the oscillator, but after the sync separator if there is one. (Test Point 40)

V drive This signal provides vertical drive. Use it to substitute into the vertical stages between the oscillator output and vertical output. (Test Points 41 and 42)

H sync This signal provides horizontal sync, timed with the video output signal. Use it to substitute into the horizontal stages before the oscillator, but after the sync separator if there is one. (Test Point 50)

H drive This signal provides horizontal drive. Use it to substitute into the horizontal stages between the oscillator output and the base of the output transistor. (Test Points 51 and 52)

To inject substitute drive signals

1. Set the Digital Display switch to "Drive Signal."
2. Set the Drive Level control to "Oil."
3. Select the desired drive signal with the Drive Signal switch.
4. Connect the Direct Test Lead to the Drive Output jack and connect the test clips to the circuit test point and ground.
5. Set the Drive Range control to the lowest range that includes the required signal level.
6. Adjust the Drive Level control to match the level and polarity of the signal normally at the test point into which you are injecting.

Note: Remember to connect the monitor you are servicing to an isolation transformer before making any test equipment connections.

Using auxiliary tests

Ringer test Once you have used signal substitution or signal tracing to isolate problems to the deflection or power supply circuits, you can use the CM2125 ringer test to check for shorted turns in the yoke, flyback, or switching power supply transformer. The ringer test is a simplified check of the coil's quality or "Q", and locates shorted turns that cannot be detected by other troubleshooting techniques.

To ring a yoke or transformer, connect the direct test lead across the coil to be tested and set the digital display switch to either "Yokes & Flybacks" or "Switching Xformers" to match the device you are testing. The digital display shows the number of times the coil rings before it damps out. A reading of 10 or more is good and means that the coil does not contain a shorted turn. A bad reading, less than 10 rings, indicates a shorted turn. (If any winding of a transformer tests good, the transformer does not contain a shorted turn.)

DVM The autoranged DVM portion of the digital display section measures external dc and peak-to-peak voltages to 2000 volts. Use the DVM DCV or PPV functions to aid you in troubleshooting any section of the monitor, including measuring at the collector of the horizontal output transistor to verify proper supply and pulse voltages.

Use the digital display switch to select the desired measurement. Use the supplied DVM test leads to connect the external voltages to the PPV and DCV input jacks. The digital display readout displays the voltage levels.

Connecting the computer monitor

There are three steps to connecting a computer monitor to the CM2125 and getting a pattern on the CRT:

1. Setting the parameters

2. Setting the video format

3. Hooking up the correct connector

Setting the parameters

Four main parameters determined the performance capabilities of a computer monitor: horizontal frequency, horizontal pixels, vertical frequency, and vertical pixels (lines). Here is a brief explanation of each. Refer to Fig. 8-19.

Horizontal frequency This is the number of times per second the electron beam travels horizontally across the CRT and back (horizontal scan).

Horizontal pixels These are the number of dots or picture elements that can be displayed horizontally. A pixel is the smallest dot or picture element the monitor can produce.

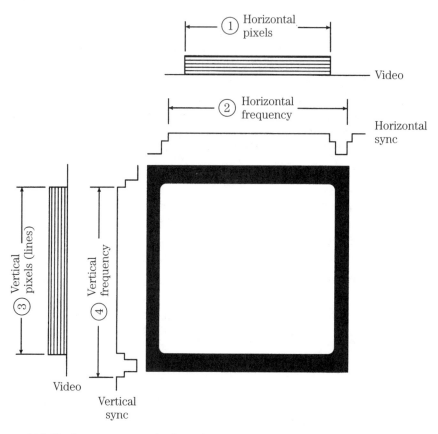

■ 8-19 *A computer monitor's performance capabilities can be defined by four parameters: horizontal pixels, horizontal frequency, vertical pixels, and vertical frequency.*

Vertical frequency This is the number of times per second the electron beam travels from the top of the CRT to the bottom and back (vertical scan).

Vertical pixels These are the number of picture elements that are displayed vertically on the CRT. Vertical pixels are also referred to as *lines*.

These four parameters are generally found in the computer monitor's service literature. If you do not have the service literature, you can identify the computer monitor type and find parameter information in the CM2125 Pull Chart.

After making the proper set-up, the CM2125 is generating the horizontal and vertical sync frequencies and pixel resolutions required by an EGA computer monitor. The numbers in the parameters display should match those shown in Fig. 8-20.

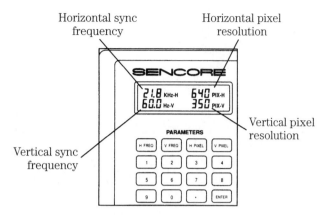

Horizontal sync frequency

Horizontal pixel resolution

Vertical pixel resolution

Vertical sync frequency

■ **8-20** *This is how the display should look after you've entered the parameters for an EGA computer monitor.*

Setting the video format

The second step to hooking up to a computer monitor is setting the correct video format. This includes setting: the monitor type, the polarity of the video, horizontal and vertical sync signals, the sync adder, interlace, and the video outputs.

Let's now briefly look at each of these settings

Type Monitors require either digital or analog input signals. This button sets all the sync & video output video signals to digital levels (LED "on") or analog levels (LED "off").

Polarity The polarity format buttons establish the polarity of the video, horizontal sync, and vertical sync signals at the sync & video output jacks. The LED indicator lights for "+" polarity and is not lit for "–" polarity. Most monitors require "+" video polarity. Incorrect sync polarities may have no effect on some monitors and may cause loss of sync in others. Some monitors use different sync polarity combinations to select operating modes.

Sync adder The sync adder buttons select the video line to which the sync information is added. Selecting R, G, or B adds both the vertical and horizontal sync (composite sync) to that signal line. Sync is added to a line when the corresponding LED indicator is lit. Sync can only be added to analog monitors.

Interlace This button switches the vertical sync between interlaced scan (LED "on") and progressive scan (LED "off"). Set it to match the monitor type you are servicing. Most monitor types use progressive scan.

Video output   Use these buttons to make the R, G, B, and "I" output lines active (LED "on") or inactive. The "I" (intensity) line is used by some digital monitors to provide an additional signal level step between on and off.

Using the memory store & recall functions

The parameter values and video format settings of the most common computer monitor types are stored in the CM2125 permanent memory. This memory function saves you the hassle of having to enter all of the setup data on each monitor you service. It allows you to quickly recall complete monitor setups, by entering the storage location of the desired setup.

The memory presets consist of three groups:

1. Standard setups

2. User setups

3. Computer interface setups.

All the setups can be recalled from the front panel keypad, but only the "User Setups" can be programmed from the front panel.

Standard setups   Presets 0 through 19 are the setups for the most common monitor types. You will find them in the pull chart beneath the equipment. These setups are preprogrammed into permanent memory and cannot be erased or changed by the user.

User setups   Presets 20 through 39 can be programmed from the front panel keypad using the store button. Use these presets to store special setups used in your servicing. The setups will not be lost when the power is turned off.

Computer interface setups   Presets 40 through 59 can only be programmed via the interface accessory jack, but can be recalled from the front panel recall button. The setups will not be lost when power is turned off.

Recalling the setup for an EGA computer monitor

1. Find the memory storage location of an EGA monitor from the pull chart table.

2. Press (RECALL) (2) and then (enter)

The CM2125 is now generating the correct parameters and video format required for an EGA computer monitor. The parameter display and the LEDs on the video format buttons should be the same as those in Figs. 8-20 and 8-21.

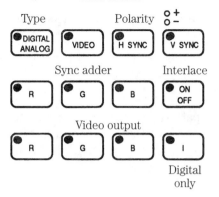

Video format

Type | Polarity

| DIGITAL ANALOG | VIDEO | H SYNC | V SYNC |

Sync adder | Interlace

| R | G | B | ON OFF |

Video output

| R | G | B | I |

Digital only

8-21 *Here's how the VIDEO FORMAT buttons should look for an EGA computer monitor.*

Hooking up the correct connector

Now that the CM2125 is generating the correct signals out of the sync & video output jack, you are ready to hook up the computer monitor.

There are quite a number of different monitor input connectors and wiring configurations. Some take a 9 pin D-sub; and still others BNC connectors. Building a connector for each computer monitor type can be a time-consuming task.

Along with the CM2125, there are connectors available for hooking to the most common computer monitor types. A listing of the available connectors is shown in Fig. 8-22. This chart also appears as a pull chart. These connectors convert the output of the CM2125 to match the required input of the monitor you are servicing.

CM2000 Connector Chart	
Connector	*Computer Monitor Type*
1	CGA, MDA, Hercules
2	EGA
3	PGC
4	VGA, PS/S SVGC, XGA
5	Apple or Mac
6	BNC Input
Universal	Adapts to match any computer monitor type

8-22 *Connectors are available for hooking the most common computer monitor types to the CM2000.*

291

Choosing the correct connector for an EGA computer monitor

1. Find the type on monitor to be serviced on the CM2125 pull chart.

2. For an EGA computer monitor hook up the monitor cable to connector #2 and the connector to the sync & video output jack of the CM2125.

You should now have a pattern on the computer monitor screen. If you do not, make sure the MC2125 is generating the correct signals for the computer monitor being tested. Also, make sure you are using the correct connector.

Testing with the Multiburst pattern

Resolution on computer monitors has been improving steadily since the late seventies. While early computer monitors produced fuzzy images, today's mainstream monitors produce a very sharp, clear picture.

Let's now look at a number of key terms related to bandwidth calculation, and see how to use the CM2125's Multiburst pattern for testing a computer monitor's bandwidth.

Key definitions

Pixel The smallest picture element possible. One of the dots that makes up the displayed image.

Horizontal frequency The number of times per second the electron beam scans horizontally across the screen and back.

Horizontal pixels The number of dots that can be displayed horizontally across the screen.

Vertical pixels The number of dots that can be displayed vertically on the CRT. The number of vertical pixels is similar to the number of scan lines in television terminology.

Vertical frequency The number of times per second the electron beam scans from the top of the screen to the bottom and back.

Resolution The number of transitions made between a pixel being on (light) and a pixel being off (dark) on the display.

Bandwidth The fastest transition between a pixel being on and off, that the monitor circuits are capable of passing and displaying.

292

The higher the bandwidth, the more resolution and clarity in the picture.

Calculating bandwidth

Vast improvements in computer monitor picture resolution have been made by increasing the horizontal scanning frequency and increasing the number of pixels displayed in one horizontal scan. In other words, more pixels are displayed in less time.

A computers monitor bandwidth is best checked with a pattern that produces vertical lines that are a single pixel wide (see Fig. 8-23). If the monitor can display a crisp distinct line, the video circuits have the bandwidth needed to turn on a single pixel at a time. A fuzzy, nondistinct line means the video amplifiers do not have the bandwidth needed to pass the test signal. The signal is not amplified adequately as it travels through the video circuits as illustrated in Fig. 8-24.

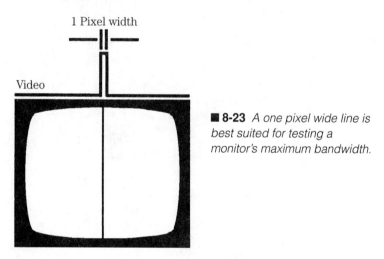

■ **8-23** *A one pixel wide line is best suited for testing a monitor's maximum bandwidth.*

The area of concern in a bandwidth test is the area across the display that is seen by the viewer. This area is called active video. Active video uses about eighty percent of the total horizontal scan time. The rest of the time is spent in blanking—the electron beam is shut off and is moving back across the display as shown in Fig. 8-25.

For example, let's calculate the required bandwidth of a VGA computer monitor. The VGA standard has 640 horizontal pixels and the horizontal scanning frequency is 31.5 kHz.

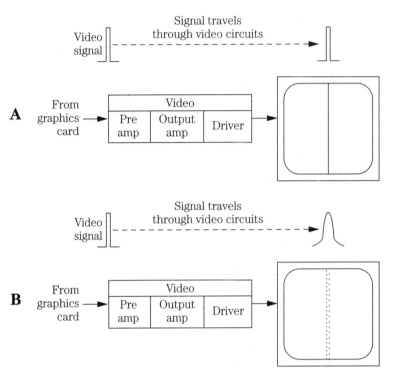

■ **8-24** *A) A crisp, distinct line shows that the monitor has the bandwidth needed to turn on a single pixel at a time. B) A fuzzy line means the monitor does not have the bandwidth needed to pass the signal.*

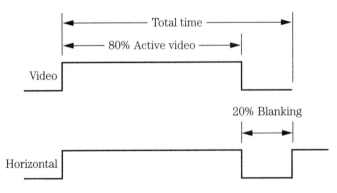

■ **8-25** *One scan line is made up of active video and blanking.*

Inverting the horizontal scanning frequency gives a total horizontal scan time of 31.7 microseconds. About 80% of this is active video (what's seen on the monitor) and about 20% is blanking. So 25.4 microseconds is active video and 6.3 microseconds is blanking.

If 640 pixels must be fit into the 25.4 microsecond active display time, we can find the amount of time it takes to turn on one pixel by dividing 25.4 microseconds by 640 pixels. This shows that each pixel is on for 39.7 nanoseconds (39.7×10-9 seconds). If we invert 39.7 nanoseconds, we get a frequency of 25.2 MHz. So, in order to see a crisp distinct line of one pixel width at the VGA resolution of 640 horizontal pixels, the bandwidth of the video amplifiers must be 25.2 MHz or greater.

Testing bandwidth with Multiburst pattern

The CM2125's Multiburst pattern is used for testing a computer monitor's resolution and bandwidth because it has a series of horizontal and vertical lines of varying pixel widths. The sets of vertical lines test horizontal pixel resolution and the sets of horizontal lines test vertical pixel resolution. The lines in each set are grouped according to pixel width. The lines in the first group are one pixel wide, the second group two pixels wide, the third group three pixels wide, etc. The groups of lines that are one pixel wide test the computer monitor to its maximum bandwidth. Each of the lines should be individually discernible on a properly operating monitor.

Because bandwidth is a product of the horizontal scanning, active video time, and the number of horizontal pixels; the bandwidths of the groups of vertical lines in the Multiburst pattern are different for each computer monitor format. For example, the bandwidth of the "1 pixel on, 1 pixel off" group of vertical lines for a Super VGA computer monitor is 36 MHz.

The Multiburst pattern also tests vertical resolution. With vertical resolution, we are not concerned with the bandwidth of the signals because these signals are of such lower frequency. We are instead concerned that we can see each of the sets of lines of 1, 2, 3, and 4 pixels. Refer to pattern shown in Fig. 8-26.

There are a number of circuits that will keep a computer monitor from being able to display a clear, focused, Multiburst pattern. The monitor may have a problem in the focus or high voltage circuitry, the video circuits, or the CRT.

Troubleshooting monitor H V regulation problems

Computer monitors require excellent high voltage regulation to prevent the raster from changing size as the display brightness levels change. Let's now use the Computer Monitor Analyzer to

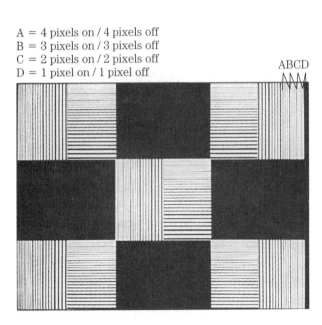

A = 4 pixels on / 4 pixels off
B = 3 pixels on / 3 pixels off
C = 2 pixels on / 2 pixels off
D = 1 pixel on / 1 pixel off

ABCD

■ **8-26** The Multiburst test pattern.

test a monitor's high voltage regulation and how to troubleshoot the monitor to locate the source of regulation problems.

The need for high voltage regulation

The brightness of a monitor's display is controlled by the signals sent to the monitor from the computer. These signals control the CRT bias, which in turn controls the amount of current flowing from the CRT cathodes to the phosphor screen. This current is supplied by the high voltage, which is driven from the horizontal scan circuit.

A brighter CRT display draws more current from the high voltage supply, tending to load down the high voltage. If the high voltage decreases, the raster size increases because the electrons flowing from the cathodes to the phosphor screen move slower and are more easily deflected by the yoke's magnetic field. Regulation is needed to hold the high voltage and raster size constant at all CRT brightness levels.

High voltage regulation operation

Horizontal scan circuits use a switching transistor (the horizontal device) to convert the low supply voltage (generally 65 to 120 volts) into an ac signal. This ac signal is stepped up by the output transformer (flyback) and rectified to produce the CRT high voltage (generally 15 to 25 thousand volts). As long as the low voltage supply to the horizontal circuits is held constant and the flyback circuit is functioning properly, the high voltage output remains fairly constant over a wide range of brightness levels. The circuit used to regulate the low voltage supply to the horizontal circuit is usually a switching regulator.

Testing high voltage regulation

The best way to test high voltage regulation is to switch the display between the extremes of brightness, black and white, and note how much raster size changes. The Monitor Analyzer raster pattern, which includes a white border, makes this very easy to see.

To test high voltage regulation

1. Connect the CM2125 to the monitor-under-test as described in the pull chart.
2. Select the raster pattern.
3. Adjust the monitor's brightness control for maximum brightness without blooming.
4. Switch the "video polarity" button between and "+" and "−." This causes the raster to alternate between white (maximum load) and black (minimum load).
5. Note the size of the raster, defined by the surrounding white border line.

On a monitor with perfect high voltage regulation, the raster size would not change at all as the display brightness changed. On a typical monitor, however, the raster size increases as much as twice the width of the border line in all directions as the raster is switched from black to white. Any raster size increase greater than this indicates a problem with the monitor.

Troubleshooting poor high voltage regulation

The following procedure will help you determine whether poor high voltage regulation is due to poor low voltage regulation or defective components in the high voltage supply circuit.

If the display indicates a regulation problem, measure the dc voltage at the collector of the horizontal output transistor while repeating the regulation test.

To measure the dc voltage at the horizontal output collector

1. Connect the DVM test leads to the DCV & PPV input jacks.
2. Connect the black DCV & PPV input test lead to ground.
3. Connect the red DCV & PPV input test lead to the collector of the horizontal output transistor.
4. Set the digital display control to "DCV."
5. Note the voltage readings on the LCD display as you switch the video polarity switch from "+" to "−."

If the horizontal output collector dc voltage changes more than 1% while changing the video pattern polarity, troubleshoot the low voltage regulator circuit.

If the PP and dc voltages remain stable, measure the CRT high voltage while repeating the regulation test.

Warning

Measuring high voltage exposes you to the possibility of a severe shock hazard if you do not follow test methods. Do not measure the high voltage until you completely read and understand the following warnings and instructions.

☐ Never measure more than 2000 volts without a high voltage probe. Use the TP212/10 KV probe to measure voltages in the 2000 to 10,000 volt range. Use the HP200 50 KV probe for voltages near or over 10,000 volts.
☐ Remove power to the circuit before connecting or disconnecting the high voltage probe.
☐ Connect the ground lead so that it cannot become detached during the test. If the ground lead comes loose, immediately remove the ac power to the monitor.
☐ Connect the correct ground point. Some chassis use a separate ground for high voltage.
☐ Immediately remove power from the monitor if the high voltage probe comes loose. Do not touch the high voltage probe until power is removed.
☐ If you must hold the high voltage probe, use extra caution. Be sure the connections to the probe and ground lead are firmly attached. Hold the probe behind the molded safety rings to

prevent the possibility of contacting the high voltage test point and to prevent arcing across the probe to your hand.

To measure the monitor's high voltage

1. Turn the monitor off.
2. Set the CM2125 Digital Display switch to "DCV."
3. Connect the DVM Test Leads to the DCV & PPV Input jacks.
4. Slide the red DVM Test Lead into the optional HP200 50 KV high voltage probe. **Note:** Be sure the tip is firmly seated in the connector inside the HV probe so that it will not detach during the measurement.
5. Connect the black DVM Test Lead to the monitor's HV ground point.
6. Connect the HP200 HV probe to the CRT high voltage connection so that the HV probe does not need to be held during measurement.
7. Turn on the monitor and note the voltage readings on the LCD display as you switch the video polarity switch from "+" to "−."
8. Multiply the readings by 100 when using the HP200 High Voltage probe.
9. Turn off the monitor before disconnecting the HP200.

If the high voltage decreases more than 3% when you switch from black to white raster, but the dc voltage at the collector of the horizontal output transistor was stable, look for problems in the high voltage secondary of the horizontal output transformer.

A common problem is the ground return capacitor on the low end of the high voltage secondary winding, especially if an electrolytic is used (typically in the 1 microfarad range). Check the cap for value, ESR, and dielectric absorption.

If the high voltage remains stable when you switch from black to white raster, but the raster size increases more than twice the width of the border line, check the video or sync circuits for changing levels.

Testing composite NTSC video monitors

Some computer monitors, as well as video monitors, use a composite input signal that conforms to the NTSC standard rather than having separate video and sync signals that conform to a particular computer display standard. You can test these monitors, plus all other computer monitors, with the CM2125 Computer Monitor Analyzer.

Selecting the input signal

The CM2125 is able to provide the standard 1 V_{PP} composite video signal normally present at the input of a composite monitor. The bandwidth of the signal can be adjusted to match any resolution monitor. Adjust the CM2125 as follows to obtain a standard composite video signal.

Setting the video format switches

Refer to the push pad illustration in Fig. 8-27.

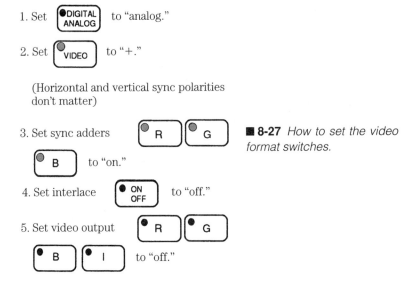

1. Set [●DIGITAL ANALOG] to "analog."

2. Set [VIDEO] to "+."

(Horizontal and vertical sync polarities don't matter)

3. Set sync adders [R] [G] [B] to "on."

■ **8-27** *How to set the video format switches.*

4. Set interlace [ON OFF] to "off."

5. Set video output [R] [G] [B] [I] to "off."

Setting the signal parameters

Refer to the push pad illustration in Fig. 8-28.

Note: 325 horizontal pixels at the NTSC scan rate is equivalent to a 3.0 MHz video input signal for a 40 column monitor. To adjust the number of horizontal pixels for different resolution NTSC monitors, see Fig. 8-29.

At this point the CM2125 is producing a signal you can connect to the composite monitor you wish to test. However, when you enter monitor scan parameters, such as these, that don't correspond to a standard the CM2125 recognizes, it automatically sets the blanking timing to a default condition. The default blanking timing is

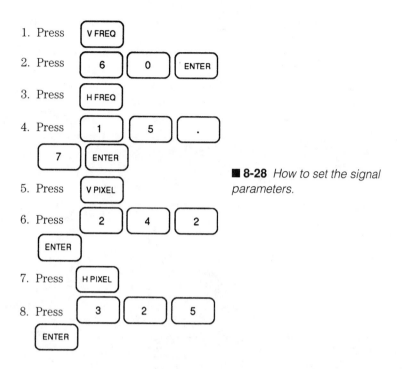

1. Press [V FREQ]

2. Press [6] [0] [ENTER]

3. Press [H FREQ]

4. Press [1] [5] [.]
   [7] [ENTER]

5. Press [V PIXEL]

6. Press [2] [4] [2]
   [ENTER]

7. Press [H PIXEL]

8. Press [3] [2] [5]
   [ENTER]

■ **8-28** *How to set the signal parameters.*

Video bandwidth	H pixels
3 MHz (40 col)	325
4 MHz	430
5 MHz	540
6 MHz (80 col)	650
7 MHz	760

■ **8-29** *Horizontal pixels for various resolution NTSC monitors.*

80% active video time and 20% blanking time, with blanking time divided equally among front porch, sync, and back porch. This blanking timing will give you a usable display on the monitor, but the patterns may be slightly off center.

You have two options. First, you can use the new composite signal format you have created with the default timing parameters, which may result in your test pattern being slightly off center. If you wish to do so and want to connect the CM2125 to the monitor now, skip to the section titled "Hooking Up To The Monitor." Second, if you wish to see the pattern positioned exactly as it will be for the user, you can easily change the blanking timing parameters as follows.

Changing blanking timing parameters for a composite monitor

The CM2125 has a manual blanking timing mode that allows you to easily customize the blanking timing for a monitor that does not use one of the preprogrammed formats in memory locations 0 thru 19. This mode allows you to set the blanking timing to exactly match NTSC standards. Figure 8-30 lists the complete NTSC format.

H Scan	15.7 kHz
V Scan	60 Hz
H Pixels	See Fig. 1
V Pixels	242
V Front porch	0.191 msec
V Back porch	0.892 msec
V Sync	0.191 msec
H Front porch	1.5 usec
H Back porch	3.2 usec
H Sync	4.7 usec

■ **8-30** *Composite NTSC format.*

Changing to NTSC blanking timing parameters

Disconnect any adapter from the sync & video output jack. Refer to Fig. 8-31.

You must enter each of the three parameters for either vertical or horizontal blanking timing before those parameters take effect. Once you have entered values for all three, you can then go back and modify any of the three parameters you wish. To recall a blanking timing parameter to see what you have entered, press Store, the location # of the parameter, and Enter.

Also, anytime you wish to switch from the manual blanking timing parameters you have just entered, back to the default blanking timing mode, just repeat the keystrokes Recall, 8, 0, Enter. To return to the manual blanking timing parameters you have entered, enter the keystrokes Store, 8, 0, Enter. Three eights in the right hand display when you attempt to recall a blanking timing parameter indicates you are in the default blanking timing mode.

Once you enter the manual blanking timing mode, the vertical sync frequency is automatically calculated from the horizontal sync frequency, vertical pixel number, and blanking timing parameters you enter. If you attempt to set the vertical sync frequency while in the manual blanking timing mode, the error code "E 1" will appear in the right hand digital display.

1. Disconnect any adapter from the sync and video output jack

2. Press [STORE] [8] [0] [ENTER]

(Switches to manual blinking timing mode.)

You are now ready to enter your desired vertical sync parameters in locations 81 thru 83.

3. Press [STORE] [8] [1] [ENTER]
   [.] [1] [9] [1] [ENTER]

(Enters vertical front porch time in milliseconds.)

4. Press [STORE] [8] [2] [ENTER]
   [.] [8] [9] [2] [ENTER]

(Enters vertical back porch time in milliseconds.)

5. Press [STORE] [8] [3] [ENTER]
   [.] [1] [9] [1] [ENTER]

(Enters vertical sync time in milliseconds.)

You are now ready to enter your desired horizontal parameters in locations 84 thru 86.

6. Press [STORE] [8] [4] [ENTER]
   [1] [.] [5] [ENTER]

(Enters horizontal front porch time in microseconds.)

7. Press [STORE] [8] [5] [ENTER]
   [ENTER] [3] [.] [2] [ENTER]

(Enters horizontal back porch time in microseconds.)

8. Press [STORE] [8] [6] [ENTER]
   [4] [.] [7] [ENTER]

(Enters horizontal sync time in microseconds.)

■ **8-31** *To change to NTSC blanking timing parameters.*

303

Storing the new format

Once you have created a new format (by manually entering horizontal and vertical sync frequencies and pixel rates, and at your option blanking timing parameters), you can store the new format for later use in one of memory locations 20 thru 39. To store a new format in location 20, for example, press Store, 2, 0, Enter. The format you currently have entered in the CM2125 will be stored at memory location 20 can be recalled for use at a later time by pressing Recall, 2, 0, Enter.

Hooking up to the monitor

Attach connector cable #6 (39B272) to the CM2125 sync & video output jack. If the monitor uses an RCA phono jack as its video input connector, use a BNC to RCA adapter to connect the green BNC connector from cable #6 to the monitor's video input jack. If the monitor uses a BNC jack as its video input connector, connect the green BNC connector from cable #6 directly to the monitor's video input jack.

Selecting video patterns

The video pattern you select for testing composite monitor's will be the same as those you use for testing any other monitor, with one exception. The color bars pattern will be monochrome on both monochrome and color monitors. This is because the CM2125 does not produce the chroma subcarrier signal required by a color NTSC monitor to produce color. Also, since the monitor is being fed from just a single color output line, green in this case, the full monochrome signal normally seen from color bars is not present. The upper half of the screen will contain two half-intensity rectangles and the lower half of the screen will contain two full-intensity rectangles, with the remainder of the screen being dark.

Programming sync timing parameters

Let's now look at the importance of proper timing for video monitors. The horizontal and vertical sync signals fed to a monitor are responsible for synchronizing the horizontal and vertical oscillators to the incoming video signals. The oscillators in turn feed the driver and output stages which move the electron beam up and down and back and forth across the face of the CRT.

The timing of the sync signals in relationship to the video establishes the position of the picture that is displayed on the CRT. If the sync and video timings are incorrect the displayed picture will be the wrong size, will be shifted up or down, or will be shifted to the left or right. See drawings in Fig. 8-32.

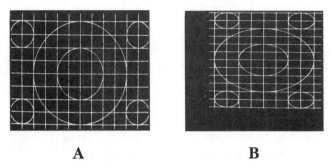

A　　　　　　　**B**

■ **8-32** *A) The display is properly sized and centered. B) Display is schrunched and shifted because of incorrect timing between the sync signals and video.*

Four sync parameters

The horizontal and vertical sync signals each have four parameters; front porch time, sync time, back porch time, and active video time. The combination of front porch, back porch, and sync times make up blanking time. Blanking time plus active video time equals the total scan time. Refer to Fig. 8-33.

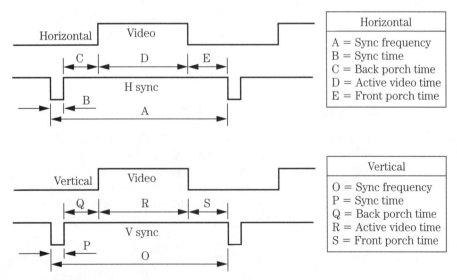

■ **8-33** *Four timing parameters: front porch, sync, back porch, and active video, establishing the size and centering of the raster on the CRT.*

When to program sync parameters

Memory locations 0–19 in the CM2125 contain the setups for the most common computer monitor formats. These setups contain the correct horizontal and vertical sync frequencies and pixel counts, as well as the timing parameters for vertical and horizontal front porch, sync, and back porch.

If you enter the scanning frequencies and pixel rates for a computer monitor format the CM2125 does not recognize, the scan and sync parameters will automatically default to 80% displayed video and 20% blanking. The blanking pulse time will be divided evenly between front porch, sync, and back porch. If the computer monitor does not use a 80% video and 20% blanking timing format (with blanking divided into thirds), a locked pattern will appear on the display, but it will not be centered.

You can center the pattern on the display by changing the timing of the vertical and horizontal front porch, back porch, and sync to the values the computer monitor has been designed to receive. You can change the timing of these parameters from the front panel of the CM2125.

Programming the sync time parameters

In order to change any of the timing parameters, you must enter a series of keystrokes that puts the CM2125 into the "programming" mode, you can start entering the timing values for the horizontal and vertical front porch, sync, and back porch parameters. The values you enter will appear in the right-hand display located above the digital display switch. The following key sequences are used to program vertical and horizontal sync time.

Programming vertical blanking parameters

In the program mode, the vertical sync frequency is automatically calculated from the horizontal sync frequency, vertical pixel number, and sync time parameters you enter. If you attempt to set the vertical sync frequency while in the programming mode, the error code "E4" will appear in the right-hand display. Refer to key pad drawing in Fig. 8-34.

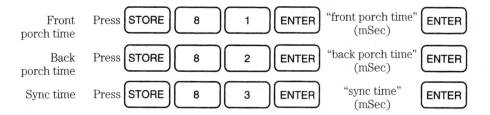

Front porch time	Press STORE	8	1	ENTER	"front porch time" (mSec)	ENTER
Back porch time	Press STORE	8	2	ENTER	"back porch time" (mSec)	ENTER
Sync time	Press STORE	8	3	ENTER	"sync time" (mSec)	ENTER

■ **8-34** *Keystrokes for programming vertical timing parameters.*

Programming horizontal blanking parameters

You must enter all three parameters (front porch, sync, and back porch) as a group for either vertical or horizontal sync timing before those parameters take effect. Once you have entered values for all three, you can go back and modify any of the three parameters individually. Note the key pad illustration in Fig. 8-35.

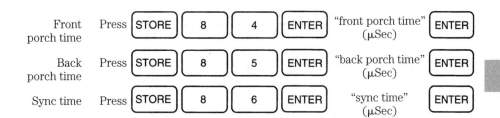

Front porch time	Press STORE	8	4	ENTER	"front porch time" (μSec)	ENTER
Back porch time	Press STORE	8	5	ENTER	"back porch time" (μSec)	ENTER
Sync time	Press STORE	8	6	ENTER	"sync time" (μSec)	ENTER

307

■ **8-35** *Keystrokes for programming horizontal timing parameters.*

If an "E9" appears in the right-hand display when you attempt to store a timing parameter, the "sync time" programming mode has not been enabled. Press Store, 8, 0, and then Enter and begin again.

Storing the new format

Once you have entered the timing parameters for the new setup, you can store them for future use. Storage locations 20–39 are available for user setups. All six timing parameters will be stored in the same memory location. The CM2125's memory is nonvolatile so the setup will not be lost when the unit is shut off or unplugged.

Checking a timing parameter

You may want to check the time you have entered for one of the parameters. This can be done by recalling the location where the parameter is stored. The value will appear in the right-hand display. You cannot recall the timing values of the setups stored in memory locations 0–19. If you attempt to do this, three 8's will appear in the right-hand display.

Programming examples

The following illustrations in Fig. 8-36 contains the timing parameters for a computer monitor. Follow steps 1–9 to program this information into the CM2125. In this example, the setup is stored in memory location 20. When Recall, 2, 0, and Enter are pressed, the CM2125 will generate signals with the timing values you have

Parameter	Horizontal	Vertical
Frequency	65.2 kHz	61.7 Hz
Resolution	1024 pixels	1024 pixels
Front porch	.360 μSec	.300 mSec
Sync	.770 μSec	.114 mSec
Back porch	.770 μSec	.114 mSec
Polarity	+	−

Set [H FREQ] to 65.2 kHz [H PIXEL] to 1024 [V FREQ] to 61.7 Hz [V PIXEL] to 1024

Press [STORE] [8] [0] [ENTER] ("scan time" program mode)

Press [STORE] [8] [1] [ENTER] [.] [3] [ENTER] (vertical front porch)

Press [STORE] [8] [2] [ENTER] [.] [1] [1] [4] [ENTER] (vertical back porch)

Press [STORE] [8] [3] [ENTER] [.] [1] [1] [4] [ENTER] (vertical sync)

Press [STORE] [8] [4] [ENTER] [.] [3] [6] [0] [ENTER] (horizontal front porch)

Press [STORE] [8] [5] [ENTER] [.] [7] [7] [0] [ENTER] (horizontal back porch)

Press [STORE] [8] [6] [ENTER] [.] [7] [7] [0] [ENTER] (horizontal sync)

Press [STORE] [2] [0] [ENTER] (Store in memory location 20)

■ 8-36 The keystrokes required to set the timing parameters for a computer monitor.

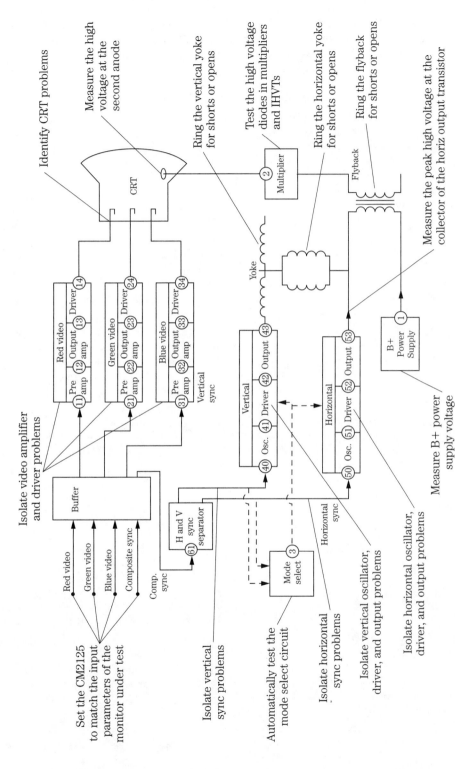

Identify CRT problems

Measure the high voltage at the second anode

Ring the vertical yoke for shorts or opens

Test the high voltage diodes in multipliers and IHVTs

Ring the horizontal yoke for shorts or opens

Ring the flyback for shorts or opens

Measure the peak high voltage at the collector of the horiz output transistor

Isolate video amplifier and driver problems

Set the CM2125 to match the input parameters of the monitor under test

Isolate vertical sync problems

Automatically test the mode select circuit

Isolate horizontal sync problems

Isolate vertical oscillator, driver, and output problems

Isolate horizontal oscillator, driver, and output problems

Measure B+ power supply voltage

CRT

Multiplier ②

Flyback

Yoke

Red video — Pre amp ⑪ Output amp ⑫ Driver ⑬⑭

Green video — Pre amp ㉑ Output amp ㉒ Driver ㉓㉔

Blue video — Pre amp ㉛ Output amp ㉜ Driver ㉝㉞

Vertical sync

Vertical — Osc. ⑩ Driver ㊶ Output ㊷㊸

Horizontal — Osc. ㊿ Driver ㊶ Output ㊾㊽

B+ Power Supply ①

Buffer

H and V sync separator ㉛

Mode select ③

Red video
Green video
Blue video
Composite sync

Comp. sync

Horizontal sync

309

■ **8-37** *Test point for isolating video amplifier problems in a computer monitor with the sencore CM2125 analyzer.*

programmed. If you will now refer to Fig. 8-37, you will see how easy it is to troubleshoot a computer monitor from the input connector to the CRT with the Sencore CM2125 Computer Monitor Analyzer.

Information in this chapter is courtesy of Sencore, Inc.

"Real world" microprocessor troubleshooting

9

This chapter leads off with a brief overview of microprocessor fundamental operation and functions.

Then we will look at some quick and easy tips for quickly pin pointing problems in the microprocessor with the Sencore SC3100 Waveform Analyzer. These applications include using the "Auto Tracking" digital functions and "Delta" measurement techniques.

We will also cover the computer automated Bus operation for the SC3100 scope. Then onto a Zenith microprocessor and video processor PIP circuit operation. And we'll finish up with some analog-to-digital conversion information.

Some microprocessor fundamentals

The microprocessor is constructed as a large-scale monolithic integrated (LSI) on a chip that functions as a central processing unit (CPU) that is the heart of a personal computer (PC) and other electronic devices. The MPU is made of the arithmetic-logic unit (ALU), instruction decoder and control, timing, accumulators, registers, address buffers, and input/output ports.

No doubt the integration of the main functions of the stored-program digital computer on a small silicon chip tops the twentieth century technical invention.

The MPU is a universal LSI circuit capable of replacing lots of standard logic IC chips and other expensive custom LSI circuits. In some cases, MPU's are performing functions that could not have been constructed in hard-wired logic. The MPU can do a wide variety of various functions with less trouble than arrays of logic devices.

The MPU is the computing component in a microcomputer and is usually coupled by input/output ports (I/O) to many devices to the outside world. Also, these external devices provide input signals and are controlled by the MPUs output. The MPU responds to inputs and produces outputs as set by the program or sequence of instructions which are stored in memory for the microprocessor. Even the basic microcomputer based system, the MPU requires more read only memory (ROM) to handle instructions, read/write memory (RAM) to handle data, input/output (I/O) ports, and a clock oscillator and timer.

MPUs are available with 8-, 16-, and 32-bit architecture. They should not be confused with microcontrollers (MCU) or single-chip microcomputers available with 4-, 8-, and 16-bit architectures. Both classes of devices have similar origins but different architecture and applications. The microcontroller has more of the functional elements of a complete computer on a single monolithic chip than the microprocessor, but the microcontroller does not have as high a performance. The microcontrollers are optimized for real-time, intensive applications such as those in automobile engine controls, motor controls, and PC keyboards.

The newer 32-bit microprocessor features instruction and data caches, relatively high-speed, on-chip memory for holding the most recently used instructions and data for future re-use by the CPU. A memory management unit (MMU) provides protection by allowing programmers to use system resources without considering the actual size of the memory in megabytes. The MMU also allows multiple programs and operating systems to be used simultaneously.

The electronics industry has accepted 8-, 16-, and 32-bit microprocessors. The most concentrated efforts relate to finding new applications for the 32-bit devices. MPUs designed and built by Motorola Semiconductor and Intel Corporation dominate the world market. These are the 68000 family processors from Motorola (68020 and 68030) and the iAPX286 and 386 from Intel (80286 and 80386).

The process of selecting a microprocessor for a new product is complicated by a lack of compatibility between the leading 32-bit products. Because of its compatibility with software developed for earlier and very popular Intel 8-bit and 16-bit microprocessors, many users want to stay with the Intel MPUs. However, the Motorola microprocessors have been successful in the popular workstation marketplace and are compatible with the more versatile Unix operating system.

Scoping the troubled microprocessor

Many technicians think that the microprocessor is difficult to troubleshoot. This is probably because you think of microprocessors as computers. Yet most microprocessors systems are used as controllers, not as computers. Examples of controllers are found in VCRs, microwave ovens, TV receivers, and most microprocessor-controlled test equipment. Once you know this, servicing microprocessors can seem a lot less difficult.

Let's start with a practical piece of advice: do not change the microprocessor too quickly. Time and time again, technicians admit that changing a microprocessor does not help a problem which looks like it "might" be caused by a defective micro P. However, microprocessors rarely fail. They are protected from static discharge and power line surges by filtered power supplies and by buffering transistors and ICs. The best line of attack is to leave it on your list of suspects, but be sure to interrogate all the other likely culprits first.

You can quickly isolate most microprocessor-related problems by using the Sencore SC3100 Waveform Analyzer, (see photo in Fig. 9-4), and five quick tests that will be covered a little later. First, let's see how a microprocessor used as a controller differs from one used as a computer, so that you can see why microprocessor servicing has very little to do with "computer servicing."

The computer vs the controller

The biggest difference between a microprocessor used in a computer and one used as a controller has to do with programming. A computer can be reprogrammed as needed, usually by entering information from a magnetic disk or tape. Refer to drawing in Fig. 9-1. The controller lives a relatively boring life—playing the same program over and over again. Reprogramming rarely happens once the system has left the factory. This main difference leads to several other differences as well. Note controller set-up in Fig. 9-2.

Computers (whether desk-top personals or large main frames) handle large volumes of assorted data. One batch may be numbers for a payroll, and the next may be a document from a word processor. Controllers, by comparison, deal with much smaller volumes of data. The data is repetitive and predictable, often representing inputs from simple switches and sensors within the system.

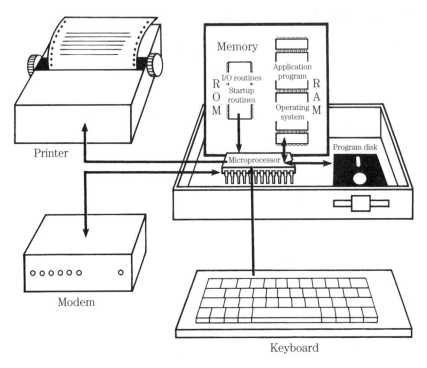

■ **9-1** *The main thing that sets a computer apart from a controller is that the computer gets new programs from a disk or tape. It also has external memory, and complex inputs and outputs.*

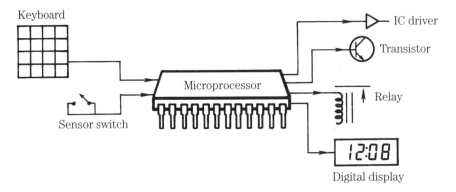

■ **9-2** *The microprocessor used as a controller is programmed one time at the factory. It uses simple switches and sensors for inputs, and transistors, ICs, relays, and digital displays for outputs.*

The microprocessor used in a computer connects to thousands or millions of bytes of external random-access-memory (RAM), each byte containing 8 memory locations. This RAM may require dozens of external memory chips. The microprocessor used as controller only needs a small amount of memory—often inside the microprocessor chip itself.

Lastly, a computer has complex inputs and outputs. Inputs come from typewriter keyboards, disk drives, or modems. Outputs feed printers, plotters, CRT displays, or other computers. The controller only has inputs from a few switches or sensors. It only feeds a few ICs, relays, and a simple digital display.

Servicing controller-type microprocessors does not need to be any more complicated than servicing any integrated circuit. The limited environment of the controller means you do not have to know many things you might think you need to know.

The simplified system

One of the biggest differences between servicing computers and controllers is that you do not have to worry about software problems in controllers. You do not need to know programming or ASCII codes. If you suspect a software problem, you have only one option; change the program chip.

Second, you do not have to sort through rows and rows of memory chips. This means you do not need a $20,000 logic analyzer or an 8-channel scope to view each byte of data separately in order to locate a defective memory location. If an internal memory location is bad, you have to change the microprocessor. See Fig. 9-3.

Finally, the controller has limited inputs and outputs—generally no more than 8 of each. You can test each one separately to confirm whether the problem is coming from inside the microprocessor or from an external component.

Once you stop worrying about software, memory, and complicated interface systems, the microprocessor takes on a whole new look. You can find most problems by testing the following items using the Sencore SC3100 Waveform Analyzer (see Fig. 9-4):

☐ The power supply.
☐ The clock.
☐ The input and output lines.
☐ The reset circuits.
☐ The grounds.

Let's now look at the ways to do these tests with the SC3100.

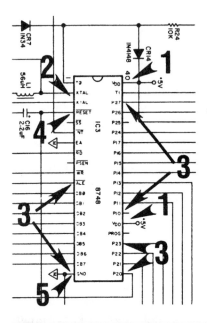

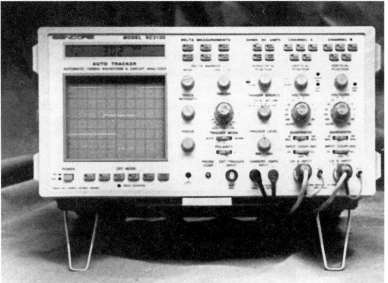

■ **9-3** *Most defects are caused by problems outside the microprocessor. Test the microprocessor inputs and outputs in this sequence to isolate external problems before substituting with a new one.*

■ **9-4** Locating a short on a microprocessor PC board.

1: Testing the power supply

Always test the power supply(s) first, whether the problem is a totally dead micro or one with erratic operation. Start with the DC level. Press channel "A" Digital Readout "DCV" button, so that you can monitor the dc level, while you watch for ac problems on the CRT.

Touch the channel A probe to the power supply pin. Glance up at the digital display to confirm the dc voltage (usually 5 to 10 volts) is correct. Your voltage should be within about 0.2 volts of the correct level.

But, do not stop at this point, as noise often enters the microprocessor through the power supply, causing it to act erratically. Look at the CRT to confirm the signal is clean. Press the "PPV" button to measure its actual value. You should see less than 0.1 volts of ripple.

You may see 60 Hz ripple from a bad filter or regulator. Or you may may see high frequency digital noise from another stage, which can cause the micro to freeze as the noise pulses intermix with the normal input signals. If so, suspect a bad filter or decoupling capacitor on the power supply line, or a bad IC on the same line which is loading the supply.

If the microprocessor has more than one power supply pin, check each one in the same manner.

2: Test the clock

A problem in the crystal-controlled clock can cause intermittent operation. Watch for the following conditions as you probe one, then the other, of the microprocessor pins connected to the clock input pins, usually coming from the crystal.

First reach over and press the "freq" button. The SC3100 auto-ranged frequency function displays the operating frequency with six full digits of resolution, so that you can be sure of the results. If the frequency is wrong, suspect a defective crystal.

Next, press the "PPV" button, and look up at the digital readout to confirm the signal has the correct amplitude. Although the crystal might be putting out the correct frequency, the micro may not know it, because the amplitude is just below the point that gives reliable operation.

The last check is a look at the CRT waveform to make sure the clock does not include extra "glitch" signals. These extra signals may cause the microprocessor to intermittently skip a program step, or may cause the whole system to run to fast. The clock should be a clean sine or square wave.

3: Test the input & output lines

Inputs

Generally, input defects affect only a few functions. Try every function controlled by the micro and note which ones work correctly and which ones have troubles. Then, determine which input pins are associated with the bad functions. For example, one or two switches might provide an input to a single function and not be used with any other of the micro's inputs.

Connect the SC3100 scope probe to the pins associated with the questionable functions and observe the trace as you cycle the input switches. Press the "DCV" button, and note the dc level with the switch contact open and with it closed to be sure the level properly changes between the "one" and the "zero" logic levels. Be sure that neither level falls into the "undefined" area between the two levels, or the micro may not be able to decide whether a high or a low condition exists. Refer to the drawing in Fig. 9-5.

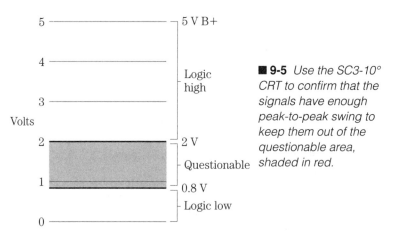

■ **9-5** *Use the SC3-10° CRT to confirm that the signals have enough peak-to-peak swing to keep them out of the questionable area, shaded in red.*

Check contact resistance or pull-up resistors if the levels are wrong. Watch for noise or glitches which may cause the micro to interpret a single switch operation as two or more separate switch closures. Check the switch contacts, decoupling capacitors, and switch buffer circuits to isolate noise conditions.

Outputs

Next, test all data (output) lines to be sure one is not stuck at logic high or logic low. Touch your probe to each microprocessor output pin, one at a time. Do not worry that the signal shows a blur of lines—seemingly out of sync. This is simply because of the asynchronous (random) data coming from the microprocessor.

Set the SC3100's vertical input to the "dc-coupled" mode to confirm that the low points on the waveform are below the minimum level for a "zero" and the high points are above the minimum level for a "one." Suspect a defective pull-up resistor or IC outside the micro if the signals are falling between logic levels.

If the signals at a pin remain cemented to ground or to B+, look at the schematic to see when that pin is used. You might have to trace the pin to a relay or an IC to find out which function(s) it controls. Then, force the microprocessor into a function that uses this pin by pressing a button or cycling a sensor.

If the signal at the pin does not change, isolate the pin from the external circuits by carefully removing the solder between it and the foils on the printed circuit board. Connect the SC3100 to the isolated pin and again check for toggling. If the pin toggles with its load removed, the problem is most probably outside the micro. An external component is holding the pin high or low. Isolate each component on that line, one at a time, until the line toggles. Then replace the defective part.

If the pin remains stuck after being isolated, it's beginning to look more like a defective microprocessor, but do not unsolder the legs yet. You have got two more checks to make.

4: Test the reset circuit

Microprocessors need an external reset pulse at turn-on. Without the reset pulse, the microprocessor starts in the middle of the program, resulting in totally unpredictable operation.

Take advantage of the SC3100's CRT to check the reset pulse. Set the trigger "Source" switch to channel A, the Trigger "Mode" switch to "Norm" and the Trigger "Level" control to zero in the center of its rotation. Refer to circuit shown in Fig. 9-6.

Connect the device containing the microprocessor to a switched ac outlet strip, so that you can turn the power off and on. Do not rely on the device's power switch, since the microprocessor often receives power independent of the power switch. In fact, many "power" switches are simply one of the microprocessor inputs, and do not interrupt power.

Turn off the power and connect the SC3100 channel A probe to the reset pin. The SC3100 CRT should show no trace. Watch the CRT as you apply power to the system. If you see the trace flash across the CRT, you know a reset pulse occurred and triggered the SC3100 sync circuits. If there is no trace, repair the reset circuits.

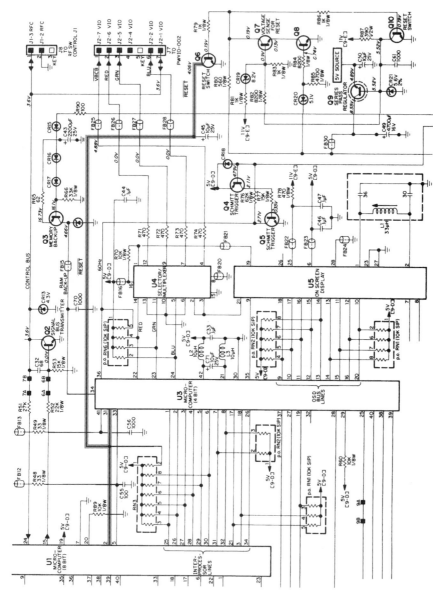

■ **9-6** Watch for a reset pulse when you first apply power. Defective reset circuits make the microprocessor appear defective, because it did not start at the beginning of the program.

"Real world" microprocessor troubleshooting

5: Check the grounds

Now, the microprocessor is highly suspect. But, do not unsolder it yet. First, check every grounded pin. Each should show zero volt dc and zero volts ac. If any grounded pin has a signal on it, it will cause the microprocessor to act as though the micro itself is bad. The presence of a signal tells you there is an open in the grounded path—either a broken P.C. foil or a poor solder connection. Repairing the bad ground will probably clear up your problems.

If the grounds are good, you are ready to substitute the microprocessor. You have already confirmed that all the inputs and outputs are normal. And, as we mentioned earlier, one of these other circuits will usually be the cause of the poor operation.

Using the SC3100 Auto-Tracking digital functions

The Auto-Tracking digital tests provide ac voltage, dc voltage, and frequency measurements of the signal applied to either the channel A or B inputs at the push of a button. These digital parameter measurements are called Auto-Tracking because the readout constantly and automatically follows the input signal without you needing to adjust any controls or set measurement cursors. In fact, the signal does not even need to be displayed on the CRT to use the Auto-Tracking tests. The signals for both the CRT display and digital readout are applied through the same probe.

Most of your waveform measurements can be done using either the Auto-Tracking digital tests or the SC3100's Delta tests. The Auto-Tracking digital tests measure parameters of the entire waveform, while the Delta tests are used to measure a portion of the waveform. The SC3100 measurement buttons are shown in Fig. 9-7.

■ **9-7** *The Auto-Tracking™ digital tests provide peak-to-peak, dc voltage, frequency, ACV and dBm measurements at the push of a button.*

Digital readout & CRT controls

The signal takeoff to the digital circuits (both the Auto-Tracking and Delta tests) is made ahead of the CRT controls, such as the vertical and horizontal position controls, vertical and horizontal vernier controls, and input coupling switches. This allows you to set the CRT display to any convenient size without affecting the digital tests. Because the digital tests are independent of the circuits, they are also much more accurate than CRT-based measurements.

The Auto-Tracking digital tests operate properly without the CRT trace locked or displayed. This allows you to use the digital readings to help set the CRT controls.

The digital frequency and peak-to-peak readings, for example, can be used to set the TIME/DIV and VOLTS/DIV controls.

Note: The digital tests for channel A and channel B share some common circuitry but also use some different circuitry. While the two channels are closely matched, each channel may show a slightly different reading if you were to connect both probes to the same test point. This is due to the normal tolerances, and is similar to the difference you would see if you used two different pieces of test equipment.

Voltage measurements (dc)

You can measure the dc voltage at the test point by simply pushing the "DCV" button of the corresponding channel. The DCV function is fully autoranged and operates independent of the CRT display. You may adjust the CRT display to any convenient size or set the input coupling switch to any position (even "GND") without affecting the dc reading.

The dc function measures average dc voltage. Average dc voltage is the same value that is indicated on schematics and is the power supply or B+ voltage, for example, that a DVM measures. Sometimes you may need to measure the instantaneous or absolute dc + ac voltage at a waveform point, such as the logic high or low level of a digital signal.

In addition to the 10X Low Capacity probe, you can use an optional direct probe, or a dc voltage probe to supply signals to the scope inputs. The dc voltage probe allows you to measure the dc voltage at a test point independent from the CRT input and also allows you to use the optional probes to measure dc voltages higher than 2 KV.

To measure dc volts

1. Connect the dc signal to the CH A or CH B dc volt jack.
2. Press the channel A or B "DCV" digital readout button.
3. Read the digital display for correct voltage.

Peak-to-peak voltage measurements

The SC3100 provides a direct readout of the peak-to-peak amplitude of any signal applied to the input. You just press the "VPP digital readout" button for the corresponding channel. Specially designed circuits allow you to make VPP measurements on low duty cycle, low frequency signals to 20 Hz as well as high frequency signals up to 120 MHz.

Delta measurement applications

The applications of a waveform and circuit analyzer/oscilloscope such as the Sencore SC3100 "Auto tracker" are limitless. Most measurements can be made faster and more accurately using the SC3100. Let's now look at some of these applications that you can use for digital/logic troubleshooting.

Determining logic levels

Digital circuits operate with logic high and logic low signal levels. These logic levels must be correct or the circuit will confuse one level for another. You can easily determine if a signal is at the correct logic level by using the Delta DCV function.

A questionable area exists where the digital circuits cannot determine if the signal is a high level or a logic low level. This questionable area depends upon the type of logic. The drawing in Fig. 9-8 shows the logic low, high, and questionable areas for the most common types of logic circuits, TTL, and CMOS.

TTL circuits operate with a supply voltage of 5 volts and have a questionable area from 0.8 to 2.8 volts. Levels that are 0.8 volts or less are a low, while levels 2.8 volts and higher are a high.

CMOS devices operate over a wider range of power supply voltages. Because of this the questionable area for CMOS logic is a

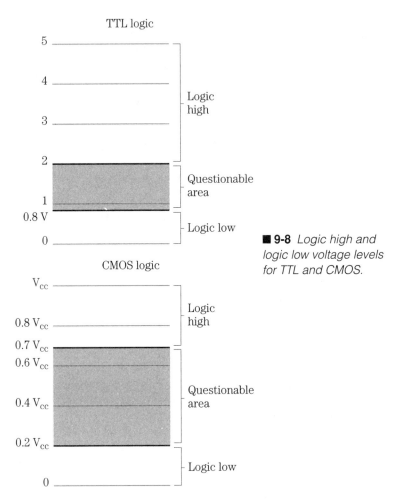

TTL logic

5
4
— Logic high
3
2
— Questionable area
1
0.8 V
— Logic low
0

CMOS logic

V_{cc}
— Logic high
$0.8 V_{cc}$
$0.7 V_{cc}$
$0.6 V_{cc}$
— Questionable area
$0.4 V_{cc}$
$0.2 V_{cc}$
— Logic low
0

■ **9-8** *Logic high and logic low voltage levels for TTL and CMOS.*

percentage of the power supply voltage, rather than a fixed voltage level. The questionable area for CMOS logic is between 20% and 70% of V_{cc}. If a 10-volt power supply is used, for example, the questionable area would be between 2 volts and 7 volts. A logic high would be 7 volts or higher and a logic low would be 2 volts and less for this example.

To determine logic levels

1. Properly lock in the waveforms on the CRT display.
2. Set the TIME/DIV and VOLTS/DIV Controls to display the entire waveform. Use the "Auto" position, if desired.
3. Press the Delta DCV button of the channel corresponding to the signal to be measured.

■ Table 9-1 Signal tracing the circuit in Figure 9-8A with short from conductor between pin 6 and pin 9 to +5 volts.

Connect pulser to IC pin	Connect probe to IC pin	Probe indication	Conclusion
1	8	Blinks	
2	8	Blinks	Gate 1 OK
4	8	Off	
5	8	Off	
9	8	Off	
Isolated 9	8	Blinks	Gate 3 OK
4	Isolated 6	Blinks	
5	Isolated 6	Blinks	Gate 2 OK External short to +5 V

■ Table 9-2 Signal tracing the circuit in Figure 9-8A with open in conductor between pin 6 and pin 9.

Connect pulser to IC pin	Connect probe to IC pin	Probe indication	Conclusion
1	8	Blinks	
2	8	Blinks	Gate 1 OK
4	8	Off	
5	8	Off	
4	6	Blinks	
5	6	Blinks	Gate 2 OK
9	8	Blinks	Gate 3 OK
4	9	Off	
5	9	Off	External open between pins 6 and 9

4. Adjust the "DCV" delta marker control to position the dc marker at the logic low or logic high point on the waveform.

5. Confirm that the voltage displayed in the digital readout matches the logic level shown in Fig. 9-8.

Measuring time delay of logic pulses

The Delta Time function of the SC3100 simplifies measuring the time difference or delay between two signals. Setting the beginning and ending points of the intensified Delta Bar on one trace also sets the beginning and ending points of the Delta Bar on the other trace.

To measure the time delay between two signals you simply set the Delta Bar to highlight the time between the start of one cycle on one channel and the start of the same cycle on the other channel. The digital display shows the time difference of the two points, which is the time delay between them.

Determining the time delay

1. Properly lock the waveforms on the CRT display.
2. Set the TIME/DIV and VOLTS/DIV controls to display both waveforms. Use the "auto" position if desired.
3. Position the waveforms so that an identifiable transition, such as the start of a cycle, is visible for both.
4. Press the Delta Time button.
5. Adjust the intensity control for good contrast between the Delta Bar and the remainder of the trace.
6. Adjust the "Begin" and "End," delta marker controls to intensify the on-time of the waveform.
7. Adjust the "Begin" delta marker control until the start of the Delta Bar is positioned exactly at the selected transition in one of the waveforms.
8. Adjust the "End" delta marker control until the end of the Delta Bar is positioned exactly at the same transition point in the other waveform.
9. Read the digital display to determine the amount of time delay between the two channels.

Setting a desired time delay

Many adjustments, however, require you to set pulse width time or adjust the time delay between two signals. The Delta Time function can simplify these adjustments.

Use the Delta Bar to "preset" the time window. Then adjust the circuit so that pulse width is the same as the intensified area, or until the required signal transition falls within the intensified area of the Delta Bar.

Adjusting a circuit to a predetermined time

1. Properly lock the waveforms on the CRT display.
2. Set the TIME/DIV and VOLTS/DIV controls for the desired waveform display. Use the "auto" positions if desired.
3. Position the waveform(s) so that the desired interval is visible.
4. Press the "Delta Time" button.

5. Adjust the intensity control for good contrast between the Delta Bar and the remainder of the trace.

6. Adjust the "Begin" delta marker control until the Delta Bar begins at the start of the waveform interval to be adjusted.

7. Adjust the "End" delta marker control until the digital display reads the desired time.

8. Adjust the circuit until the waveform just fills the area intensified by the Delta Bar, or until the signal transition falls within the intensified area.

Measuring phase shift

The Delta Frequency function provides a fast and accurate method for determining the phase between two signals that are the same frequency.

Measuring phase shift is similar to measuring the time delay between two signals. The time delay is converted to the equivalent frequency by pressing the Delta Freq button. This frequency is then compared to the frequency of one full cycle. The ratio of these two frequencies is the fractional part of 360 degrees represented by the phase shift between channels.

327

Using Delta VPP to locate interference

Sometimes the digital peak-to-peak reading is significantly higher than the waveform that is displayed on the CRT. This is an indication that the fast digital peak-to-peak circuits are detecting a noise spike or glitch that is not noticed on the scope's CRT. You can use the Delta VPP function to locate the portion of the waveform that contains the interference, because it only measures the amplitude of the intensified portion of the trace.

To locate a glitch

1. Lock in the waveform display on the CRT.

2. Position the Delta Bar to cover a narrow portion of the waveform. The digital display should read very close to the approximate amplitude indicated by the CRT. If it does not, you are already highlighting the portion of the trace that contains the interference.

3. Using the delta marker controls, slowly widen the area of the trace that is intensified by the Delta Bar while watching the digital display.

4. As soon as the meter reading jumps to a higher voltage, you have just highlighted the portion of the trace that contains the noise or glitch.

5. You can now use the CRT controls to expand this portion of the trace to make the interference visible.

Note: Delta VPP readings that randomly change are caused by random noise spikes, or by interference that is not synchronized to the triggered waveform.

Computer automated bus operation

The Sencore SC3100 can be used for computer controlled automated testing. Under computer control a program can be developed that automatically sets up any of the front panel measurement controls and reads the digital display. The front panel controls that are not computer controlled are power, delta markers, focus, intensity, trigger level, vertical position, vertical vernier, horizontal position, and horizontal vernier.

The SC3100 can be used with either IEEE-488 or RS232 control. Use the optional IB72 accessory for IEEE-488 operation and optional IB78 accessory for RS323 control. Both accessories connect to the INTERFACE ACCESSORY jack located on the rear of the SC3100.

The SC3100 functions as a Talker/Listener. In the listener mode, the computer can set the SC3100's front panel controls via the interface bus. As a talker the SC3100 sends all of the digital measurements to the controller on command.

Hooking up the controller

The signal at the SC3100's interface accessory jack must be translated to the desired standard by one of the Sencore interface accessories. The interface accessory is connected between the controller and the SC3100. The interface accessory connects to the controller using a standard IEEE488 or RS232 cable.

When used on an IEEE-488 bus system the SC3100 must be assigned an address that is separate from other addresses on the system. This allows the controller to select which instrument it is communicating with. The instructions provided with the IB72 provide additional connection information and details on setting the address. A special address is not needed when using the IB78 RS232 interface bus accessory.

Connecting the SC3100 to an automated test system

1. Remove the power from the SC3100, the interface accessory, and the computer/controller.

2. Set the slide switches on the rear of the IB72 IEEE-488 bus interface accessory for the desired address. This step is not needed with the IB78.

3. Connect the interface accessory's male DIN connector to the interface accessory jack located on the rear of the SC3100.

4. Connect the proper cable from the Interface Accessory to the computer.

5. Supply power to all units in the automated system and verify that all units are on.

Zenith video microprocessor

The IC6000 Zenith video control microprocessor (see circuit in Fig. 9-9), is a 52 pin CMOS processor in a DIP package. Keyboard commands are tied directly to the microprocessor at pins 41 and 43 thur 49. IR commands are tied to pin 36. Control of brightness, color, contrast, tint, and sharpness is at pins 30, 29, 24, 22, and 9 respectively. The output of these pins is coupled to IC1200, the video processor for controlling these functions.

Video processor/PIP

IC1200 (see Fig. 9-10) is the audio IF, video IF, sync separator Horizontal/Vertical drive, RGB generator/driver, and RGB mixer for the on-screen displays. The LSI (Large Scale Integrated) circuitry allows combining a great many functions into one chip. All consumer controls are addressed through the microprocessor and sent to the video processing IC as pulse width modulated signals. The horizontal of the sync/scan processing circuit employs a dual PLL loop system with a horizontal coincidence detector to control the gain of the phase detector for optimum performance. The coincidence detector is used for fast signal acquisition during channel change or loss of signal. The vertical section of IC1200 employs a narrow range countdown circuit. The operating range for vertical synchronization is 60 Hz ± 10%. This system differs from previous circuits; in the absence of a signal, the default vertical frequency is 60 Hz. This will result in a minimal change of vertical size and on-screen menu positions in the absence of a signal. Vertical sync/drive out is on pin 28, while horizontal drive out is on pin 23.

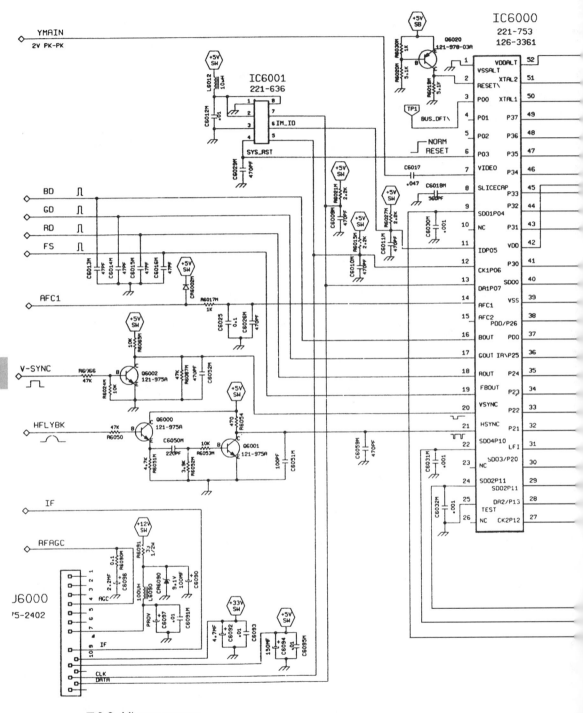

■ 9-9 *Microprocessor.*

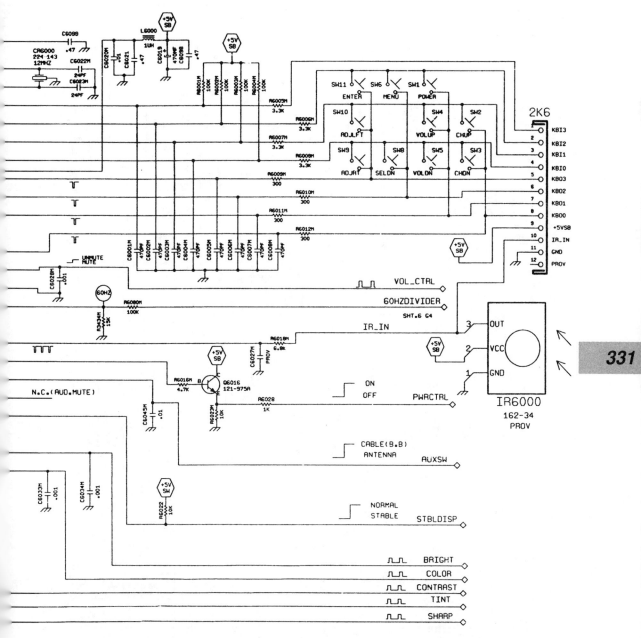

331

Video processor/PIP

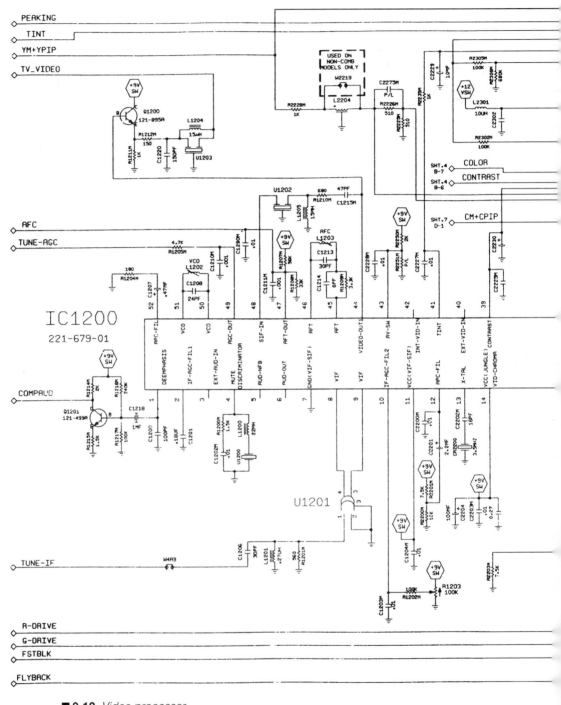

■ 9-10 *Video processor.*

"*Real world" microprocessor troubleshooting*

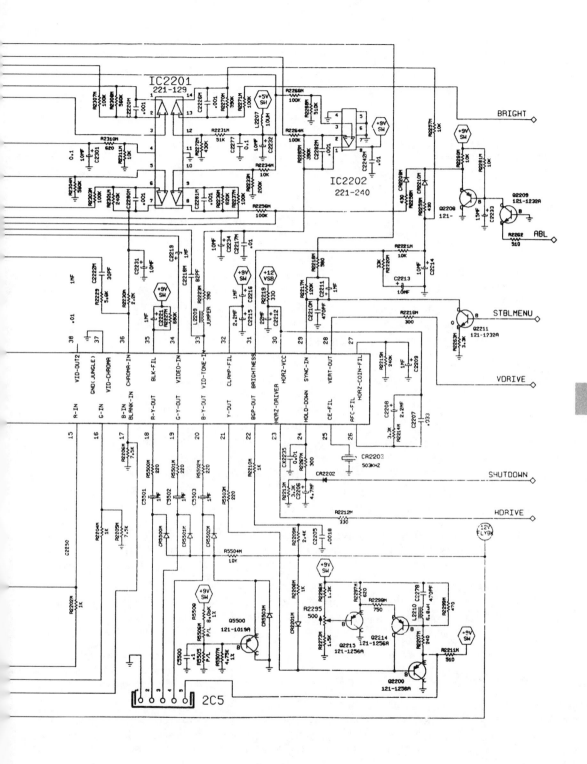

The luminance processing section is similar to the current Zenith C10 circuit. Video IF from the tuner comes in on pin 8 and 9. Video is processed by the IC and exits at pin 44. It passes through emitter follower Q1200 and is coupled to pin 3 of IC2200. See Fig. 9-11. It exits IC2200 on pin 14 and is coupled through emitter follower Q2210. For models without comb filter, the signal passes through transistors Q2203, Q2204, Q2205, and Q2206 before re-entering IC1200 on pin 34. On these models with comb filter and PIP, the output of emitter follower Q2212 is processed through DL2200 before being applied to pins 1 and 3 of 4D9 on the PIP module. PIP video is processed through transistors Q2206 and Q2207 and is applied to pin 6 of 4D9. The main and PIP luminance signal exits the PIP module on 4C9 pin 3 and enters IC1200 on pin 34. The main and PIP chroma signal exits the PIP module on 4C9 pin 5 and enters IC1200 on pin 36. The Y out signal is on pin 21. R-Y, G-Y, and B-Y out are on pins 18, 19, and 20. Sound IF input is on pin 48. Composite audio output on pin 48. Composite audio output is on pin 1. Video and audio switching is included in the video processor. Switching is controlled by pin 43.

Video output

As with other Zenith C series chassis, the video output module is a break away portion of the main printed circuit board. Use care during this operation to avoid damage to the circuit board foil pattern. Luminance information from the main module comes in on connector 5C2 pin 1. Chroma information comes in on connector 5C2 pins 2, 3, and 4. Luminance is processed by transistor Q5106 before being applied to the emitter of the three output transistors.

Chroma is processed by transistors Q5100, Q5101, and Q5102 before being applied to the base of the output transistors. Three drive controls are used to adjust the Black and White tracking. R5103 is the Blue drive control, R5104 is the Red drive control and R5105 is the Green drive control: B+ of +9 volts and +245 volts enter on connector 5A3 pins 2 and 3. Filament voltage for the CRT is on connector 5F2.

Analog to digital conversion

When an analog signal, either a voltage or a current, has to be expressed in digital form, the conversion is very often first done by transforming the analog signal into an analog time interval. The analog time interval, in turn, can be easily measured with a clock.

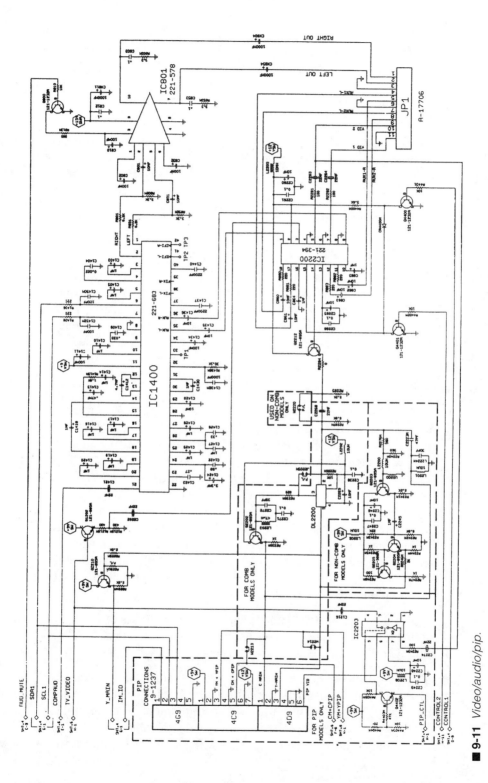

■ **9-11** *Video/audio/pip.*

Analog to digital conversion

The time displayed by the clock, when the clock period is correctly chosen, is also a digital expression of the analog value. Another way to do an analog-to-digital conversion (A/D conversion) is to increment or decrement a digitally controlled and known analog signal and to compare it with the analog signal to be digitized. At coincidence of both signals, the digital value of both signals is equal.

The sophistication of an A/D converter will depend on required performance such as the following:

- [ ] Accuracy
- [ ] Speed
- [ ] Noise Immunity
- [ ] Polarity Handling
- [ ] Dynamic Range

The reverse process is the digital-to-analog conversion (D/A conversion). A digital signal or multi-bit word has to produce an analog voltage or current. The design considerations for both D/A and A/D are very similar, except that the noise problem does not exist for the D/A conversion.

The staircase converter

A staircase converter circuit is shown in Fig. 9-12. The +V input is the analog signal to be digitized. A clock gives a start signal that causes a staircase ramp generator to begin to generate a 1 millivolt step with each clock pulse. Assume that the input = +5.753 V. This voltage will be inverted by the impedance converter and then applied to the comparator. After 5753 clock pulses, the staircase ramp will have a value of +5753 mV. The comparator will detect the zero crossing at point A and will stop the clock. The display will indicate 5753 clock pulses, or with a decimal point, a value of 5.753. The measurement resolution depends only on the magnitude of each staircase ramp step. For a higher resolution, each step could be 100 microvolts or less.

The staircase converter cannot handle + and − inputs directly. Either a + and a − ramp must be generated, or one inverting and one non-inverting impedance converter must be provided in the input.

The disadvantage of this type of A/D converter is its low conversion speed and sensitivity to noise. For example, assume that the dc voltage to be measured has an ac component, such as ripple from a power supply. As shown in Fig. 9-13, coincidence of the input voltage value and staircase ramp will not always happen at the

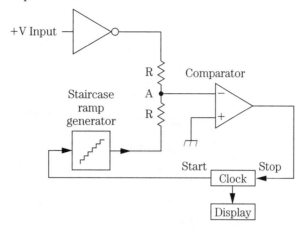

Impedance converter

+V Input

Comparator

R

Staircase
ramp
generator

A

R

Start   Stop

Clock

Display

■ **9-12** *Simple staircase A/D converter.*

same level for each measurement. A difference between two measurements can be as high as the peak-to-peak value of the ripple voltage. A possible improvement would be to connect a low-pass filter in the signal input. However, such a filter would considerably reduce the speed at which measurements can be made.

A/D converter

If A/D conversions must be repeated at a fast rate, such as hundreds, or possibly thousands-per-second, the staircase converter would be too slow. For a 3½ digit display, the staircase converter may need up to 1999 clock pulses. The basic principle in the successive approximation ADC is the unknown voltage (input) compared to a sequence of known reference voltages developed by an internal digital-to-analog converter. The value of the comparison voltage at any step is dependent on the result of previous comparisons.

A simple ADC

The comparison of the input voltage and the reference voltages, which are stepped in binary-coded-decimal (BCD) weighted voltage sets, is made at point A, which is also the input of a comparator. Each voltage set is generated in a 8, 4, 2, 1 sequence and collectively represents a significant digit of the display. The output of the comparator drives the switches that turn the BCD voltage steps on and off. If the switched-in BCD level is more than the input, it is rejected and the next step is checked.

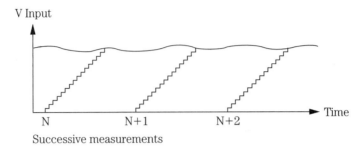

■ 9-13 *Effect of noise on successive measurements.*

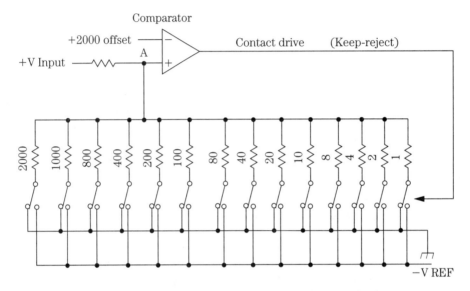

■ 9-14 *Successive approximation A/D converter with negative input capability.*

For example, as shown in Fig. 9-14, if the input voltage is 165.5 mV, the ADC first compares the input value with the 1000 mV step. Since the input value is lower, the 1000 mV step is rejected. The input is compared with the next step voltage, in this case 800 mV. The 800 mV step is also rejected for the same reason. This comparison shows that the input is higher so the 100 mV step is saved. The next step voltage is now added to the 100 mV step just saved and compared with the input. The total of 100 mV and 80 mV is more than the input voltage, so the 80 mV step is rejected. Then the next step, now 40 mV, is added to the 100 mV previously kept and the new comparison is made at 140 mV.

The input voltage is more than 140 mV so the 40 mV is also kept and now the reference is 140 mV. This process continues through steps 20 mV, 10 mV, 8 mV, etc. The remaining approximation is easy to follow. All other steps will be rejected. The display logic now checks which BCD steps have been retained and digitally expressed the value of the analog input.

The difference between the converted 165 mV and the known input of 165.5 mV is known as quantizing error. This error results because there is no combination of step voltages in this particular ADC that will yield the precise value, that is, the ADC cannot "resolve" the value of 0.5 mV. While another ADC with greater resolution could be used, it may not be as fast.

Effect of noise

If there is noise on the input to the ADC, it will destroy the integrity of the reading. Any ripple voltage superimposed on the input will also produce a reading error. This tells us that we must hold the input voltage constant before making the analog-to-digital conversion: there must be a good sample and hold circuit in front of the ADC.

Portions of this chapter are courtesy of Sencore.

339

Signature analysis techniques

10

This chapter introduces microprocessor system troubleshooting by the signature analysis (SA) technique developed by Hewlett-Packard. It begins with the need for and concept of SA testing methods. Next, design testability and fundamental techniques will be explained.

The chapter continues with how SA can make field troubleshooting much easier for the technician, and then describes the Hewlett-Packard SA test for microprocessor-based systems.

The chapter concludes with how free-running SA testing techniques simplify microprocessor troubleshooting. See Table 10-1.

341

■ Table 10-1 A look-up fault table.

5 Vdc signature	Course of action
UCF4	**ROM is good. Proceed to RAM check.**
U789	**Replace hybrid processor A15U13.**
05C7	U34
095A	U3
0F25	U31
2986	U35
2HP3	U29
31HP	U32
34P5	U33
394U	U5
512U	U2
5PUC	U36
61A0	U7
6HF5	U6
77A0	U4
78FP	U1
CH44	U30
CPUI	U8

Signature analysis concepts

To keep troubleshooting in step with the state-of-the-art, Hewlett-Packard developed the SA technique as well as a signature analyzer test instrument line for component-level troubleshooting of microprocessor-based devices. A signature analyzer detects and displays the unique digital signatures associated with the data nodes in a circuit under test. By comparing these actual signatures to the correct ones, a troubleshooter can back-trace to a faulty node. By designing or retrofitting SA into digital products, electronics manufacturers can provide test and field service procedures for component-level repair without needing to stock expensive exchange boards. Thus, the total microprocessor system must be designed with SA in mind.

The current trend in digital system design is toward bus-structured machines that rely heavily on LSI components, such as microprocessors, ROMs, RAMs, and various interface devices. Because interaction between bus devices is controlled, much of the dedicated hardware logic previously associated with performing complex signal- and data-processing tasks yields to software data manipulation. However, when logic signals are replaced by data bit streams in, say, a microprocessor system, the functional operating characteristics of the circuit are not necessarily associated with specific hardware components and are much more difficult to characterize and define because of the long complex data streams that are present. Another complication is that many of the devices connected to the bus are bidirectional and can input and output data on the same bus pins.

Unlike random logic circuits, all but the most trivial microprocessor systems defy fault analysis unless they are heavily supported by documentation and extensive use of circuit isolation techniques. For this reason, servicing of microprocessor sections of equipment has been handled by exchange of boards, and most service technicians have been reluctant to troubleshoot microprocessors. Even when an experienced service technician is armed with logic analyzers and other specialized service instruments, finding faulty components in a microprocessor or bus system requires detailed knowledge of the circuitry and can be quite time-consuming.

In many cases, the test instruments may provide either too much or too little information. Generally, what is required for component-level field repair is a means of compressing the long data streams in a system running at its normal operating speed into a concise, easy-to-interpret readout. The readout need not tell any more than whether a particular circuit node is operating correctly.

Until SA was developed, the best way for finding component-level faults was by a technique known as "transition counting," where the number of changes of logic state or node during a given time interval were counted and compared to the number recorded for the same node on a known good circuit. Transition counting, however, has practical limitations. An external stimulus is often required to provide logic activity on circuit test nodes. Also, numerous transitions must occur to produce statistically usable information, because counts produced are not time dependent. In other words, the correct number of transitions might occur, but at the wrong time.

The basic makeup of SA is *data compression* and *circuit-generated stimulus*. Both of these features exist, to some degree, in transition counting, but in SA they are refined in a way that gives better overall performance in terms of locating faults in complex digital circuitry.

Data compression is accomplished in the signature analyzer by probing a logic test node from which data is input for each and every circuit clock cycle that occurs within a circuit-controlled time window. Any change in the behavior of this node—even a transition that is one clock cycle late or skewed with respect to the clock—will produce a different signature, indicating a probable circuit malfunction. A single logic state change on a node is all that is necessary to produce a meaningful signature. And, because of the compression algorithm chosen, measurement intervals exceeding 2^{16} clock cycles will still produce valid, repeatable signatures.

The signal that causes the node to produce a signature is the *stimulus*. In SA, the stimulus is supplied by the product itself. By doing this, a controlled environment can be created wherein selected circuit portions can be tested independently of others while maintaining full dynamic operation. Additionally, synchronization and measurement intervals for the signature analyzer can be controlled by the product under test. In microprocessor systems, the stimulus is nothing more than a program (generally in ROM) that exercises the rest of the system. If the data manipulative capabilities of microprocessors are used advantageously, generating good stimulus patterns that exercise individual devices in the product is usually not very difficult. Indeed, it is often true that the more complex the system the greater the benefit derived from using SA.

The technique can take much of the uncertainty out of trouble-shooting microprocessors and other bus-structured products.

Equipment test design

Electronic equipment needs good testability. For example, breaking a system's circuitry into minimally interdependent modules, each on its own PC board, makes for a good design. This makes the unit easier to understand and repair than a massive jumble of interwoven functional circuits on a few large PC boards. Usually, micro-processor systems generally lend themselves well to orderly partitioning. However, when SA is included in their design, large boards become much less of a servicing disadvantage, and the savings in the overall production costs of the equipment can be substantial.

Another useful concept is *self-test* or *performance verification*. This usually is in the form of exercises and measurements performed by the product on itself to check out as much of its circuitry as practical. The self-test sequence can be initiated automatically when the power is turned on, or by pushing a test button on the front panel.

A typical sequence results in a go/no go "confidence" indication visible to the operator. Additionally, the self-test can provide some degree of failure diagnostic information if so desired. In most cases, it is not possible or cost-effective to self-diagnose beyond the board or function level.

The main advantages of self-test are as follows:

1. Alerting the operator to a possible operational problem.
2. Assuring the operator that even though you may be having trouble getting the unit to perform, it's really OK. This advantage can save the frustrated technician from sending a good (but probably complex) module in for unneeded service or repair.

Once a unit is found to be faulty, it must be repaired or discarded. Since most electronic products are not yet disposable, the objective is to find the fault and fix it. If the equipment has been designed with good serviceability in mind, almost any fault can be localized quickly and repaired. This is where the payoff can come from a good application of SA, partitioning, and documentation.

The design SA capability is usually a shared responsibility between the design and service engineers. There is actually no clear line between them when it comes to designing a good serviceability product. Usually, the designer takes care of making sure the hardware is compatible with good SA practices, and the service engineer prepares the service documentation. Both participate in writing the test stimulus programs and overall troubleshooting strategy.

As with any new concept, it follows that the learning curve principle applies to how effectively a design engineer can utilize SA in a new product design. The "tricks" he picks up from the first SA application will likely make the second one easier and of even greater benefit for that equipment.

The signature analyzer

The signature analyzer uses a unique data compression technique that reduces any long, complex data stream pattern on a logic node into a four-digit signature. When placed on a logic node whose correct signature is known (having been determined from a known good device), a comparison can be made, with the circuit running at full operating speed, to determine good or bad circuit operation. By probing various nodes, finding bad signatures, and then tracing them back to the functional origin, you can find the actual fault. The signature analyzer is more than just a transition counter, because its internal feedback shift register circuit is both data and time dependent, allowing for a signal reduction algorithm that produces highly reliable results.

In actual operation, signals fed to the signature analyzer start and stop a measurement time period or window gate. A clock input synchronizes and controls the data sample rate of the probe input so that data is input to the signature analyzer and processed every clock cycle within a start/stop interval. The start and stop inputs are individually selectable for logic 1 or 0 levels. The clock input is edge triggered and can be selected for either rising or falling edges.

General comments

1. The measurement window framed by the start and stop signals must be unique and synchronized to all the nodes tested so that consistent signatures are produced. The number of clock edges enclosed must be a constant for each test setup condition.
2. Data must be synchronous with a stable signal during the triggering edge of the clock. Data setup time must be included.

3. Start and stop can be physically tied together with any of the four logic-level select combinations permitted. This minimizes the number of connections to the test circuit and is thus a desirable practice.

4. Although a single start/stop sequence produces a valid signature, troubleshooting is faster with continuous cycling.

Figure 10-1 illustrates the timing involved in a measurement window.

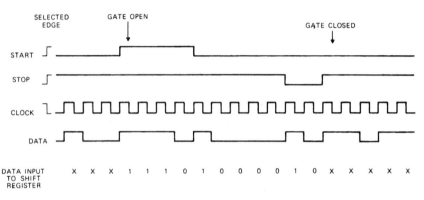

■ **10-1** *Typical data input to the signature analyzer.* Hewlett-Packard Co.

The most common connection point for the signature analyzer clock is the clock hase of the circuit under test where address and data lines are stable.

Start and stop signals that define the data sampling interval can be taken from address lines, state pointers, software-controlled output ports, or any other signals that identify the presence of a unique data stream for the particular set of circuit nodes of interest. Keep in mind, however, that the more circuitry involved with generating these signals, the higher the probability that a fault will be present in that circuitry. You should verify these individual circuit components so that any faults in them can be found.

The clock and the start/stop signals generally remain on the same circuit points through many, or even all, signature analyzer probe readings. In this way, much of the signature gathering process can be simply a matter of moving the signature analyzer input probe from node to node on the circuit under test. By minimizing the number of test setups requiring unique start, stop, and clock connections and edge selections, you can spend less time troubleshooting. The degree to which this can be done depends on the circuit's design structure.

The data input of the signature analyzer consists of a dual-threshold, (logic 0 and logic 1) comparator circuit. In effect, these comparators sample the input at the time of the selected clock edge. To the node under test, the input looks like a 50-KΩ resistor pulled to a nominal 1.4-V reference. Because 1.4 V lies between the two threshold voltages, a change from an active logic level to a floating (or high-impedance) condition will not cause a change in the logic state input to the signature analyzer. Figure 10-2 illustrates how this input circuit reacts to various signals. The major benefit derived from this technique is the ability to obtain a stable and repeatable signature from a tri-state node. If the input had instead been pulled toward V_{CC}, stray test node capacitance could delay the transition to the high state and cause inconsistent signatures.

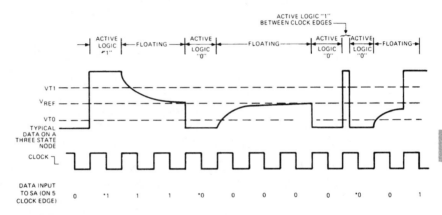

■ 10-2 *Floating nodes retain the logic state of the last valid data clocked in.*
Hewlett-Packard Co.

The input algorithm does not require that the first bit of the data stream be a hard 0 or a hard 1. If, however, the first data input to the signature analyzer following a start signal is a nonvalid logic level (floating), then the last valid logic state present during a clock time (preceding the start signal) will be the first logic state input to the signature analyzer. (Depressing the reset button on the signature analyzer has the same effect that a 0 last valid logic state has.)

Basic techniques

The underlying concept of SA is the *wiggling line* (a logic node that changes from one logic state to another). Only a limited amount of information can be derived from a logic node that never changes state during a particular test sequence. It doesn't get "exercised." This applies to nodes on PC boards as well as the logic nodes internal to an IC. On the other hand, if a node actively changes state in a proper manner at the correct time for that circuit, much more valid information and confidence results. Statistically, it often doesn't matter much "what" caused the node to wiggle in order to obtain useful diagnostic information. A truth table exercise on the components, however, is generally more exhaustive and will catch a greater number of failures:

☐ Getting the circuit to run in a repetitive loop
☐ Using only a minimum number of the circuit's logic components required for the task
☐ Causing the maximum number of logic nodes in the circuit to wiggle.

For microprocessors, controllers, sequencers, and ASMs, free-running is often accomplished by opening the data (or instruction) input bus and then forcing in an instruction (such as NOP) or control that causes a continuous cycling through the entire address or control field. The circuitry doing this cycling is often referred to as the *kernel*. It is usually the origin or heart of the system. If it doesn't work, neither will the balance of the circuit.

Taking signatures while in the free-running mode can verify the kernel, much of the combined circuitry on the address or control lines (especially address decoders and the data in the ROMs), and the operation of the data bus. But in most cases free-running alone cannot sufficiently exercise all devices and circuit nodes. For example, RAMs, most sequential and LSI circuits and most microprocessors are not well exercised by mere free-running.

To exercise this class of components, specific test stimulus algorithms should be generated that produce as many multi-gate-level logic changes as practical. Often these can be subroutines in the self-test program. The key thing to keep in mind, and one of the advantages of SA, is that the logic stimulus is programmed internally by the circuit itself. For microprocessors, this is usually done by writing an SA stimulus program in a portion of ROM. The intrinsic data manipulative capabilities of microprocessors makes this a powerful stimulus control, yet a relatively straightforward task to implement in the design. Typically, this code is much less complex and easier to generate than the product's operating code. Other types of systems, less capable of generating stimulus algorithms, may require a higher level of firmware commitment. And with many classes of random logic systems, the whole SA approach may not be practical, due to the very high hardware overhead required to provide good stimulus and data feedback control.

Most applications of SA will be with bus-structured systems. Bus structures offer very definite design advantages, but they can make fault analysis difficult. The tough question is, which element is putting the bad data on the bus? There are several major classes of faults that can make bus fault location difficult. The key things to mention at this time are the two techniques used with SA to deal with buses:

☐ The ability to disable buses and bus elements
☐ The ability to open feedback loops

Although the signature analyzer is primarily a service and production troubleshooting tool, it can prove valuable on the design bench for checking out prototype and pilot production run equipment, once the good signatures are known. You can sometimes diagnose timing errors and excessive node settling times by varying the system clock rate and observing any change or instability of the signature.

Checking the processor

The microprocessor's ability to help verify and troubleshoot extends from the A/D portions of an instrument. When a processor entirely controls an instrument, you must determine whether the processor is functional before attempting to isolate faults in the rest of the equipment. In multiprocessor-based equipment, isolating the faulty processor is especially crucial.

Thus, the primary function of a processor's self-test program is to verify the processor and its digital circuitry, or as much of it as possible. Either a self-test routine will activate every time the instrument comes on, or an instrument preset key or test switch will initiate the test routine. The routine generally includes a pattern test of the processor's internal registers, a checksum verification of the program in ROM, a pattern test of the system RAM, a visual test pattern shown on the instrument's display (CRT, LEDs, etc.), and a check of some of the I/O devices. The go/no-go results of self-test are displayed on the front panel by LEDS or by a turn-on message on the CRT.

In operation, a preset/power-up line forces the main processor to its reset condition while turning on red check LEDs on the front panel. See Fig. 10-3. The processor then performs a read-write pattern check of its internal accumulators and registers, performs

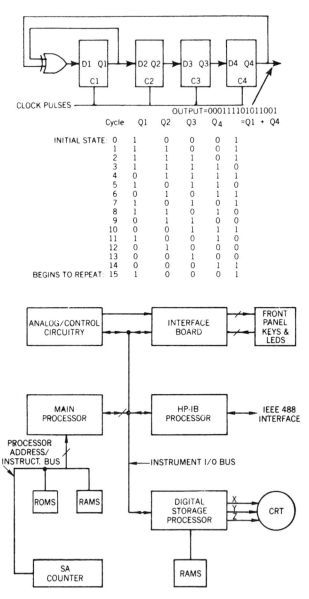

■ 10-3 *Block diagram of digital section of a spectrum analyzer.* Hewlett-Packard Co.

a checksum of each of the 16 program ROMs and a pattern check of the 16 RAMs, executes a read-write check on the display RAM memory through the digital storage processor, and reads the status of the front panel keys from the interface board.

If all tests pass, the check LEDs (two in this case) are turned off. Both LEDs on indicates a problem with the ROM, RAM, or main processor. One LED on indicates a likely problem in the digital storage processor or its display RAM; the other LED on indicates an unexpected bit from the interface board.

The HPIB processor board has its own self-check routine and front panel LED. In addition, the digital-storage processor verifies both itself and its RAM (via an internally selectable self-test pattern) and generates a CRT test pattern independent of the main processor and the I/O bus of the instrument. Usually, then, from the front panel it's possible to both detect a fault and isolate it to one of the three processors or the I/O bus.

Both the front panel keys and the self-check routine itself can be checked by keeping a key depressed during the main self-test routine. Problems will be detected when the interface board is read. And one check LED will be kept on to ensure that the two check LEDs are not turned off improperly.

At times, the processor's self-check routine can also isolate faults. For example, when checking the program ROMs, the routine generates a checksum for each ROM, which enables the processor to tell you which ROM is defective. One way to find this out is to display the faulty IC number on the CRT, but you would need a known good I/O bus, digital-storage processor, and display RAM.

There is an easier way. Write the ROM checksum routine so that the time required to execute unambiguously indicates the faulty ROM. See Fig. 10-4. Here, checksums are generated for the upper and lower bytes of the first two words. If the sums agree with that stored in the first ROM, then the program continues to the next pair of ROMs; if they do not agree, the routine terminates.

Signature analyzer as a monitor

To monitor the execution time of this routine, a 4-bit ring counter hangs on the memory address bus and is cleared and clocked by the main processor, using appropriate addresses. Before starting the routine, the processor clears and clocks the counter once, then does it again when the routine is terminated. The time between the rising edges of the first two counter outputs can then be monitored.

A signature analyzer makes a good monitor here, because with a steady 1 at its data probe, the unit generates a unique signature that depends on the number of clocks between the start and stop

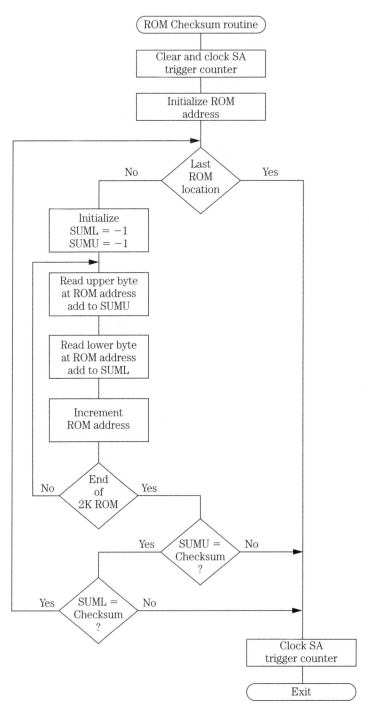

■ **10-4** *A checksum routine verifies that all program ROMs are OK.* Hewlett-Packard Co.

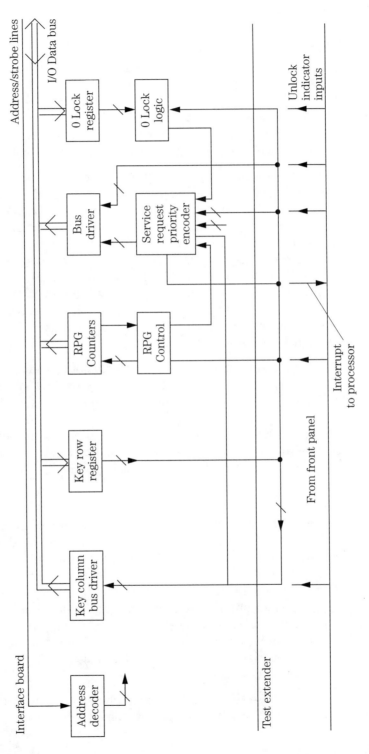

Interface board

Address/strobe lines

I/O Data bus

Address decoder

Key column bus driver

Key row register

RPG Counters

RPG Control

Bus driver

Service request priority encoder

0 Lock register

0 Lock logic

Unlock indicator inputs

Interrupt to processor

From front panel

Test extender

■ 10-5 *Block diagram of spectrum analyzer board shows mating technique of signature analysis.* Hewlett-Packard Co.

inputs (see Fig. 10-5). You can then reference the signatures to the defective ROM using a fault table.

For example, a signature of 6HF5 indicates that U6 is bad; UCF4 indicates that all ROMs are good. You can similarly isolate faulty RAMs with their pattern-check routine and another fault table, using the next pair of counter outputs as the start/stop control lines. The complete self-check routine can be forced to repeat continually by grounding a status line into the processor. Not only does this simplify testing, but it helps isolate intermittent failures.

Self-test obviously has its limitations. To run the routine just to check the program ROMs requires that some part of the ROM and a good portion of the processor be operating properly. If the routine does not run, you will need an additional test, usually called a *free-run* check, to isolate the first ROM, containing the self-test program, from the processor. The best way to do this is break the feedback path from the ROM back to the processor, thus forcing a NOP instruction and continually causing the processor to increment the memory address. You can then verify the actual outputs of the ROM, chip select lines, and memory address lines by using the signature analyzer.

If the processor's memory output lines do not sequence properly, you may have to do some additional troubleshooting with an oscilloscope to verify the processor's clocks, reset, and power-supply inputs. If these fall within specs, you have isolated the fault to the processor chip. If the ROM outputs are good, but the self-check routine still does not run when the ROM outputs are reconnected, the processor is defective.

Other test aids

Of course, troubleshooting this way will not always pin down exactly which processor function has failed. You may need a scope, logic analyzer, or other debug device in this design phase in order to troubleshoot the actual program steps or to determine precisely what a processor is (or is not) doing. This test, however, will give a go/no-go indication of the processor's performance at its full operating speed and in its true environment. And once the basic kernel of the processor and first ROM are verified, you can use the kernel to test the remaining ROM and RAM, which in turn can help you test the I/O and other digital circuitry.

Self-testing also shows its limitations when you attempt to isolate faults in the I/O or other circuitry not directly connected to a processor bus. The processor cannot always read the outputs of the I/O device-self-test requirement, though in some cases it is worth adding the circuitry required to read back the output of an I/O port.

In other situations, the processor cannot exercise all the inputs required to verify an I/O device thoroughly in its normal configuration. Or it may be able to verify a section of circuitry but not easily pinpoint the faulty device. A good way to find out if the input or output buffer is defective is to team up the processor with the signature analyzer.

A routine in the processor's program generates the stimuli for the various I/O peripherals; the analyzer verifies the logic circuitry and traces bad signals to their starting points. The stimulus program usually differs from the self-test program in that the stimuli must not change because a device is good or bad.

Besides designing the stimulus program, you may have to modify the I/O to accommodate a test configuration. The two following tips should be helpful:

☐ Either avoid asynchronous timing signals, or disable or ignore them during test modes.
☐ Disable feedback paths, such as interrupts to the processor or circuit under test, because a failure anywhere in the loop will make all logic signals appear bad and make isolation impossible. Disabling is easiest when software performs the feedback functions, because a software "path" is easily opened.

To disable a hardware feedback, you can generally add a strategic test point to be grounded during testing or a jumper to be removed. Or you can connect an unused processor-controlled output to a point in the loop that allows the feedback path to be disabled. Proper board partitioning is always helpful in troubleshooting, because some feedback paths can be broken and bus-loading problems isolated simply by removing certain boards.

We also need to provide some way to stimulate those I/O inputs that are not under processor control. Jumpering those inputs to processor-controlled outputs (which can be independently verified) usually provides the best stimulus, yet it may be enough to manually connect a line alternately to ground and 1, and then to verify both results.

The finale

The spectrum analyzer interface board is a good example of SA coupled with a stimulus test program. See Fig. 10-6. The board contains the logic required to interface the main processor with the instrument's front panel. It also handles the service request logic, including lock/unlock indicators, keydown indication, HPIB requests, and so on. Communication with the processor takes place via the bidirectional 16-bit data bus, an address bus, a strobe line, and an interrupt line.

During the self-check routine, the processor can check the board only minimally. To do so, it clears the rotary pulse generator (RPG) counter, reads the outputs to verify all 0's, and reads the key column lines to verify all highs. But to check the circuitry thoroughly requires a repetitive, synchronous stimulus to all the various inputs. Because of the number of inputs, you may need a special-purpose test extender to disconnect the normal inputs and to reconnect them to the key row outputs. The processor can now control all the inputs by outputting bit patterns to the key row register.

The test extender also does other things. It breaks several feedback loops on the board and opens the interrupt feedback from the service request logic to the processor. And because the clear line on the one-shot in the RPG control block is connected to a key row line, the one-shot can be cleared by the processor to avoid the timing ambiguity of its pulse width.

Another feedback path around the RPG counter detects the overflow state and inhibits any further clocks. A grounded test point connected to an otherwise unused gate input opens the feedback, thereby isolating the two counter stages.

Once you have taken care of the test configuration, write the test stimulus program. In many cases, especially with an 8-bit processor, all it takes to cover all possible bit patterns is a simple increment/output loop from 0 to 255.

Test pattern requirements

With a 16-bit processor, however, the cycle time to count through all possible states becomes excessive. In addition, the service request priority logic may require that a particular sequence of bit patterns test all possible states.

Testing the spectrum analyzer interface board and the other devices on the bus requires a test pattern with several rotate/output

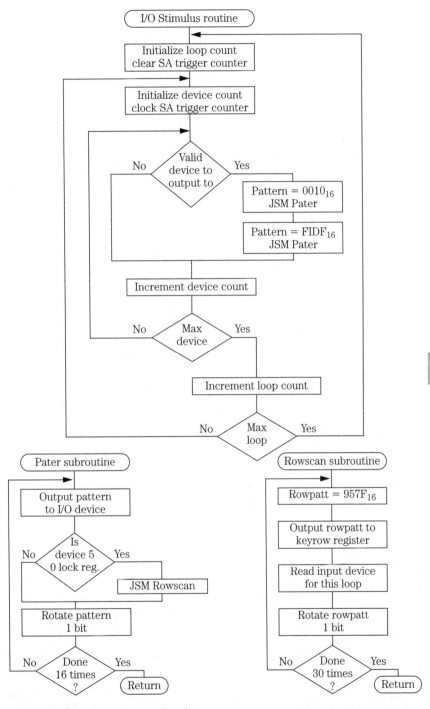

■ **10-6** *Stimulus program drawing.* Hewlett-Packard Co.

patterns like those shown in Fig. 10-7. For most I/O bus devices, a fairly simple test stimulus suffices—one generated in the program by cycling two different patterns through all valid I/O devices. One pattern is simply a 1 rotating through the 16 bit positions. The other pattern rotates 0's through the word.

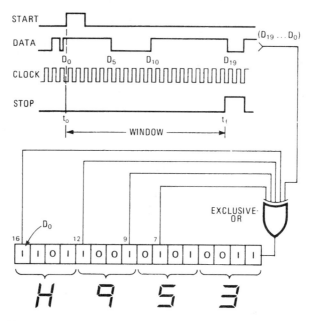

■ 10-7 *This 4-place hexadecimal signature is a compression of the 20-bit data stream entering the linear-feedback shift register.* Hewlett-Packard Co.

To check the more complex service request logic, a third pattern sequence stimulates the key row register whenever the device address indicates the phase-lock register. During this sequence, an I/O input device is read into the processor; which device is read depends on the loop count.

The first time through the loop, the input device acts as the processor's accumulator, so no actual I/O read occurs. During that loop, all information on the bus depends only on the processor. So even with all I/O devices removed, the bus signatures can be verified. The key row register outputs are also checked during the first loop.

During the second loop, the processor reads the RPG/SRQ word. Any faults now appearing on the bus can be traced back through those logic blocks. During the third loop, the key column word is read onto the I/O bus, and so on.

Generally, you will need one setup for each driver because it is not possible to trace a fault if two unverified devices are driving the bus during the same measurement window. However, by indexing the read address and changing the start/stop inputs, you can make one software routine test all the I/O devices.

It is easy to overlook verification of a test program, but please don't. Does the program really test all the states of the priority encoder? Taking the time to question the capability of critical sections of the test program with a logic analyzer can save time in the long run:

☐ Does the program properly test the pattern sensitivity of the RAMs and I/O devices?
☐ Are the same signatures obtained on all known good boards, or is there some marginal timing in the test pattern sequence?
☐ Is an indeterminate open logic input affecting some signature?
☐ If power is cycled off and on, does the test generate the same results or does the test rely on an undefined input from another board?
☐ Does inducing faults by jumping signals to ground or supply show up on the verification outputs?
☐ Does the test stimulus rely on some hardware that has not yet been verified?
☐ Does the input stimulus remain unchanged when failures are induced on the board, or are there still feedback paths that make fault isolation impossible?

As you now go through the checklist, you will be one step away from SA. The last stop is documentation. Good signatures must be documented so that those troubleshooting the board will know if a particular node signature is good or bad. One way is to include all the signatures in a flowchart, an approach that can work well for overall troubleshooting down to the module level but becomes risky and cumbersome when extended to the IC level.

Another approach is to make notations on the schematic with signatures rather than the familiar analog voltage levels and waveforms. An obvious advantage is that all the information is on one document: the signature tells if a node is good or bad and the schematic shows the node connections and what inputs affect that node.

Signature notations on the schematic, especially on a medium to complex board or on one requiring more than one test setup, can be not only difficult to lay out, correct, and update but be hard to use. An alternative prints the signatures on a component layout diagram. Although this cannot replace the schematic, additional color-coded information along with the signature minimizes the need to switch continually from the board to the schematic while tracing a fault.

A verification path (arrow) guides you through the nodes. Checked here are the service requested interrupt to the processor, the I/O data output lines from the RPG/SRQ circuitry, and, with a different start/stop setup, the I/O data outputs from the key column drivers. When a bad signature is found, the colored numbers next to the signature indicate the IC and the pin number of the source of that signal.

At the IC, a black pad represents an output, a colored pad an input. Colored lines connecting inputs and outputs indicate which inputs affect only a certain output. Isolated colored pads indicate inputs that control multiple outputs, such as clock or clear. With this information, you can trace a bad output signature to its origin, where the inputs to a device are good but the output signature is incorrect.

360

Glossary

Active elements   Those components in a circuit that have gain or in which direct current flows: diodes, transistors.

Active state   The state in which the logic circuit performs its particular function. For example, the active state of the power set (initializer) circuit provides a reset function when power is initially applied, therefore, the logic levels should be shown for this active state.

Activity   The presence of active signals. These signals are then detected in the activity checker which generates an activity signal.

Adder, logical   Switching circuits that generate an output (sum and carry bits) representing the arithmetic sum of two inputs.

Adder, resistive   A method for converting multi-bit digital information to an analog level by sourcing/sinking current from a fixed-voltage supply through a resistor network.

Address   A code designating the particular unit (vehicle, decoder, teleprinter, radiotelephone, etc.) that must respond to an incoming message. When used with computers, it is a code which designates the location of information or instructions in the main storage, peripherals, etc.

Analog computer   A continuous-variable computer, or nondigital computer. A differential analyzer. Measures the effect of changes in one variable on all other variables in a system. Its operation is analogous to a slide rule.

Analog switch   A device that allows transfer of signals in both directions whenever the switch is enabled. When the switch is not enabled, it offers a high impedance.

And gate   *See* Gate, AND.

Astable multivibrator A free-running electronic circuit that generates pulses that can be used as timing signals or other similar signals.

Asynchronous Operation of a switching network by a free-running signal that triggers successive instructions; the completion of one instruction triggers the next.

Binary A system of numerical representation that uses only two symbols, 0 and 1.

Binary Coded Decimal (BCD) Four bits of binary information that are used as a unit to encode one decimal digit. When a decimal digit is encoded in this way, it is called a Binary Coded Decimal (BCD).

Bistable *See* Flip-Flop.

Bit Abbreviation for Binary Digit.

"Black box" A description used for an electronic circuit that concerns itself only with the input and output, ignores the interior elements, discrete or integrated.

Buffer A non-inverting stage, such as an emitter follower, that provides isolation and is sometimes used to handle a large fan-out or to convert input and output levels.

Bus transceiver A three-state device that provides 2-way asynchronous data transfer. Data transfer capability is in either direction but not both simultaneously. Direction of data transfer depends upon the logic level of the Direction Input.

Byte A group of eight bits considered as an entity. Instruction sets for 8-bit microprocessors are defined in multiples of bytes.

Chip A single substrate on which all the active and passive elements of an electronic circuit have been fabricated utilizing the semiconductor technologies of diffusion, passivation, masking, photo resist, and epitaxial growth. A chip is not ready for use until it is packaged and provided with terminals for connection to the outside world.

Clear To restore a memory or storage device, counter, etc., to a "standard" state, usually the "zero" state. Also called reset.

Clock A pulse generator that controls the timing of switching circuits and memory states, and determines the speed at which the major portion of the computer or timing circuits operates.

362

(The pulse generated is referred to as the clock pulse; sometimes shortened to clock.)

Clocked RS flip-flop The clocked RS flip-flop has two conditioning inputs that control the state to which the flip-flop will go at the arrival of the clock pulse. If the S (set) input is enabled, the flip-flop goes to the "1" condition when clocked. If the R (reset) input is enabled, the flip-flop goes to the "0" condition when clocked. The clock pulse is required to change the state of the flip-flop.

Comparator A device used to determine if two bits of information are in the same state (both 0 or both 1).

Complement The complement of a variable or function is the binary opposite of that variable or function. If a variable or function is 1, its complement will be 0. If a variable or function is 0, its complement will be 1. The complement of 011010 is 100101.

Counter A device capable of changing states in a specified sequence upon receiving appropriate input signals. Or A circuit that provides an output pulse or other indication after receiving a specified number of input pulses. (See specific counters as follows.)

Counter, binary A series of flip-flops having a single input. Each time a pulse appears at the input, the flip-flop changes state; sometimes called a "T" flip-flop.

Counter, nonsynchronous (ripple) A number of series connected flip-flops that divides (counts-down) the input into a series output occurring at a lower rate. The actual division depends upon the number of flip-flops and their specific connections.

Counter, programmable An integrated circuit, containing series connected flip-flops, into which a binary number (within the counter range) can be programmed. The counter then counts the input pulses starting at the programmed number until the counter is full and resets. The cycle then repeats.

Counter, ring A loop or circuit of interconnected flip-flops so arranged that only one is "ON" at any given time and that as input signals are received, the position of the "ON" state moves in sequence from one flip-flop to another around the loop.

Counter, shift A number of clocked series connected flip-flops in which the flip-flops do not change with each clock. Instead, each flip-flop only changes once for each cycle of the counter. That is; in a 3-stage shift counter, the flip-flops only change once every three clocks; once every four clocks in a 4-stage shift counter, etc.

Counter, synchronous A number of series connected flip-flops in which the next state of each depends upon the present state of the previous, and all state changes occur simultaneously with a clock pulse. The output (or equivalent count of input pulses) can be taken from the counter in parallel form.

DCTL (Direct Coupled Transistor Logic) Logic is performed by transistors.

D-type flip-flop A D-type flip-flop propagates whatever information is at its D (data) conditioning input, prior to the clock pulse, to the Q output on the leading edge of a clock pulse. If the data input is 1, the Q output becomes 1 on the leading edge of the next clock pulse. If the data input is 0, the Q output becomes 0 on the next clock.

Decimal A system of numerical representation that uses the symbols 0, 1, 3 ...9.

Decoder A device used to convert information from a coded form into a more usable form (i.e., binary-to-decimal, binary-to-BCD, BCD-to-decimal, etc.).

Delay Undesirable delay effects are caused by rise time and fall time that reduces circuit speed, but intentional delay units may be used to prevent inputs from changing while clock pulses are present. The delay time is normally less than the clock pulse interval.

Digit A digit is one character in a number. There are 10 digits in the decimal number system. There are two digits in the binary number system.

Digital circuit A circuit that operates like a switch; it's either "on" or "off."

Discrete Electronic circuits built of separate, finished components, such as resistors, capacitors, transistors, etc.

Divider, programmable *See* Counter, programmable.

DTL (Diode-Transistor-Logic) Logic is performed by diodes. The transistor acts as an amplifier; and the output is inverted.

Enable A gate is enabled if its input conditions result in a specific output. The specific output varies for different gating functions. For instance, an AND gate is enabled when its output is the same level as its inputs, whereas, the NAND gate is enabled when its output is the complement of its inputs. In some cases, function enabling inputs allow operation to be executed on a clock pulse after the function enabling input is enabled with the correct logic level.

Encoder A device that takes information in one code and encodes it into another (e.g., the decimal-to-binary encoder, decimal-to-BCD, etc.).

Eraseable Programmable Read Only Memory (EPROM) Similar to a PROM, except that the previous information can be erased and new information can be written in.

Exclusive "OR" The output is true only when the two inputs are opposites (complementary) and is false if both inputs are the same.

Exponent of a number The number of times the base number is to be used as a factor.

Fall time A measure of the time required for a circuit to change its output from a high level to a low level.

Fan-in The number of inputs available on a gate.

Fan-out The number of gates that a given gate can drive. The term is applicable only within a given logic family.

Flip-flop An electronic circuit having two stable states, and having the ability to change from one state to the other upon the application of a signal in a specified manner. Specific types follow this entry.

Flip-flop, "D" D stands for data—a flip-flop the output of which is a function of the input that appeared one pulse earlier. If a 1 appears at its input, the output one pulse later will be 1. Sometimes used to produce a one clock delay.

Flip-flop, "JK" A flip-flop having two inputs designated J and K. At the application of a clock pulse, a 1 on the J input will set the flip-flop to the 1 or "ON" state, and 1's simultaneously on both inputs will cause it to change state regardless of what state it has been in. If 0's appear simultaneously on both inputs, the flip-flop state remains unchanged.

Flip-flop, "RS" A flip-flop having two inputs designated R and S. The application of a 1 on the S input will set the flip-flop to the 1 or "on" state, and 1 on the R input will reset it to the 0 or "off" state. It is assumed that 1's will never appear simultaneously at both inputs. (In actual practice the circuit can be designed so that a 0 is required at the S and R inputs.)

Flip-flop, synchronized "RS" A synchronized RS flip-flop having three inputs, R, S, and clock (strobe, enable, etc.) The R and S inputs produce states as described for the RS flip-flop above. The clock causes the flip-flop to change states.

Flip-flop, "T" A flip-flop having only one input. A pulse appearing on the input will cause the flip-flop to change states. A series of these flip-flops make up a binary ripple counter.

Gate A circuit having two or more inputs and one output, the output depending upon the combination of logic signals at the inputs. There are five gates called: AND, EXCLUSIVE OR, OR, NAND, NOR. The following gate definitions assume that positive logic is used.

Gate, AND All inputs must have 1-stare signals to produce a 1-state output (in actual practice some gates require 0-state inputs to produce a 0-state output).

Gate, Exclusive OR The output is true only when the two inputs are opposites (complementary) and is false if both inputs are the same.

Gate, NAND ALL inputs must have 1-state signals to produce a 0-state output (in actual practice some gates require 0-state inputs to produce a 1-state output).

Gate, NOR Any one or more inputs having a 1-state signal will yield a 0-state output (in actual practice some gates require 0-state inputs to produce a 1-state output).

Gate, OR Any one or more inputs having a 1-state signal will yield a 1-state output (in actual practice some gates require 0-state inputs to produce a 0-state output).

Half-add The half-add is performed first in doing a two-step binary addition. It adds corresponding bits in two binary numbers ignoring any carry information.

High-level AND gate An AND gate that is activated when all inputs have 1-state output.

High-level NAND gate A NAND gate that is activated when all inputs have 1-state signals applied to produce a 0-state output.

High-level NOR gate A NOR gate that is activated when one or more inputs have a 1-state signal applied to produce a 1-state output.

High-level OR gate An OR gate that is activated when one or more inputs have a 1-state signal applied to produce a 1-state output.

Integrated circuit The Electronics Industries Association defines semiconductor integrated circuit as "the physical realization of a number of electrical elements inseparably associated on or within a continuous body of semiconductor material to perform the functions of a circuit."

Inverter The output is always in the opposite logic state of the input. Also called a NOT circuit.

Leading edge The leading edge of a pulse is defined as that edge or transition that occurs first (i.e., the leading edge of a high pulse is the low-to-high transition).

Logic A mathematical approach to the solution of complex situations by the use of symbols to define basic concepts. The three basic logic symbols are AND, OR, and NOT. When used in Boolean Algebra these symbols are somewhat analogous to addition and multiplication.

Low-level AND gate An AND gate that is activated when all inputs have 0-state signals applied to produce a 0-state output.

Low-level NAND gate A NAND gate that is activated when all inputs have 0-state signals applied to produce a 1-state output.

Low-level NOR gate A NOR gate that is activated when one or more inputs have a 0-state signal applied to produce 1-state output.

Motherboard The circuit board on which the CPU, RAM, ROM, and other chips are connected.

Mouse A small input device that you roll on your desk top to move a cursor (or pointer) around the computer screen and which sends commands to the CPU.

Negative logic The reverse of positive logic; the more negative voltage represents the 1-state and the less negative voltage represents the 0-state.

"NOT" A Boolean logic operator indicating negation. A variable designated "NOT" will be the opposite of its "AND or "OR" function. A switching function for only one variable.

Octal The octal number system is one that has eight distinct digits: 0,1,2,3,4,5,6,7.

Parallel operation Pertaining to the manipulation of information within logic circuitry, in which the digits of a word are transmitted simultaneously on separate lines. Parallel operation is faster than serial operation but requires more circuitry.

Parity Parity is a method by which binary numbers can be checked for accuracy. An extra bit, called a *parity bit*, is added to numbers in systems using parity. If even parity is used, the sum of all 1's in a number and its corresponding parity bit is always even. If odd parity is used, the sum of 1's in a number and its corresponding parity bit is always odd.

Passive elements Those components in a circuit that have no gain characteristics: capacitors, resistors, inductors.

Pcm: Pulse-code modulation A method for representing analog values in digital form. Each digital output code represents a finite range of analog values.

Peripheral Interface Adapter (PIA) A device that provides means of interfacing peripheral equipment to a microprocessor unit (MPU). All control signals for the PIA are originated by the MPU and some are supplied via certain lines (chip select) on the address bus.

Positive logic The more positive voltage represents the 1-state; the less positive voltage represents the 0-state.

Programmable Read-Only Memory (PROM) A ROM device into which information can be written by means of special equipment.

Propagation delay A measure of the time required for a change in logic level to propagate through a chain of circuit elements.

Pulse A change of voltage or current of some finite duration and amplitude. The duration is called the pulse width or pulse length; the magnitude of the change is called the pulse amplitude or pulse height.

Radix The number of symbols used in the number system. (For example, the decimal system has a radix of ten.)

Random Access Memory (RAM) A static or dynamic memory device that data can be written into, or out of, from a specific location. The specific RAM location is selected by the address applied via the address bus and control lines. Data is stored in such a manner that each bit of information can be retrieved in the same length of time.

Resistor-Capacitor-Transistor-Logic (RCTL) Same as RTL except that capacitors are used to enhance switching speed.

Read-Only Memory (ROM) A non-volatile memory device containing permanent pre-programmed digital data. Data can only be read out of this device on the data bus whenever the proper location address is applied to the ROM address bus input and control lines. The ROM can be controlled either by a microprocessor or other device capable of generating the proper address. The ROM is preprogrammed at the time of manufacture.

Register A device used to store a certain number of digits within the computer circuitry, often one word. Certain registers may also include provisions for shifting, circulating, or other options.

Reset See Clear.

Rise time A measure of the time required for a circuit to change its output from a low level to a high level.

Resistor-Transistor-Logic (RTL) Logic is performed by resistors. The transistor produces an inverted output from any positive input.

Schmitt trigger A fast acting pulse generator that produces a constant amplitude pulse as long as the input exceeds a threshold dc value. Used as a pulse shaper, threshold detector, etc.

Serial operation Pertaining to the manipulation of information within logic circuitry, in which the digits of a word are transmitted one at a time along a single line. Though slower than parallel operation its circuitry is considerably less complex.

Set To restore a memory or storage device, counter, etc., to a "standard" state, usually the "one" state. Always the complement of clear.

Shift register An element in the digital family that utilizes flip-flops to perform a displacement or movement of a set of digits one or more places to the right or left. If the digits are those of a numerical expression, a shift may be the equivalent of multiplying the number by a power of the base.

Strobe A sampling pulse that is used to enable a register, flip-flop, counter, etc.

Summing amplifier circuit A circuit consisting of an amplifier (usually an op amp) with a multiple-wired OR input and a single combined output. The output signal is the analog sum of all inputs.

Synchronous Operation of a switching network by a clock pulse generator.

Three-state device Any integrated circuit device in which two of the states are conventional binary (1-0) states; and the third state is a high-impedance state. When in the third state these devices present a high impedance to their respective output lines to reduce power drain and allow access to the common bus lines by other devices.

Trailing edge The trailing edge of a pulse is that edge or transition that occurs last. The trailing edge of a HI clock pulse is the HI to LO transition.

Transistor-Transistor-Logic (TTL) A modification of DTL that replaces the diode cluster with a multiple-emitter transistor.

Universal Asynchronous Receiver Transmitter (UART) A device that provides the data formatting and control to interface serial asynchronous data. Input serial data is converted to parallel data for transfer to the microprocessor or microcomputer via the data bus. Conversely, output parallel data, from the data bus, is converted to serial data in the output.

Word The term "word" denotes an assemblage of bits considered as an entity. For example, a 16-bit address word contains 16 bits.

Index

Illustrations are in **boldface**

375

377

Other Bestsellers of Related Interest

Maintaining and Repairing VCRs, 3rd Edition
Robert L. Goodman
This is a 50,000-copy bestseller—the #1 guide for technicians and advanced do-it-yourselfers—covering the latest VCR technology from General Electric, RCA, JVC, Zenith, Panasonic, Sony, and more. Goodman offers professional tips and techniques for keeping VCRs operating trouble-free—and for fixing them when they don't—using pinout diagrams and exploded-view photographs to illustrate procedures.
ISBN 0-8306-4080-0, #023970-3 $19.95 Paperback
ISBN 0-8306-4079-7, #023969-X $39.95 Hardcover

The Complete Book of Oscilloscopes, 2nd Edition
Stan Prentiss
This revised edition of the bestselling Complete Book of Oscilloscopes provides an up-to-date look at all of the latest oscilloscope equipment and advanced testing procedures developed during the last five years. Professional technicians and electronics hobbyists will find detailed information on all types of oscilloscopes and their applications.
ISBN 0-8306-3908-X, #157781-5 $19.95 Paperback

Troubleshooting and Repairing Compact Disc Players, 2nd Edition
Homer L. Davidson
Updated to cover all the latest CD player makes and models, this bestselling guide provides all the information professionals need to diagnose and fix the most common problems in today's players.
ISBN 0-07-015670-0 $24.95 Paperback
ISBN 0-07-015669-7 $44.95 Hardcover

Troubleshooting and Repairing Computer Monitors

Stephen J. Bigelow

The technician's guide to maintaining, aligning, troubleshooting, and repairing both CRT and flat-panel computer monitors.

ISBN 0-07-005408-8 $42.95 Hardcover

Troubleshooting and Repairing Consumer Electronics Without a Schematic

Homer L. Davidson

Indispensable for electronics technicians, students, and advanced hobbyists, this hands-on guide comes to the rescue for all those times when no schematic diagram is available.

ISBN 0-07-015650-6 $22.95 Paperback
ISBN 0-07-015649-2 $34.95 Hardcover

Troubleshooting and Repairing Solid-State TVs, 2nd Edition

Homer L. Davidson

A complete workbench reference for electronics technicians and students. Packed with case study examples, troubleshooting photos, and diagrams for every kind of TV circuit, this popular guide is just what technicians need to diagnose and repair virtually any TV malfunction.

ISBN 0-8306-3893-8, #157677-0 $24.95 Paperback
ISBN 0-8306-3894-6, #157678-9 $36.95 Hardcover

How to Order

Call 1-800-822-8158
24 hours a day,
7 days a week
in U.S. and Canada

Mail this coupon to:
McGraw-Hill, Inc.
P.O. Box 182067
Columbus, OH 43218-2607

Fax your order to:
614-759-3644

EMAIL
70007.1531@COMPUSERVE.COM
COMPUSERVE: GO MH

Shipping and Handling Charges

Order Amount	Within U.S.	Outside U.S.
Less than $15	$3.50	$5.50
$15.00 - $24.99	$4.00	$6.00
$25.00 - $49.99	$5.00	$7.00
$50.00 - $74.49	$6.00	$8.00
$75.00 - and up	$7.00	$9.00

EASY ORDER FORM—
SATISFACTION GUARANTEED

Ship to:

Name _____

Address _____

City/State/Zip _____

Daytime Telephone No. _____

Thank you for your order!

ITEM NO.	QUANTITY	AMT.

Method of Payment:

☐ Check or money order
enclosed (payable to
McGraw-Hill)

☐ VISA   ☐ DISCOVER

☐ AMERICAN EXPRESS Cards   ☐ MasterCard.

Shipping & Handling charge from chart below	
Subtotal	
Please add applicable state & local sales tax	
TOTAL	

Account No. ☐☐☐☐☐☐☐☐☐☐☐☐☐☐☐☐

Signature _____ Exp. Date _____
Order invalid without signature

**In a hurry? Call 1-800-822-8158 anytime,
day or night, or visit your local bookstore.**

Code = BC15ZZA